W9-BRU-281

I LIKE TO BACKPACK. THERE'S MAGIC WITHIN THE TRAIL, I'VE FOUND. I'VE ALSO LEARNED THAT OUR CORNER OF MICHIGAN – THE NORTHWEST CORNER OF THE LOWER PENINSULA – CAN CAST A SPELL PRETTY DARN QUICK.

The other day I was hiking within the Brown Bridge Quiet Area just southeast of Traverse City. I was practicing for a much bigger hike the next week. I carried my backpack, 40 pounds full. My hiking poles were pumping like pistons. The Boardman River, high from spring rains, surged to my left. A marvelous day.

Then came the prettiest little fiddle tune through my ear phones . . . an Adrienne Young piece called "Sgt. Early's Dream." And I lost it. The music, the sun's glitter off the Boardman rapids, the thick green of the spring forest, the curvaceous sandy-brown path beckoning me "this way!" — they all combined to cause this quiet hiker to dance a jig, polls raised skyward, eyes to the sky, skipping along on my own Riverdance. And then, with a big grin, I shouted to no one, and everyone, "OH GAWD, HOW I DO LOVE THIS PLACE!"

MAGIC!

It was from a guidebook a tad like this one that I first learned of Brown Bridge. (We discuss Brown Bridge and other great trails on page 110.)

But this guidebook is bigger. Better. And that's our promise to you, dear reader. You hold in your hand a unique collection of pure, magical escapes — your path to doors not opened, trails not explored, little-known nooks and crannies of rich delight, all across the Grand Traverse region.

It's not a boast that this is, indeed, the true insider's guide to UpNorth. The authors, combined, including our own Heather Lee Shaw, who organized the book, have more than two centuries of living in these parts. And it's not a boast that this is a "Complete Guide." We challenge you to find one as thorough, and as full of fabulous secrets, as this.

So venture on. Enjoy these many pages. We're confident your copy of *Inside UpNorth* will soon be dog-eared as it becomes your indispensable go-to road map to all things wonderful in Northwest Michigan.

Oh . . . and don't miss the splendid stories by local authors Bob Butz, Michael Delp and Todd Mercer that flow across the bottom of each page. It makes turning to the next page, and the next, all the more rewarding.

See you on the trail!

Doug Weaver
Mission Point Press

INSIDE UPNORTH:
THE COMPLETE TOUR, SPORT AND COUNTRY
LIVING GUIDE TO TRAVERSE CITY, TRAVERSE
CITY AREA AND LEELANAU COUNTY
by Heather Shaw, Jodee Taylor and Tom Carr
© 2017 by Mission Point Press

No part of this book may be reproduced, stored
in a retrieval system, or transmitted in any
form or by any means electronic, mechanical,
photocopying, recording or otherwise, without
the prior consent of the publisher.
Readers are encouraged to go to www.
MissionPointPress.com to contact the authors or
to find information on how to buy this book in
bulk at a discounted rate.

Design by Heather Shaw
Front cover photo by Tom Haxby

Published by Mission Point Press

2554 Chandler Lake Rd.
Traverse City, MI 49686
(231) 421-9513
www.MissionPointPress.com

ISBN: 978-1943995240

Library Of Congress: 2016962832

Printed in the United States of America.

ABOUT OUR COVER ARTIST: TOM HAXBY
lives in Kingsley, MI, and presently serves on
the Board of Directors of the North American
Nature Photography Association (NANPA)
and is a member of the Traverse Area Camera
Club (TACC). His experience includes time as
an Artist-In-Residence in the Great Smoky
Mountains National Park (2016), which
resulted in a first book, *A Special Place —
Great Smoky Mountains National Park*. Tom
has been published in numerous publications,
including the covers of *Michigan Blue
Magazine*, and photos in *Traverse Magazine*.
His website is www.tomhaxbyphotos.com.

• CONTENTS •

SUMMER FESTIVALS CONCERTS FAIRS & SALES

TC 4 and area

STOP BY THE TRAVERSE CITY VISITOR'S CENTER TO MEET REAL PEOPLE WHO CAN HELP YOU PLAN YOUR UPNORTH ADVENTURE.

FOR THE LATEST IN UPDATES, CHECK OUT WWW.TRAVERSECITY.COM

MAY

Monty Python's Spamalot || TC Old Town Playhouse || April 28 – May 20
Artist Charles R. Murphy || TC Opera House || May 1 – 31
Sara Hardy Downtown Farmers Market opens Wednesdays and Saturdays from 7:30AM til Noon
Downtown Art Walk || TC || May 5
"My Fair Lady" || Interlochen Center for the Arts || May 12 – 13
Old Mission Peninsula Blossom Day || TC || May 13
Empire Asparagus Day || Empire || May 20
Musicians Seth Bernard and Mark Lavengood || TC Opera House || May 24
Cherry Capital Comic Con || Acme || May 26 – 27
Author Andrea Petersen at the National Writers Series || TC || May 26
"Vanya and Sonia and Masha and Spike" || TC Old Town Playhouse || May 26 – June 9
Antrim County Petoskey Stone Festival || Eastport || May 27
Michigan Beer and Brat Festival || Thompsonville || May 27
Bayshore Marathon || TC || May 27

JUNE

Author Mary Roach at the National Writers Series || TC || June 7
"Young King Arthur" || TC Old Town Playhouse || June 9 – 11
Leland Wine and Food Festival || Leland || June 10
Colantha Walker Dairy Festival || TC || June 11
Wings Over Northern Michigan || Gaylord || June 17 – 18
The Bottle Rockets || TC Opera House || June 17

Adventure Fest || TC Open Space || June 22
TC Garden Club Standard Flower Show || TC || June 23
Charlevoix Summer Art Show || June 24 – 25
Old Town Arts & Crafts Fair || TC || June 25
Author Julia Glass at the National Writers Series || TC || June 25
Cedar Polka Fest || Cedar || June 29 – July 2
"King Lear" || Interlochen Center for the Arts || June 30 – July 1

JULY

Frankfort Carnival and Art in the Park || July 1 – 4
Manitou Music Festival || Glen Arbor || July 3 – August 15
Charlevoix Art and Craft Show || July 8 – 9
Dune Climb Concert — The Jimmys! || Glen Arbor || July 9
BlissFest || Cross Village || July 7 – July 9
National Cherry Festival || TC || July 1 – July 8
Traverse City 4th of July Fireworks || July 4 at sundown
Great Lakes Equestrian Festival || Williamsburg || July 5 – July 30
Author Bruce Cameron at the National Writers Festival || TC || July 7
"Madagascar, Jr." || TC Old Town Playhouse || July 14 – 15
Leelanau Peninsula Wine on the Water Festival || Suttons Bay || July 15
Traverse City Garden Walk || July 20
Traverse City Film Festival || TC || July 25 – July 30
Crooked Tree Outdoor Art Fair || TC || July 29
Parallel 45 presents "45 Plays for 45 Presidents" || TC || July 19 – 23

AUGUST

Friday Night Live in TC begins the first Friday of the month || 5:30 – 9 PM
Elk Rapids Harbor Days || Elk Rapids || August 2 – 5
"Evita" || Interlochen Center for the Arts || August 3 – 6
Traverse City Street Sale || August 4
Boats on the Boardwalk || TC || August 5
Northwest Michigan Fair || TC || August 6 – 12
"Hockey — The Musical!" || TC Opera House || August 9 – 12
Lake Leelanau Street Fair || August 15
Buckley Old Engine Show || August 17 – 20
Hoxeyville || Manistee || August 18 – 20
Frankfort Art Fair || August 19 – 20
Pshawbestown Pow Wow || August 19 – 20
Benzie Fishing Frenzy || Frankfort || August 26 – 28
Vineyard to Bay Run || TC || August 27

DON'T FORGET TO PUSH THE BUTTON FOR 30 MINUTES OF FREE PARKING IN TC.

SEE FALL / WINTER EVENTS ON PAGE 138

KIDTOWN
DOWNTOWN
TC

TC GETS A LOT OF PRESS FOR BEST SMALL TOWN, BEST RETIREMENT, BEST FOR BEER LOVERS AND BEST FOOD DESTINATION, BUT <u>ONE OF TC'S BEST, REALLY BEST QUALITIES IS THAT KIDS LOVE IT.</u> HOW CAN YOU GO WRONG WITH BEACHES, A SPLASH PAD, PLAYGROUNDS, TOY STORES AND KID-FRIENDLY RESTAURANTS ALL WITHIN THE WALKING DISTANCE OF A TWO-YEAR-OLD?

PLAY

#1 on the fun-list has to be the **SPLASH PAD** and playground at Clinch Park. Great for kids of all ages. Ample shade and seating for parents. Refreshments right next door at **Bayside Bites**.

In a tie for #1 is the **CLINCH PARK BEACH.** Tired of the Splash Pad, head 20 paces east for half a mile of sandy beach. Paddleboards, kayaks, bikes and float rentals all on site from **Paddle TC**. Lifeguards from mid-June through August.

THE DOGMAN by BOB BUTZ ¶ *A couple of campfires ago, in the darkest hours between midnight and dawn,*

SHOP

Forget your baby's bathing suit? No worries. **SWEET PEA** and **BOYNE COUNTRY SPORTS** have you covered.

Diapers, etc., are available downtown at **PETERTYL DRUG**.

TOY HARBOR has buckets, shovels, balls, games and everything you need to build the sand castle of your dreams.

EAT

There really isn't a single restaurant downtown in TC that frowns on kids. That said, some spots are just more fun.

LITTLE FLEET — a mostly outdoor establishment — offers food truck victuals and loads of room for running around. Full bar. Dogs also welcome.

BUBBA'S is a family-style burger joint with lots of finger-licking menu items kids will like. Full bar.

CHERRY REPUBLIC goes all-out to wow the young and old with its hyper-cherry-themed resort atmosphere.

Dine in or take out, **THE DISH** has sandwiches and wraps, veggie and vegan items.

REST

The **STATE THEATER** screens 25 cent matinees on Tuesdays, Thursdays and Saturdays all summer long.
The basement of **HORIZON BOOKS** is a great spot for quiet time.

 NEED A TIME-OUT DURING LUNCH?

• **SWEET PEA** has a play area with kitchen and Wendy house in the back of its store.

• **TOY HARBOR** is good for play all day. Open until 9 PM during the summer months.

• **CHILDREN'S WORLD** in the Arcade is almost a museum with its crowded shelves of old-timey toys and games.

• Older kids will love **TRAINS AND THINGS HOBBIES**.

EAT NAP PLAY EAT NAP PLAY EAT NAP

---

a drift of us were sitting around, caveman-style, in a merry discussion about trout. There we sat, passing the

KIDTOWN ADVENTURE WALK DOWNTOWN TC

THE BOARDMAN RIVER WINDS AROUND THROUGH DOWNTOWN TC, AND IN MOST PLACES THERE ARE PATHS ALONG ITS SHORE. <u>BE CAREFUL, THOUGH,</u> AS MANY OF THE PATHS ARE OLD AND CRUMBLY. THEY CAN ALSO BE SLIPPERY IN THE RAIN. BUT IT'S GREAT GOOD FUN FOR ALL AGES! THIS 9-BLOCK WALK EXPLORES DAMS, FISH LADDERS AND THE WEIR. TAKE A PICNIC OR EAT IN THE WAREHOUSE DISTRICT.

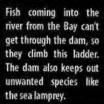

Fish coming into the river from the Bay can't get through the dam, so they climb this ladder. The dam also keeps out unwanted species like the sea lamprey.

BOARDWALK 2

2. Follow the boardwalk to where it ends. Keep right. You'll see the dam and fish ladder just ahead. Got a fishing pole? Here's the place to bait your hook.

3. There's a rocky, weedy path that winds around the southern edge of the river. Be careful! Climb the stairs to the Union Street bridge. Cross the street at Union and Sixth. You'll see a statue of lumber baron Perry Hannah on the corner. (To avoid the river edge walk, just head across the parking lot to the corner of Sixth and Union.)

CASS

1

3

WATCH YOUR STEP!

FRONT 5

1

1. Start on the corner of Front and Cass, next to **THE FRANKLIN.** Walk away from the Bay (south) along Cass. Cross State, cross the bridge. Walk around the bridge railing (in front of **FIREFLY**) and down the stairs to the boardwalk.

4

PERRY HANNAH made his fortune about 150 years ago by cutting down trees and selling them for lumber. He built the biggest house in town, on the corner of Sixth and Pine. The house was made by hand — nope, no power tools as there was no electricity then.

BOARDMAN FISH WEIR

Every fall, thousands and thousands of female salmon come in from the Bay to the river where they were born. They make a little nest in the gravel, lay their eggs, cover up the nest with more gravel … and die. The weir captures these salmon before they lay their eggs. Too many dead salmon make for a very stinky city. The captured fish are used for human food, cat food and bait.

The DNA gives free tours of the weir.

SIXTH

WADSWORTH

UNION

4. Get off the Sixth Street sidewalk and head down to the river. There's a path through the woods that will take you a couple of blocks to Wadsworth. Turn right (north) and follow Wadsworth to Front. Cross the street and turn right (east) on Front. Walk on the sidewalk until you see the new pedestrian bridge. It's right next to **J&S HAMBURGER**. Cross the bridge. You're now in the Warehouse District. Get some lunch here, check out the Boardman River Fish Weir or make yourself a cookie jar at **HANDZ ON ART**.

FRONT

UNION

HALL

5. To get back to where you started, follow the path along the north side of the river. Go under the bridge to cross Union, then up the stairs. Stay on Union until you're on the other side of the river, then follow the sidewalk (west) along the river. Sometimes you can see the female salmon laying their eggs here. Use the crosswalk behind **KILWIN'S** and you're back on Front. Take a left and the corner of Front and Cass is straight ahead.

5

TEENTOWN

TC

bike

There are over 60 miles of TART trails connecting the TC area and Leelanau County. A good day-ride for young blood starts on the trail that runs along the beach in TC and heads 17 miles north to Suttons Bay. Plenty of spots for lunch up there before turning around. No hills, but it's generally downhill all the way back to TC. Groomed in winter for skiing and fatbikes. Check out **TraverseTrails.org** for more info.

Rent a bike downtown at the **River Outfitters**, **Paddle TC** or **City Bike Shop**.

Paddle

Start your tour of the Bay by renting at Clinch Park's **Paddle TC**, or head over to **The River Outfitters** in the parking lot across from the Open Space. Both spots offer kayaks, canoes, paddleboards, floats and tubes.

play

There are classic arcade games at **The Coin Slot** on East Front Street. $7 for an hour or $10 for the whole day.

---

unmistakable clamor of a 17-foot Grumman canoe being wrapped like a bow-tie around a birch tree. ¶ "What

Open Space

The **Open Space** is the big, treeless area next to the Clinch Marina and West End Beach—perfect for Frisbees and kites. Get everything you need right inside the front door at **Toy Harbor** on Front Street.

volleyball

There are three, sand volleyball courts at West End Beach, and plenty of opportunities for a pick-up game. Need a ball? Get one at **Boyne Country Sports**. They have bikinis, too.

Yoga

Think you can chew gum and walk at the same time? How about yoga on a paddleboard? Sign up for a class at **Paddle TC, Yen Yoga** or **The River Outfitters**.

jet ski

If you must make all that noise, these are available for rental on the beach at the **Bayside Resort**.

parasail

To fly over the Bays alone or with your buds, get your parents to check out the rates at **Grand Traverse Parasail, East Bay Parasail** or **Traverse Bay Parasail**.

Maritime

Walk down Clinch Park beach, then around the corner in front of the Bayshore Resort, and you'll see the **Great Lakes Maritime Academy** dock and pier ahead. There are only seven of these training centers in the US, and this is the only one located on fresh water. The Academy's training ship was once an ocean submarine surveillance vessel, built to tow sonar arrays for tracking Soviet submarines during the Cold War. The Academy also has a sailing fleet of Flying Scots, and the team participates in regattas across the country.

There's a tunnel next to the Bayshore Resort that crosses under the Parkway and drops you off on Front Street next to cupcake heaven, **Morsels. Peace, Love and Little Donuts** plus the **Traverse City Guitar Company** are nearby.

Disc golf

You'll need a ride to get to TC's two parks. The closest one is at **Hickory Hills** on the west side of town. **Mt. Holiday**, on the far east side of town, also has a course — and a zipline. **Tilley's Party Store** has a good selection of discs if you forgot yours — or if your dog chewed up your old one.

Skateboard

TC opened a 25,000 square-foot skate park at the **Civic Center** in 2001. Public outcry about boarder degeneracy led to a 12-foot chain-link corral. Times have changed and the fences are gone. The park is tolerant of all ages and provides a pleasant, shady place to sit and watch the show. No fee.

While you're there, check out the Indian bent tree trail marker. It was made about 150 years ago and points the way to Mackinaw City.

To walk there from downtown, take State Street (east) all the way to the end. Use the school cross-walk at Garfield. The Civic Center is on the other side. Soft-serve ice cream is available down on the corner of Front and Garfield at **Bardon's**.

relax

Just want to people-watch, read a book or text your friends? **Brew** is the closest thing TC has to a college coffee shop — and it's pretty, darn close. For outdoor lounging, get a hammock at **Create TC Lounge** and hang it between the pines at the beach. You won't be the only one.

BIKES, BEERS, BOATS, AND MORE BEERS.

ADULT DOWNTOWN FUN

On THE RIVER OUTFITTERS KaBrew tour, you'll cycle, paddle, and sweat from brewery to brewery—there's no better way to earn your pint! With four stops on the tour, this one is not for the faint of liver.

For a more tight-knit spin on pubhopping, book a ride with TC CYCLE PUB. Their Circle Cycle, for 4-6 riders, and Cycle Pub, for 8-14, are available for charter to local bars and breweries. You can choose where you want to carouse, or ask your trusty navigator to steer you in the right direction!

If you're not the sort to drink while you exercise (or exercise while you drink), you can rent a kayak, paddleboard, or bicycle from PADDLE TC in Clinch Park. Explore more than sixty miles of TART Trails, or pilot your craft across the West Bay or down the Boardman River!

Can't get enough yoga? If you really want to test your balance, try a Stand Up Paddle Board (SUP) yoga class with YEN YOGA. These courses are offered mornings July 1st through Labor Day. Stretching in the beautiful East Bay, you're sure to feel one with nature!

dove for the nearest tent, leaving me and the last man knocking heads when both of us bent over to select just

GO OUTSIDE AND GET SOME COLOR.

TRAVERSE BAY PARASAILING, at the Sugar Beach Resort, offers single, double, and triple parasail rentals. Catching the wind over the waters of Grand Traverse Bay, you'll experience a one-of-a-kind view of Traverse City, Leelanau, and Old Mission Peninsula. When you land, if you're still hungry for adventure, you can rent a jet ski at a discounted rate!

Do you ever wonder what lives beneath the surface of Grand Traverse Bay? Find out on a diving trip with SCUBA NORTH! They sell snorkeling and diving gear, and provide beginner and advanced PADI Open Water Diver courses—certifications valid anywhere in the world!

The future is now! GREAT LAKES FLYBOARD rents and sells water-powered jetpacks, and provides lessons and instructor certification. Meet them at Clinch Park Beach, or—since they'll meet you at any lake in Michigan—soar over the body of water of your choice. Just don't expect a dry landing!

Want to rent a power boat or sailboat? SAIL & POWER BOAT RENTAL has them both, with a fleet of more than forty vessels to choose from! You can have your boat delivered to you, or embark on your very own nautical adventure from their West Bay location.

If you'd like to catch dinner while you're out on the water, try DAYDREAMER FISHING CHARTERS. Grab five friends, and book a four or eight-hour trip into East or West Grand Traverse Bay to catch Lake Trout, Coho Salmon, Whitefish, Walleye, and more!

If you want to try waterskiing or wakeboarding, ACTION WATER SPORTS offers watersports clinics for novices, and for those looking to improve their technique. Book a class with friends, or stop by the pro shop for all the gear you need to tear up some waves!

No sun? No problem! Grab your skates and head over to the THIRLBY FIELD ice skating rink on 14th and Pine. Or, if the weather's too brutal, skate indoors at HOWE ICE ARENA, where you can rent skates if you don't have your own. Just remember the hot cocoa!

Never skied before? The Kiwanis-Record Eagle Ski School at MT. HOLIDAY is the perfect place to learn! And if you're an old pro, head on over to HICKORY HILLS to check out their eight runs over two and a half miles of trails!

If you don't have the balance for skiing, get snug in a TIMBERLEE HILLS inner tube and go soaring down the slopes! The best part? They've got a rope tow to bring you back up to the top of the hill without breaking a sweat!

Don't let the winter weather keep you from hitting the trails! RUNNING FIT, downtown Traverse City's one-stop running gear shop, hosts a Bigfoot 5k and 10k snowshoe race every winter. Think you can break thirty with snowshoes on? There's only one way to find out!

DOWNTOWN
WALKING TOUR

TC
14

TOUR DETAILS
ON THE FOLLOWING PAGES

Traverse City in the late 1800s. Notice that the railroad became the Parkway.

to whisper a plan. The three of us would talk our way down to the river's edge using angry and pretend voices,

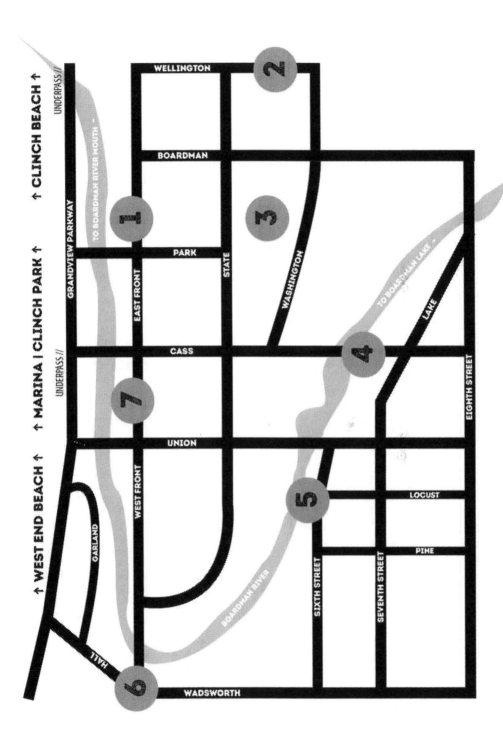

1 RIVER'S END

We're starting our tour east on Front Street, in front of the Grand Traverse Pie Company's Community Shop. Mike and Denise Busley, TC natives, learned to bake pie in California, then brought their knowledge home, opening the first store in 1996. They now own or franchise 16 stores in Michigan and Indiana. But there's something really special going on here: this Community Shop gives 100% of its profits to the Grand Traverse Regional Community Foundation for improving the quality of children's lives in TC's local community. Cheers to Mike and Denise!

Turn left out of the Pie Co., cross Park Street and continue down East Front into the River's End district. Notice the tiny brick building next to the parking deck? Les Biederman and Bill Kiker built their first TC radio control console by hand in 1939 and started broadcasting as WTCM a year later. Biederman was one of TC's most important true-believers. Not only did he bring the news to Northern Michigan, but he pushed for major expansions to Munson Hospital and led the way to higher education opportunities in TC as the

Mapleware
Lunch Set

Here's something you outdoor folk will like immensely—suitable for numberless occasions, but specially for serving your lunches on motor trips, at picnics, camping parties, yachting, etc.

Sugar Maple Dishes will carry any foods—hot, cold, semi-liquid. Each carton contains:

6 Dinner Plates—2 Long Platters
2 Deep Salad Dishes
6 Medium Side Plates
6 Butter or Salt Dishes
12 Sanitary Spoons or Spreaders
1 Table Cover—48 x 60 inches (wood fibre)
6 Large Napkins (wood fibre)

Dispenses with weight and dishwashing. Retail price, 35c. the set; 3 sets, $1.00. Trial sets on receipt of price.

THE OVAL WOOD DISH COMPANY

founder of Northwestern Michigan College.

River's End extends all the way down to where Front joins the Parkway. Its hodgepodge of building models reflects the diversity of its wares: art galleries, pastry shops, tattoos, cigars, a head shop, pizza, food trucks, people and dog grooming, fine dining, yoga and almost every single area title and mortgage broker has a place to call home. River's End doesn't get much attention from the Downtown Development Authority, but its low-slung river vibe is totally worth checking out.

2 BIG HOUSES

Turn right onto Wellington Street and walk one block. The large house on the corner of Wellington and State is the old home of John Parsons, who with Frank Stulen were the first in the US to use computer methods to solve machining problems. In 1948, their TC company was awarded a government contract to make tapered wings for military aircraft. Both MIT and IBM were subcontractors. Stulen and colleague Al Balfour went on to form the Computer Center,

crap-in-the-pants fishermen we were. ¶ Near as we could tell, it was probably a raccoon, or maybe just the

developing the first medical billing software in the country.

On the next block, on the other side of the street, you'll see the Wellington Inn and Bed & Breakfast. This house was built by W.C. Hull, the son of the inventor of the Oval Wood Dish, a kind of Tupperware of the early 1900s. An infamous shoot-out took place here in 1998, resulting in the death of a police officer. The Oval Wood Dish Company was the largest employer in the area, with 9-hour workdays and a $1.44 a day wage. The house across the street was built by Hull's father.

Take a right on Washington Street and enjoy the Victorian and Queen Anne mansions. Former state representative Jason Allen lives here, as do many other scions of TC.

Also worth noting is the Indian trail marker tree near the corner of Washington and Boardman. It points towards an ancient burial mound that long pre-dated the arrival of the first settlers. The mound was leveled, and is now the site of the County Courthouse. The tan house behind the marker tree is supposedly the oldest in TC.

3 CHURCH AND STATE

Continue down Washington Street, crossing at Boardman. The County Courthouse has dominated this corner since 1852, but that structure burned down and the one you see now didn't open until 1900. William Jennings Bryan once lectured from the front steps. In front of the Courthouse you'll find a zinc Civil War monument, a cannon, a time capsule, Spanish-American and World War I monuments and a statue celebrating the friendship between Mtskheta, Georgia, and Grand Traverse. Almost demolished in 1984,

the Courthouse was saved by the actions of concerned citizens, including Larry Hardy, for whom the downtown parking deck is named.

The Park Place Hotel, on your right, was built in 1873, then sold to lumber barons Perry

Hannah and Tracy Lay. They began tearing down the old hotel just weeks before the Great Depression began, and finished up a year later. At its grand re-opening in 1930, it was the tallest building on TC — it's still the tallest building in TC. The Park Place is a federally recognized lighthouse. The beacon at the top used to swirl around and project its rays for 25 miles. These days, the light is diminished and only points to the Bay.

Farther along Washington Street are several of the city's oldest churches, including the domed Central Methodist building across the street on Cass. For 35 years, this church has hosted a "Messiah" concert and sing-along in December.

The Congregational and Presbyterian churches were incorporated several years ago to form wings of the Robert P. Griffin Hall of Justice.

Notice the building called Ladies Library on Cass next to the church. Founded in 1869, it was one of the first monuments to civilization (education) in the area — long before the Carnegie Library, the opera houses and the Courthouse. Susan B. Anthony and Elizabeth Cady Stanton campaigned there for women's suffrage.

4 MIDTOWN

Take a left on Cass and walk to the end of the block (all the way to Lake Street) and the campus of Hagerty Insurance. Frank Hagerty began his insurance business very modestly, selling door to door in the '50s. But he had a big idea, and with the help of a couple of small loans, he and his wife, Louise, started a specialty insurance company for classic wooden boats. Genius! Hagerty is now the largest insurer of classic cars and boats in the world, and one of the largest employers in the area. The showcase on the corner always displays some kind of classic fantasy.

The Old Town Playhouse is a half-block down on Eighth Street.

Head right on Lake Ave. and you're in the Midtown District, very popular with locals for its remarkable variety of eateries and watering holes.

To continue the tour, take Lake Avenue right (west) to the corner of Union Street.

5 OLD TOWN

Old Town is so-named because it was the first area to commercialize during the lumber boom. Right in the center of converging rail lines, it was a muddy, mosquito-infected triangle of manure and sooty skies. But lumberjacks needed to eat and drink and sleep, plus other things, and this is where they did that. Novotny's Saloon (formerly Dill's, now Blue Tractor) opened in 1886 and served customers until Prohibition shut it down in the '20s. Brady's Bar, often called the oldest in TC, didn't actually get its start until the '40s.

Lumber baron Perry Hannah, whose diminutive statue stands on the corner of Union and Sixth, built his palace on Sixth Street (now the Reynolds-Jonkoff Funeral Home) only 50 feet from the railroad tracks. After the lumber boom ended, Hannah donated the riverbank across from his house for a park and the Carnegie Library. He gave St. Francis, a Catholic school, and the Traverse City Golf and Country Club the land they occupy today. An enlightened man, he also donated the property for the Beth El synagogue, said to be the oldest synagogue in the US still in service to its members.

Continue down Sixth Street to Wadsworth. Most of the

propped up against a tree had simply toppled over. Nobody really believed it was the Dogman, which has to

homes along these blocks were built under Hannah's supervision for the TC elite. This is still the case, although the neighborhood really gives back on Halloween when these few blocks dress up big-time for massive crowds of spooks and witches.

6 WEST END & WAREHOUSE DISTRICT

From Sixth Street, turn right on Wadsworth and follow that to Front Street. Once an eyesore of car lots and failed construction sites, major improvements were made to this part of the city in 2015. Specialty grocery, kitchen and wine stores, a pet store, a fly fishing shop, another Grand Traverse Pie Company, many great sandwich shops and restaurants North Peak and Little Bohemia anchor TC's West End on Front.

Crossing Front and continuing down Hall defines the Warehouse District, the fastest growing area of downtown TC. Clustered around the new Hotel Indigo — there's a roof-top bar with the best view of the Bay — are a series of old buildings re-purposed into salons, saloons, cafes and galleries. Warehouse MRKT houses boutique retail and food under one roof.

Perry Hannah built his first house on Hall, and much of TC's early industry was located here as well. The Candle Factory, on Hall, has made great use of what was the old TC Gas Company.

Take the pedestrian bridge to Front Street to head back downtown, or follow the path along the river to Union Street.

7 DOWNTOWN

Perry Hannah's commercial mark on TC begins on the corner of Union and Front streets. Hannah's clock-tower bank, now the Fifth Third bank, sits on one side. What's left of the old Hannah-Lay Mercantile is opposite (now Boyne Country and others). At one time, the Mercantile was the largest department store north of Grand Rapids. A half-block from the Mercantile, on Union, is the Weaver Building. Back in the old days, women rolled cigars on the second floor. A little farther down is Wilson's Furniture. Originally, the building hosted a skating rink on the third floor. Now, all three floors plus the basement are filled with antiques.

On Front Street, the old Steinberg Opera House has a new marquee. Community efforts refurbished the building in 1985, including

repainting the ceiling with cherubic portraits of important patrons.

On the next block down, the State Theater holds pride of place. Once upon a time (1924), the KKK set off a load of dynamite behind the theater, protesting local Catholics and immigrants.

The Martinek clock on Front once marked the locale of a jewelry store. The workings are original, and the clock must be wound by hand every three days.

READ ALL ABOUT IT

Horizon Books has a huge selection of books about the historical UpNorth.

• • • • • • • • • • • • • •

100 Years from the Old Mission by Al Barnes is short and sweet, with lovely illustrations.

Richard Fidler's *Traverse City, Michigan: A Historical Narrative*, is more comprehensive and has lots of pics.

TC WATERFRONT

If you could go back 100 years and look out over TC's downtown waterfront, you'd wonder how in the world we ever cleaned it up. Logging arrived to TC in 1847, when Capt. Harry Boardman gave his son the funds to build a small sawmill on the mouth of the river that now bears his name. The mill did not thrive, and in 1851, Boardman Sr. sailed into West Bay with a prospective buyer, Perry Hannah. Here, Hannah describes his first glimpse of the area:

" In the first days of May, 1851, I left Chicago on the little schooner Venus, in company with Captain Harry Boardman, a rich old farmer who lived in DuPage county, about five miles southeast of Naperville. Captain Peter Nelson, one of the finest Dane sailors that ever walked the deck of a ship, was master of the little schooner Venus. We had left Chicago on our journey north but two or three days when we met one of those terrible northeast gales, which were always sure to last three full days. We were well down Lake Michigan, and our brave old seaman decided that we must weather out the storm instead of returning, and never a more terrific time did I see in my life than those three days, pounding backward and forward across Lake Michigan.

" As soon as the gale subsided ... we rounded into the Old Mission harbor just as the sun was going down behind the tops of the tall maples. And on the banks of the western side sat perhaps forty or fifty old Indian hunters. I could see with my glass that each one had his pipe in his mouth and they were sitting on the bank watching the movement of our ship, chatting and talking. About the middle of the afternoon we reached our moorings alongside of the little slab dock that was built in the western part of the bay. We soon made our way up to the mill. There we met the captain's son, but all hands were taking a rest. The good natured son had stopped the mill, allowing the hands to go in and have a game of euchre. This made ... Captain Boardman more willing than ever to sell." —from *The Morning Record*, Sunday, December 10, 1899

Hannah bought the mill plus a couple of 100 more acres of land with partners Tracy Lay and "Vinegar" John Morgan for $4,500, and thus began the grand adventure. Over the next 25 years,

seventeenth century a band of French trappers ventured up river, deep into the unbroken forests then known

the population would rise from 300 to 4,000 while 400 million board feet of timber was harvested from the area. More than half the houses built in the northern states used Michigan lumber in their construction in 1867. Fifty years later, the boom was over. Every tree for miles was gone. (Lumberjacks were paid by the stump, so they cut everything.)

But Hannah had built his retirement home in TC, and he had big ideas for keeping the city on the map. Number one was ensuring that folks — like farmers to work all that cleared land — could get here, and that meant a designated stop on the railway. Then, he lobbied the state legislature for the rights to build a new mental hospital. The Northern Michigan Asylum was completed in 1884, bringing professionals to UpNorth and jobs for locals. Other industries followed, like the Oval Wood Dish Company, the Wells-Higman Basket Company and the Potato Implement Company. Now, all TC needed was tourists to fill Hannah's Park Place Hotel.

But how could dirty, industrial TC compete with pristine Petoskey and Harbor Springs? The TC waterfront was a smoky, rat-infested mud-hole and the Boardman River a stinking wash of industrial and human waste. TC needed to clean up its act, and its first response was to remove the trash from the Boardman and dump it into West Bay, making the fish no longer fit to eat. By 1920, the TC economy was also seriously in the dumps. Both industry and farmers were leaving in droves for the population centers in the south and the factories of the burgeoning auto industry.

It was about this time that TC leadership considered a national urban planning movement called City Beautiful. The idea was that beautification projects like parks and scenic views and clean water could actually result in civic virtue. You behave better when your environment looks good.

Roads were paved and sidewalks added. Then, in 1931, TC decided to take back its waterfront. Unable to pass a bond to pay for it, local citizens chipped in. For the one-day effort, businesses provided two workers each, tractors and cranes were volunteered, plus dozens of small trucks and boats. The result was so spectacular that later that year, a bond to fund the clean-up of the Boardman passed without a hitch. The Con Foster Museum (now the Bijou Theater) was added to the waterfront in 1934 as a place to showcase the native population and TC's pioneers.

Con Foster was also one of the original sponsors of the Clinch Park Zoo. Originally built on the mouth of the Boardman, it moved to the area around the museum in 1953, during the building of the Grandview Parkway. In 2007, the zoo was closed and its indigenous animal collection dispersed to refuges around the country. The 500-pound black bear caused the most problems. The Detroit Zoo lent TC a polar bear crate, and seven guys plus a forklift pushed him in. The "Spirit of TC" mini steam-engine locomotive is alive and well at the Buckley Old Engine Show. (See page 51.)

KILL THE RAT!

IN 1924, HELEN CALDWELL, A NATIONALLY KNOWN PIED-PIPER OF VERMIN, WAS BROUGHT TO TC TO SOLVE THE RAT PROBLEM. EVERY RAT TAIL WAS REWARDED WITH A DIME, POISON WAS ENCOURAGED AND WEEKLY TRASH PICK-UPS INSTITUTED CITY-WIDE FOR THE FIRST TIME.

---

only as the land of the Chippewa, now the northern Lower Peninsula. They had the white man's first run-in with

Living the Dream

TOURIST REVENUE CAN MAKE DREAMS COME TRUE FOR ENTREPRENEURS.

Maybe because TC is so far away — way up on the little finger of Michigan's mitten — it's a town that's had to reinvent itself regularly to stay on the map. What to do when you run out of lumber? Start farming. When the bottom falls out of the cherry market? Plant grapes. TC cleaned up its waterfront, bringing in tourism. But how do you make the area attractive to year-round big businesses like Hagerty and Munson Hospital? Well, for one thing, you could make TC the best foodie town north of Chicago.

It was hardly a scheme hatched out in the Chamber of Commerce. In fact, Foodtown TC is more the individual efforts of TC's rugged individualists. One of TC's best restaurants, The Cooks' House, got its start when local Jennifer Blakeslee convinced her kitchen partner, Eric Patterson, to ditch the sweat and glory of Las Vegas for a quiet room of their own. Down-staters, Amanda and Paul Danielson, and Chef Myles Anton of Trattoria Stella and the Franklin, saw an opportunity when The Commons development became a reality and jump-started the area's farm-to table movement. Amical was one of the first to dream that TC's tastes could reach beyond the burger. The popular bistro opened in 1994 with cafeteria-style service. Just in the last year, Gaijin, Mama Lu's and Alliance in the Warehouse District opened their doors and filled up their tables.

"A View of the Bay is Worth Half the Pay" was invented over 100 years ago, but it still holds true today. On the other hand, UpNorth is no rat race and the cost of living is 2% below the US average. Luring full-time professionals away from higher salaries requires creative thinking. One of these was the development of extensive, accessible bike and hiking trails. This Fit TC movement inspired some homegrown apparel industries. Lizzi Lambert of Haystacks started making clothes on her dining room table; she now has 10 stores across the US. Two brothers from Old Mission who owned a kite-boarding shop stamped M 22 on a t-shirt — the rest is history.

Bob Sutherland of Glen Arbor also started in the clothing business, selling t-shirts with the slogan "Life, Liberty, Beaches and Pie" out of the trunk of his car. The brand exploded and Sutherland's Cherry Republic now sells more than 200 products out of five stores. Graceland Fruit in Benzie County formed around the region's iconic fruit. Starting quietly in 1974, it has become one of the world's largest providers of dried, infused fruit.

Some homegrown industries make sense, like internationally renowned Quantum Sails: TC has been turning out professional sailors for as long as there have been sailboats on the Bay. Others, like Britten Banners, make fabric and vinyl banners, and patented display systems for the international market. Paul Britten (founder and CEO) returned to his native Traverse City to build a company that embraces the UpNorth culture

22

And embracing the UpNorth culture is pretty much the whole story. That, and coming up with a product that can survive the bleak, drab, chilly winters. Good ideas come and go, and so do the tourists.

a beast they described as a "loup garou," a werewolf. All but two of the French men had retired early that night,

WORK PLAY WORK PLAY

GOTTA GET STUFF DONE? THESE PLACES ARE GOOD FOR COFFEE, WIFI AND A LITTLE BIT OF PEOPLE-WATCHING.

BREW is hands-down the coolest place in town for doing business, and the steady flow of characters is a pleasant distraction. Open 7 AM to midnight every day.

MORSELS venue is smaller, quieter, and favored by local writers.

MINERVA, at the Park Place, is another quiet spot and good for lunch meetings.

SPACE rents desks by the hour, day and month. Right in downtown on Front Street.

THE TRAVERSE AREA DISTRICT LIBRARY, Woodmere Branch, is a huge, airy structure with views of Boardman Lake. Coffee and food is nearby at the Depot.

If your idea of working (during working hours) requires dark booths and beer, try the **U&I**.

MUNSON HOSPITAL, AREA SCHOOLS, GRAND TRAVERSE RESORT & SPA, TYSON FOOD, HAGERTY AND BRITTEN BANNERS ARE THE BIG EMPLOYERS IN THE AREA, BUT THAT DOESN'T STOP LOCAL RESIDENTS FROM STRIKING OUT ON THEIR OWN. INSURANCE AND THE HOUSING MARKETS ARE STRONG, AS ARE FARMING, BREWERIES AND TECH START-UPS.

HERE'S A SAMPLE:

SILIKIDS: kid-safe, silicone dishware

GROUNDWORK: helping to build a local farm and food economy

ONEUPWEB: digital marketing and strategy

DANCIN' DOGG GOLF: home golf simulator

KEEN TECHNICAL SOLUTIONS: energy efficiency and conservation solutions for the commercial and industrial sectors

PRESS ON JUICE: cold-pressed, unpasteurized juice blends

STRINGS BY MAIL: musician-reviewed strings for all instruments

If you're interested in the Upnorth technology climate, visit **TCNEWTECH.org**. The organization facilitates networking and interaction among technology enthusiasts in northern Michigan.

---

leaving the pair of them alone to keep lookout and to tend to the campfire until dawn. A couple of hours later,

THERE ARE A LOT OF PLACES AROUND THE WORLD THAT SAY, "DON'T LIKE THE WEATHER? JUST WAIT TEN MINUTES." TEN MINUTES SOUNDS ABOUT RIGHT FOR TC, TOO.

Just like on the ocean coasts, Lake Michigan and the Bays moderate land temperatures, which is the one big reason we can grow grapes and cherries. Also, if we've had a long, hot summer, winter will come a little later as the warm water keeps the chill down. Of course, if we experience a long, cold winter, spring will be delayed until the water warms up. Summers are generally hot and dry. Winters can be very snowy. The moisture rising off unfrozen lakes creates what's called lake-effect snow, and around here that averages about 6 feet.

No matter what the season, it's a good idea to watch the radar if you plan to be outside all day. Storms can come up fast. Take for example the famous storm of August 2, 2015, which knocked out power to entire counties for days. Ninety-mile-an-hour straight-line winds blew trees down from Glen Arbor to Old Mission to Yuba to Elk Lake. There had been several thunderstorms that day, and fortunately, few people were out on the water and no one was seriously injured.

 WWW.WUNDERGROUND.COM IS A GREAT APP FOR UP-TO-THE-MINUTE WEATHER WATCHING.

Lake Michigan is the #1 most dangerous of all the Great Lakes. Because of its long, vertical shape and the prevailing westerly winds, dangerous currents can spring up — even on a clear day. Rip currents arise when too much water is forced up onto beaches, particularly those with sandbars. The water has to go somewhere, and when it surges back towards the lake, that's a rip tide. Longshore currents happen frequently on Lake Michigan in the summer because we often experience winds from the south. A longshore current travels parallel to the shore and is mostly destructive to buildings close to the beach and those who like to jump off piers.

If you feel yourself caught in a current, don't panic. FLOAT WITH THE CURRENT, keep your head above water and conserve your energy. Eventually, you'll feel the current diminish and you can swim back to shore. Above all, watch for signs at beaches and get a weather app.

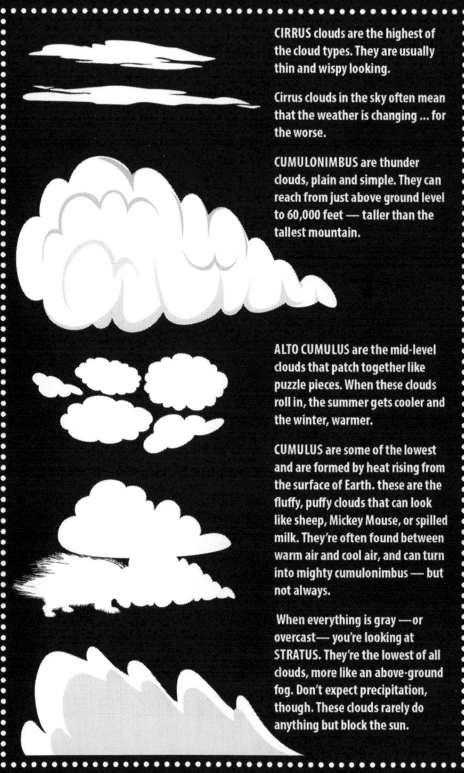

CIRRUS clouds are the highest of the cloud types. They are usually thin and wispy looking.

Cirrus clouds in the sky often mean that the weather is changing ... for the worse.

CUMULONIMBUS are thunder clouds, plain and simple. They can reach from just above ground level to 60,000 feet —— taller than the tallest mountain.

ALTO CUMULUS are the mid-level clouds that patch together like puzzle pieces. When these clouds roll in, the summer gets cooler and the winter, warmer.

CUMULUS are some of the lowest and are formed by heat rising from the surface of Earth. these are the fluffy, puffy clouds that can look like sheep, Mickey Mouse, or spilled milk. They're often found between warm air and cool air, and can turn into mighty cumulonimbus —— but not always.

When everything is gray ——or overcast—— you're looking at **STRATUS.** They're the lowest of all clouds, more like an above-ground fog. Don't expect precipitation, though. These clouds rarely do anything but block the sun.

bleu! —— in the light of the full moon, a wild dog appeared on the trail. The Dogman rose up. The Frenchie

NO WORRIES WHEN IT'S RAINING IN DOWNTOWN TC. THERE ARE PLENTY OF THINGS TO DO FOR ALL AGES.

KIDS

The **STATE THEATER** runs matinees every Tuesday, Thursday and Saturday, all summer long.

Paint some pottery at **HANDZ ON ART**. Or, build a terrarium at **DARLING BOTANICAL**. Both are located in the Warehouse District. Fun for grown-ups, too.

For older kids, a trip to **WILSON ANTIQUES** is almost as good as a museum.

Pick out a game (Pass the Pig is highly recommended) and get some lunch. **BREW** also has games in the back of their coffee house.

CROOKED TREE ARTS CENTER often has programs for kids during the day, and **BLACKBIRD ARTS** on Barlow schedules art classes all year for all ages.

NO SNORING WHEN IT'S POURING DOWNTOWN TC 26

pulled a knife. In the ensuing struggle the part-dog, part-man whatchamacallit lunged for the trapper's throat,

KIDS · FARTHER AFIELD

THE GREAT LAKES CHILDREN'S MUSEUM on M-22 has all sorts of hands-on, fun stuff to do, much of it centered around water. The museum is designed for children 1 – 10 and is open Tuesday through Saturday. You can bring a lunch and eat in the Great Lakes Room.

THE MUSIC HOUSE MUSEUM in Acme focuses on automated instruments, like music boxes and player-pianos. You can take a self-guided tour, or docents are available.

THE G.T. BUTTERFLY AND BUG ZOO is also located in Acme. Take a class or just walk around and look.

THE TRAVERSE DISTRICT AREA LIBRARY on Woodmere has a huge reading room for kids.

If you're downtown, **HORIZON BOOKS** has a huge selection of children's books and activities.

THE DENNOS MUSEUM features hands-on kid activities and exhibits year-around. Open every day.

INCREDIBLE MO'S in Grawn offers bowling, indoor laser tag and video games galore.

INLAND SEAS has terrific hands-on displays and experiential learning activities at the Suttons Bay headquarters.

ADULTS

NO SUNSHINE, NO CRY FOR GROWN-UPS, EITHER.

If you like antiques, **WILSON ANTIQUES** is a downtown mecca. Everything from jewelry to fishing paraphelia to textiles, kitchen items, books, rugs, lamps and, of course, that floor-to-ceiling, mahogany sideboard you've always wanted. Mid-century contemporary items as well. More about antiques on the next page.

Check out **NOLAN'S TOBACCO** in the River's End District. A huge selection of cigars, a walk-in humidor and a full bar where you can smoke in peace.

ROBERTSON'S Hair Center on Union is a real, old-fashioned barbershop. For the hipster, there's a handsome establishment, **BULLDOGS**, on Cass.

For the ladies, there are salons all around the downtown area. Get a manicure at **IMPRES** Salon and **TRUE ESSENCE** Salon, both on Front.

Get your fortune told at **HIGHER SELF** on Front.

Feeling impulsive? American- and Japanese-style tattoos are available at **FRONT STREET TATTOO**. They also do removals. Guest artists in the summer.

Artist Shannon Doah of **ACORN TATTOO** does intricate folkloric images with real style. Also on Front Street, consults are by appointment only.

KNIT NORTH on Union has a beautiful space for passing some knit / purl time.

For more options, the **NORTHERN EXPRESS** lists activities every week in its free publication.

---

but with one deft move of the blade, the Frenchman slashed the monster's ear clean off, sending it screaming

ANTIQUES
and other
SHOPPING

Antiques

WILSON ANTIQUES || four floors in downtown TC plus another location in Acme

WALT AND SUSAN'S OLD BARN ANTIQUES || dolls, china and "automobilia" || Nelson Road on Old Mission Peninsula

ROLLING HILLS ANTIQUES & ART || American furniture and other treasures in an old barn || Barney Road, west of TC

JUNKERS CORNER ANTIQUES || they can fix up whatever you find || Woodmere Avenue, TC

BAY WEST ANTIQUES || multiple vendors — furniture, jewelry, clothing || Garland Street in TC

ANTIQUE EMPORIUM || silver, coins, glass, paper, "tobacciana" || West Blue Star Drive, TC

GREY WOLF CREEK || Light fixtures and lamps || in the Warehouse District, TC

CHERRYLAND ANTIQUE MALL & CONSIGNMENT CENTER || 55,000 square feet || South Garfield Avenue, TC

RICKMAN'S ANTIQUE FURNITURE || American furniture || Fern Street in TC

FURNITURE MASTERS || furniture || LaFranier Road, west of TC

RE * CLEC * TIA || a consignment store full of furniture, lots of mid-century contemporary || South Garfield Avenue in TC

Other Shopping

NAWBIN || beads, rocks, fossils, and supplies || Front Street in TC

THE CANDLE FACTORY & HOME ELEMENTS || candles on one side, kitchen textiles and implements on the other || in an old factory across the street from the Indigo Hotel

MARY'S KITCHEN PORT || interesting, useful kitchen items and food || West Front Street

Clothing shops come and go in TC, but **ELLA'S** and **CALI'S** have staying power. Both shops also carry home items || downtown on Front Street

into the night. ¶ Hurrying back to camp, the man became lost, wandering in circles until the morning. With his

HOW TO
make fudge

BY JODEE TAYLOR

IT'S ALL ABOUT TEMPERATURE. AND PRACTICE. ADD CHOCOLATE.

Dave Murdick has been making fudge for 36 years. His dad is Doug Murdick, patriarch of Murdick's Fudge with locations, well, everywhere.

Dave Murdick says the basic ingredients for fudge are simple — heavy cream, sugar, maybe some corn syrup — so you may as well go for quality, especially when it comes to chocolate.

Heat the cream and sugar to around 235 degrees, stirring constantly. Murdick uses a copper pan, which looks really cool, but any heavy-bottom saucepan will work. The 235-degree mark is ballpark. For instance, the more chocolate you add, the lower the temperature will have to be. "A quarter of a degree can make a difference," Murdick says. And that's where the practice comes in. You may get all the way to the end of the process, when you pour the fudge into its final pan, before you realize it's too creamy. Raise the temperature on the next batch, Murdick advises.

The biggest mistake most home fudge-makers make is again temperature-related. After the fudge reaches the 235-ish-mark, it needs to cool. Murdick pours the liquid fudge onto marble slabs — again, it looks cool, but it actually serves a purpose because marble is a cooling surface — and lets it cool to room temperature. Home cooks can cool it in the pan or pour their fudge out on a cookie sheet to cool it more quickly.

Then whip it, whip it good. Murdick uses a long-handled paddle, but he says a home confectionaire can use a spoon. It's tough work; the fudge needs to be stirred/whipped for about 15 to

Dave Murdick whips the fudge.

20 minutes. (Murdick's biceps are stunning.) Near the end of the whipping stage is when you add the nuts, cherries, marshmallows, what have you.

Keep whipping as the fudge turns creamier but once it gets "nice and fluffy," STOP. If you overwhip, it may not set up. Murdick knows to stop when the fudge stops moving on his marble slab. "You have to watch it," he says. "As soon as it changes, stop and pour it into your pan." Let it sit for another five minutes before slicing.

The perennial bestselling flavor at Murdick's Fudge is chocolate.

 **FOR AS LONG AS ANYONE CAN REMEMBER, TC TOURISTS HAVE BEEN CALLED FUDGIES.**

The National Cherry Festival

IT'S 1928. THE LUMBER BOOM IS OVER AND INDUSTRY IS PICKING UP AND LEAVING TOWN.

Farmers are leaving, too, drawn to salaried jobs in the south that don't depend on the weather. It's a good thing that TC has always grown a healthy crop of True Believers. One of these was Frank Hamilton, who had the idea of creating a highway linking UpNorth to Detroit, Chicago and Miami. It's gone now, but here and there throughout the state, you'll see signs of what was called the Dixie Highway. New roads and cars changed everything UpNorth. Tourists no longer arrived by boat to remain cloistered in all-inclusive resorts for weeks. Now, they traveled in the family car and they wanted motels, restaurants and attractions. The Cherry Festival was invented to take advantage of this new era. In 1928, the year of the first festival, 30,000 people showed up for parades, concerts and boat races on the Bay. Two years later, the Festival committee decided to fudge things a bit, setting the Festival start-date back to the first week in July. Unfortunately, cherries are never ripe at that time and most of the fruit consumed at the Festival these days comes from Washington state.

Although locals complain of the noise and crowds, the Festival is good fun for the young at heart. This year, the U.S. Air Force Thunderbirds return for the 92st Festival Airshow. Concerts feature The Tenderloins and Cole Swindell. The big parade — the Cherry Royale — is scheduled for July 8.

IN 2016, JUST BEFORE THE FESTIVAL, BLUE ANGEL'S MARINE CAPT. JEFFREY KUSS WAS KILLED WHEN HIS F/A-18 HORNET CRASHED AT THE GREAT TENNESSEE AIR SHOW. SINCE THEN, NAVAL AIR FORCES, PACIFIC, HAVE ELIMINATED THE SPLIT-S MOVE FROM THE STUNT LINE-UP.

---

the undergrowth and collapsed before a line of ghostly faces staring down the pipes of their muskets cocked and

NATIONAL WRITERS SERIES

The Writers Series was established in 2009 by *New York Times* bestselling author and Traverse City native Doug Stanton, his wife, Anne Stanton, a former journalist who now heads the Writers Series, and Grant Parsons, a civil rights attorney. The idea for the nonprofit came after Doug began his nationwide book tour in 2008 for *Horse Soldiers*. He was startled to find several things: little face-to-face interaction between authors and the general public, a waning interest in young writers to pursue their craft, and a massive shift in the bookselling industry to online, anonymous sales. He created the Writers Series to spark meaningful conversation with authors and to support the next generation of writers.

NWS also offers year-around programs and writing classes for youth.

2017 events include presentations by author MARY ROACH in June; BRUCE CAMERON in July; TOM STANTON in August; ALICE WATERS in September.

Traverse City Film Festival

The TC Film Festival got its start by the seat of its pants in the late spring of 2005 when Michael Moore and a dozen locals gathered around a table at Amical and divvied up everything from fund-raising to copy-writing to popcorn machines. Just a couple of months later, more than 50,000 people showed up for "Just Great Movies." Today it's nearly three times that big and requires an army of volunteers.

But in 2005, the State Theater was a bit of a wreck. It was owned by Grand Traverse Rotary Charities, who'd been trying to off-load it for years. In 2007, they gifted the theater to the Film Festival. Renovations began immediately and, in 2013, the State was awarded the #1 spot as Best Movie Theater in the World by the Motion Picture Association of America.

This year, the Festival runs from July 25 – 30 and features independent films and documentaries from around the world. Don't miss the giant, inflatable screen and free movies at the Open Space.

In Memory of Lori Hall Steele

---

ready to fire. Leading the fire squad was the second man from the fire the night before, his head wrapped in a

Lithograph by Tajin Robles

ART TOWN
TC
32

THE GREAT RECESSION HAD LITTLE EFFECT ON TC, EXCEPT FOR ITS ARTISTS. TWO-DIMENSIONAL ARTISTS SUFFERED THE MOST, WITH GALLERY CLOSINGS, LOSS OF PUBLIC FUNDING AND A RELUCTANT MARKET. IT'S NO BETTER TODAY THAN IT WAS IN 2008.

bandage, wet with a crimson stain over where the ear should have been. ¶ Years later, in 1987, at a lumber

Until 2003, local public funding nationwide for the arts stayed ahead of inflation and even grew slightly during the early years of the Great Recession. But over the next four years, the Michigan Council for the Arts and Cultural Affairs lost half its budget. Even worse, funding for art is in a 25-year decline of private support as philanthropy moves to knowledge-based charities. Today, there are very few two-dimensional artists in the area who can make a living from their work.

DENNOS
MUSEUM CENTER

The Dennos, on the campus of Northwestern Michigan College, opened in 1991. The museum has a permanent collection of over 2,000 works, and one of the largest Inuit collections in the world. There are also three (soon to be five) galleries for traveling exhibits and a large (soon to be larger) sculpture garden. The Interactive Discovery Gallery offers hands-on experiences of art and science for children. A nearly 15,000-foot expansion project is scheduled to be completed in 2017.

CROOKED TREE
ARTS CENTER

Crooked Tree got its start almost 50 years ago in the basement of the Petoskey Public Library. It has grown to provide services to more than 50,000 individuals every year. In 2015, Crooked Tree merged with the TC ArtCenter and took over the old Carnegie Library on Sixth Street. Crooked Tree hosts exhibitions, juried events and classes.

PUBLIC ART IN TC

The big idea of big art in TC began with local artist and former NMC Art Department chair Paul Welch. Works come from the collection at the Dennos, the Detroit Institute of Art, and local artists. Printing is done by Britten Studios.

Art classes are available at the following: **Crooked Tree Arts Center, Painting with a Twist, Blackbird Arts, Glass Artz, Northwestern Michigan College, Interlochen Center for the Arts.**

Galleries

There's no business harder to get going than a gallery, but TC has a few that have weathered the recession.

Michigan Artists Gallery: A wonderful place with regional photography, landscape paintings and contemporary folk art.

Courtyard Fine Art: Original, pre-1900 maps and woodblock prints.

Peninsula Studios: Watch artist Debra Sanborn create her colorful landscapes.

Higher Art Gallery: A fine arts gallery with a diverse range of artists and mediums.

Art & Soul Gallery: Painting, prints, jewelry and tchotchkies in the Arcade downtown.

Bella Galleria: Floor to ceiling paintings to ogle while you enjoy your prime rib.

Shoestring Gallery: chainsaw carvings, ceramic body parts, pinball machines, oh my.

94.7 CLASSICAL RADIO
91.5 NEWS RADIO
GET THE APP AT ITUNES

34

Interlochen Center for the Arts

Back in the late 1920s, Joe Maddy had a dream of a world-class orchestra of high school musicians. When a failed resort on the shores of two small lakes in Interlochen appeared on the market, Maddy moved in. The summer camp opened in 1928 with 22 faculty members and 115 students. Incredibly, the camp survived the Great Depression and, in 1960, Chicago philanthropist Clement Stone donated the seed money for renovation and construction. Weatherized buildings meant that the camp could operate during the winter, and thus was born the Interlochen Arts Academy, the highest profile arts boarding school in the world.

Also a first-class school for academics — more young people have received the Presidential Scholars in the Arts awards than any other school in the nation — students can major in Creative Writing, Dance, Theater, Motion Picture Arts, Visual Arts, Songwriting and, beginning this summer, Fashion Design. However, Interlochen is best known for its music, and many of its students go on to professional careers in the industry.

Enrollment at Interlochen Arts Academy hovers around 500, about three times larger than most boarding schools. During the summer, the Arts Camp student body swells to about 2,500.

Notable Interlochen alumni include: Josh Groban, Felicity Huffman, Norah Jones, Larry Page, Tom Hulce, Jewel Kilcher, Jackson Rathbone, Mike Wallace, Betty Who, Joel McNeely, Rufus Wainwright and Sean Young.

High school performances through-out the year are worth attending as these are some of the most talented students in the world.

Interlochen Presents schedules main-event performances from June through August. This year's line-up includes:

JUNE 1 || ZZ Top with Austin Hanks
JUNE 29 || Paul Shaffer & The World's Most Dangerous Band
JULY 3 || The Capital Steps
JULY 8 || Shen Wei Dance Arts
JULY 12 || Tracy Atkins
JULY 19 || Diana Ross
JULY 22 || Amos Lee
AUGUST 17 Jethro Tull
Go to tickets.interlochen.org for the full schedule.

forest. They cornered the animal and upon clobbering it with a stick. The monster stood and came forth with a

Traverse Symphony Orchestra

The story of the TC Symphony begins with Elnora Milliken. The daughter of Italian immigrants, she began life in a mining town in Minnesota. Her talent as a violinist gained her acceptance to the prestigious music department at Northwestern University in Chicago. After graduating, she moved to Detroit, working in the public school system as an instructor. Then she met TC native John Milliken (brother to Michigan's longest serving governor, William Milliken) and they married in 1944.

Elnora didn't take the move to the boondocks of UpNorth sitting down. Like the other TC True Believers, she created a community orchestra by calling upon local professionals and asking each of them for $100. Just before their first concert in 1952, the *Record-Eagle* ran a story titled: "Musical Housewives Play in N.W. Symphony Orchestra."

While there may still be "housewives" playing violins, the TC Symphony became a professional orchestra in 1985, employing 60 contracted members. Kevin Rhodes has been the Music Director since 2001. The group has been perennially in search of a permanent space.

A biography of Elnora Milliken is available through the TC Symphony offices.

The Traverse Symphony Orchestra schedule runs from fall to spring. See the events on page 138 and at traversesymphony.org.

COMMUNITY MUSIC

ENCORE WINDS performs several times a year and encourages new membership or all ages.

NORTHWESTERN MICHIGAN COLLEGE has many community performance ensembles, including big band, concert band and several choirs.

TC SINGS! is a member of the Ubuntu Choirs Network and welcomes all voices and cultures.

PARALLEL 45 THEATRE

TC's only professional theater company, Parallel 45 brings nationally recognized theater artists to UpNorth. Performances are at the TC Opera House and the former InsideOut Gallery in the Warehouse District. The company also offers seasonal workshops, an intern program and, coming this year, the New Opera Project.

SUMMER SCHEDULE:
"45 Plays for 45 Presidents" runs July 19 – July 23.

OLD TOWN PLAYHOUSE

Elnora Milliken was also the force behind the Playhouse inauguration in 1960. Since then, nearly 300 productions have crossed its stages, every one of which was produced, designed, built, costumed, ushered and performed by volunteers.

The Playhouse also has a youth education program, the OTP Young Company. Performance and educational activities for preschool through secondary school include mainstage performances during December, June and August and classes and workshops throughout the year.

SEE THEIR SCHEDULE AT OLDTOWNPLAYHOUSE.COM.

---

horrible man-like scream. The story goes that every logger's hair turned white and their faces stayed ashen with

MUSICTOWN
TC

YOU'VE SEEN THE DUNES, NOW HEAR THE TUNES – BY TOM CARR

Just down the road apiece from Traverse City (about 25 minutes southwest by car) is a town that's nearly synonymous with music and the arts: Interlochen.

We'll get to that shortly, after we see that TC itself is no slouch in the music department for a city of its size. You can find several styles any given week here. Bluegrass, folk, roots music, jazz, country, rock and some friendly and lively open mics. This small town even has a symphony orchestra and some homegrown artists who are making major notes on a national scale.

A lot of musicians call this area home, though most have to tour outside the area, teach or do something else in order to make a go of it. Still, there are some standout musicians in these parts.

The small venues —— restaurants and bars, brew pubs, wineries —— are too numerous to list, and have increased, some of it along with the boom in microbreweries and cider houses. Summertime, when the fudgies flock to the north and lawns and patios open up, you can have different live music with your dinner or drink just about every night.

fear for the rest of their days. ¶ Then there's the story of the old farmer in Buckley, who, after working into the

Some of the downtown-area places that have kept musicians in pocket money for the longest include Front Street's **LITTLE BOHEMIA** and **POPPYCOCK'S**; and **UNION STREET STATION** (I'm not going to tell you what street that's on). The **MILLIKEN AUDITORIUM** at Northwestern Michigan College often hosts traveling acts and **STREETERS** on the south side of town often hosts national country, metal or rock acts.

If you're looking for bluegrass/country/roots, look for a chance to hear artists like **JOE WILSON**, who is pure Nashville when he plays steel guitar, but can also play Texas swing or rock-a-billy on an archtop. You can even hear him laying down some Chick Corea on the Dobro in an online video. He's played with several bands including the True Falsettos and the Joe Wilson Trio.

There are also a few musical festivals here and in the larger region, depending on the time of year. **THE MICROBREW AND MUSIC FESTIVAL** marries suds and sounds twice each year, winter and summer, in Traverse City. The **NATIONAL CHERRY FESTIVAL** hosts famous legacy and tribute bands each summer and the **TRAVERSE CITY FILM FESTIVAL** often has local musicians playing between movies.

If you're looking for a northern taste of the Mississippi Delta, check out **K JONES AND THE BENZIE PLAYBOYS**, with their zydeco/cajun/creole sound. From acoustic "lounge funk" to electric jazz to folk rock and jam band music, G-Snacks plays around the area and will be at **TAP ROOT CIDER HOUSE** on Thursdays for the summer. Chanteuse **MIRIAM PICO** is a favorite to all ages and can often be seen at wineries or concert stages (or singing the commercial jingle for Floor Covering Brokers)

Now, that's just a few of the stages and players with followings here and beyond. There's no way we're going to hit all of them, and there are always new artists coming up. In fact, you may even catch some talented budding stars at one of the open mics in town. Or, you may want to tote your own guitar, or accordion or whatever, along and show the room your own chops. For a consistently entertaining one, which leans toward folk, country and bluegrass but lets in other musical styles and miscellaneous acts; check out the Roundup on Thursday nights with host BILL DUNGJEN. It's at the **HAYLOFT INN** on M-72, a few miles west of TC. BLAKE ELLIOTT, whose smoky voice and smooth archtop guitar can be heard gigging around the region, has recently begun hosting a twice-monthly Sunday evening open mic at **STORMCLOUD BREWERY** in Frankfort. For years, she has hosted Open Mic Monday at **LEFT FOOT CHARLEY WINE AND CIDER** at Grand Traverse Commons. That's now hosted by singer/songwriter/guitarist ROB COONROD.

MUSICTOWN

TC

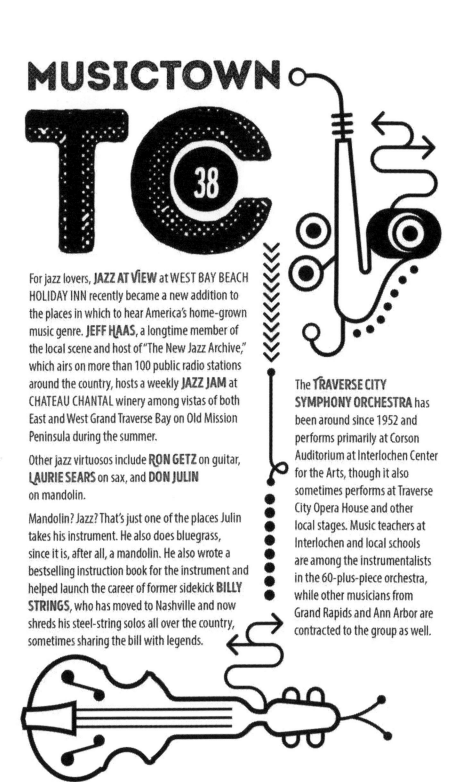

For jazz lovers, **JAZZ AT VIEW** at WEST BAY BEACH HOLIDAY INN recently became a new addition to the places in which to hear America's home-grown music genre. **JEFF HAAS**, a longtime member of the local scene and host of "The New Jazz Archive," which airs on more than 100 public radio stations around the country, hosts a weekly **JAZZ JAM** at CHATEAU CHANTAL winery among vistas of both East and West Grand Traverse Bay on Old Mission Peninsula during the summer.

Other jazz virtuosos include **RON GETZ** on guitar, **LAURIE SEARS** on sax, and **DON JULIN** on mandolin.

Mandolin? Jazz? That's just one of the places Julin takes his instrument. He also does bluegrass, since it is, after all, a mandolin. He also wrote a bestselling instruction book for the instrument and helped launch the career of former sidekick **BILLY STRINGS**, who has moved to Nashville and now shreds his steel-string solos all over the country, sometimes sharing the bill with legends.

The **TRAVERSE CITY SYMPHONY ORCHESTRA** has been around since 1952 and performs primarily at Corson Auditorium at Interlochen Center for the Arts, though it also sometimes performs at Traverse City Opera House and other local stages. Music teachers at Interlochen and local schools are among the instrumentalists in the 60-plus-piece orchestra, while other musicians from Grand Rapids and Ann Arbor are contracted to the group as well.

fright. Strange tracks, like a man's feet, but hairy and with claws, were all around the body. The same tracks

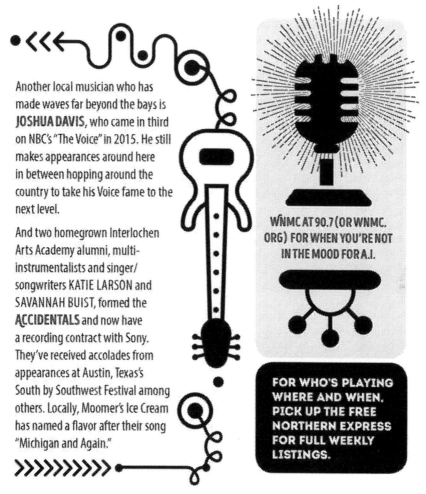

Another local musician who has made waves far beyond the bays is **JOSHUA DAVIS**, who came in third on NBC's "The Voice" in 2015. He still makes appearances around here in between hopping around the country to take his Voice fame to the next level.

And two homegrown Interlochen Arts Academy alumni, multi-instrumentalists and singer/songwriters KATIE LARSON and SAVANNAH BUIST, formed the **ACCIDENTALS** and now have a recording contract with Sony. They've received accolades from appearances at Austin, Texas's South by Southwest Festival among others. Locally, Moomer's Ice Cream has named a flavor after their song "Michigan and Again."

WNMC AT 90.7 (OR WNMC. ORG) FOR WHEN YOU'RE NOT IN THE MOOD FOR A.I.

FOR WHO'S PLAYING WHERE AND WHEN, PICK UP THE FREE NORTHERN EXPRESS FOR FULL WEEKLY LISTINGS.

SO NOW, AS PROMISED, LET'S TAKE A JAUNT DOWN TO INTERLOCHEN (AND NO, THAT'S NOT WHERE THEY MAKE JIGSAW PUZZLES).

INTERLOCHEN CENTER FOR THE ARTS is home to the Interlochen Arts Academy, which attracts top students of the arts from around the world among the woods and lakes. Pop artists Jewel and Norah Jones are among the famous alumni.

It's also home to Kresge open-air and Corson indoor auditoriums. Ever since the Elvis of American marches, John Philip Sousa, conducted here a couple times in the 1930s, the famous and even legendary have made appearances. Count among them Yoyo Ma, Bob Dylan and B.B. King. The big time for top artists to appear is in the summer. That's when the stars hit the Kresge and boaters often anchor in Green Lake behind the stage and listen in. (See more on page 34.)

So you see, if you can't find some good music here in the summer, you might need a Q-tip to clean out your ears. **TC**

were found in 1906, after an old widow confided to friends about the nightmares she was having, in which a

Driving Home from Gigs

JANUARY · MIDNIGHT · NEW YORK
"Hey you guys want to party?" says the cold miniskirted hooker in her fuzzy jacket as John and I load up his Saab after an ... open mic

(GRAND CENTRAL)

1980

Hoot Night audition at a club on 3rd where we waited with other sensitive songwriters and bad comics for our names to be called from the list.
Heckler to comic: "Next! You suck!"
Comic: "Oh... well... Do you know what Steve Martin would say about that if he were here?"
Heckler: "No. Get out. You suck!"

AFTER A REHEARSAL IN A LOFT DOWNTOWN John finds his car double parked in. Rather than blow his horn 'til someone comes, he naps. He wakes to find two suits outside his window. One has a 20 lb. dog food bag; the other has a fat envelope. John slouches lower in the seat.

One summer I tried to leave enough time to fish for an hour on the nearest river to a gig. I never left enough time. Then if I actually saw fish, well, how frustrating was that. Once the jeep sort of slid off the side of the road into the ditch as I pulled out. Then of course there was the late night incident with the beaver.

We are speeding through the mountains between Faenza and Firenze in a Volvo stuffed with the four of us plus amps, accordion, mandolin, and bass protruding into the front seat. Wes brakes after a sharp corner, jumps out and pees off a cliff. At Lamberto's Jazz Club they listened to every note. Fed us and wined us then brought us the grappa then fed us dessert, then took our pictures to go in a book they will publish. Wes somehow knows these narrow roads with no guard rail and I gaze out the back window at little villas that poke out of the rocks and stone bridges over creeks that trickle hundreds of feet below. We aren't in Kansas, or Michigan anymore.

After gigs at the Park Place I would follow the sax player out along Silver Lake and flash my brights if I thought she might fall asleep.

→ see "THE RIVER HOME" J. DENNIS

Canad

pack of dogs that howled at the moon with human screams tried to get into her home. Townsfolk later found

"Driving Home from Gigs" by Glenn Wolff. Glenn Wolff grew up in TC and has worked as an illustrator for the New York Times, the Village Voice, the Central Park Conservancy, and the New York Zoological Society. His work is part of the permanent collection at the Dennos Museum Center.

her dead of a heart attack, a ghoulish expression of fear on her face, and the tracks of the Dogman pressed in

FOODTOWN

TC 42

NO DOUBT ABOUT IT, TC AND AREA HAVE <u>THE BEST FOOD IN THE WORLD</u> SEZ MARIO BATALI: "HANDS DOWN, TRAVERSE CITY IS MY NUMBER ONE DESTINATION, ANY TIME. IF YOU VISIT, YOU'LL UNDERSTAND THERE'S NOTHING THAT'S THIS CLOSE TO SCRATCHING ALL THOSE ITCHES LIKE TUSCANY AND SONOMA... THIS PLACE JUST BECAME A GASTRONOMIC DESTINATION. I'M HERE AS A TESTIMONIAL: TRAVERSE CITY IS REAL AND I LOVE IT. IT'S A REMARKABLE PLACE." [FODOR'S]

EAT TC

INSIDER PICKS FOR THE BEST AREA DINING

the snow outside her open window. ¶ Less than a quarter of a century ago, a Cadillac raccoon hunter named

BREAKFAST

**BLUE HERON 2
CAFE & BAKERY**
hearty, wholesome food
with local ingredients

FRENCHIES FAMOUS
made by scratch with a
"whole lotta love"

PATISSERIE AMI
beignets and eggs Benedict
full bar

THE TOWNE PLAZA
good people-watching
and a "passion for pig"
full bar

BRUNCH

AMICAL
crepes, omelets, French toast,
eggs Benedict
all beautifully presented
brunch only on Sundays
full bar

HARVEST
chicharrones, pulled pork
tacos, falafel
Saturday and Sunday
they also have a food truck
at Little Fleet
full bar

AERIE
dress up for
Sunday buffet with a view
full bar

RED SPIRE BRUNCH HOUSE
crabcake Benedict
red velvet pancakes

LUNCH

AMICAL
where the locals lunch
full bar

THE FRANKLIN
the charcuterie and cheese
board is almost as good
as the view
full bar

FRENCHIES FAMOUS
a pastrami sandwich to
rival even Katz's

GREEN HOUSE CAFE
if you've got no time and just
want a bowl of soup

POPPYCOCK'S
one of the oldest downtown
restaurants and still
going strong
full bar

MAMA LU'S
one single delicious taco!
can be very cozy
full bar

TRATTORIA STELLA
serves exquisite lunches
at incredible value
full bar

SLEDER'S FAMILY TAVERN
dead animal decor
and All-American eats
full bar

DISH CAFÉ
local fast food
vegetarian / vegan options

GEORGINA'S
try the tortilla bowl poke
with Thai tacos

PASTRIES

SWEET TARTLETTE
outstanding
cakes, cupcakes, pastries

PLEASANTON BRICK OVEN
the best bread anywhere
gluten-free pastries

MORSELS
tiny bites
outdoor seating

GRAND TRAVERSE PIE CO.
fruit pies, cream pies,
savory pies, pastries

**PEACE, LOVE AND LITTLE
DONUTS**
bite-sized deliciousness
made right in front
of your eyes

BEST GREASY SPOONS

RANDY'S DINER

J&S HAMBURGER

ROUND'S RESTAURANT

HAM BONZ

Fortney got a good look at the Dogman running with a pack of what appeared to be wild dogs. Fearing for his

HOTEL FOOD

REFLECT BISTRO
at Cambria Hotel & Suites
steak and seafood from
Eric Nittolo, formerly of
The Boathouse Restaurant
full bar

AERIE
at Grand Traverse Resort & Spa
fresh, local ingredients

HOTEL INDIGO
locally sourced ingredients
on top of the world

PIZZA

PAESANO'S
the local fave

PANGEA'S
another local fave

THE FILLING STATION
wood-fired pizza

PLEASANTON BRICK OVEN
flatbread pizza

TRATTORIA STELLA
thin crusts, new flavors

EAST BAY PIZZA
pizza + famous
Moomer's ice cream!
try the black cherry

44

TC IS BUSY. MAKE A RESERVATION.

TAKE-OUT

ORYANA
pre-packaged or self-serve
eat in or take out
live music in the cafe

MARY'S KITCHEN PORT
great sandwiches and salads

GRAND TRAVERSE PIE CO.
quiche and pot pies
to take home and heat

FOLGARELLI'S
full deli picnic spot

BURRIT'S
dinner items, ready to cook

LUCKY'S
a gigantic, Whole Foods-style
selection of pre-packaged
and self-serve
huge cheese selection

**NADA'S GOURMET
MEDITERRANEAN**
fresh wraps, pizza, salads

RADUNO
Home-made pasta,
charcuterie and salads

BURGERS

7 MONKS
Wagyu and Michigan beef
turkey burgers, too

GEORGINA'S
some of the best in TC

SLABTOWN BURGERS
lots of combos
paper bag packaging

U & I
in a red plastic basket

BUBBA'S
19 varieties + special sauce

SLEDER'S
buffalo burgers!

J&S HAMBURGER
where dad used to take
the kids when
mom was away

OUTDOOR

LUNCH & DINNER

The Towne Plaza

The Franklin

Little Fleet

Amical

Apache Trout Grill

West End Tavern

Firefly

North Peak

West Bay Beach / Dayclub

DINNER ONLY

Mission Table

The Boathouse

---

skin, Fortney fired a shot into the air, only to be struck dumb when from the middle of the rout something man-

DINNER

THE COOKS' HOUSE
farm-to-table
intimate atmosphere
Mario Batali's fave
dressy

ALLIANCE
small plates to share
lots of vegetarian options
best kitchen design ever
dressy

TRATTORIA STELLA
farm-to-table
wild boar, pastas, oysters
another Batali fave
dressy

AMICAL
steaks, fish, vegetarian
table d'hote fixed menu
before 5:30 PM
dressy

RED GINGER
asian fusion + sushi
rambunctious bar
dressy

GEORGINA'S
latin / asian fusion
lively, loud, youthful
casual

TOWNE PLAZA
pork belly, porchetta,
pork confit, pork wings
+ non-pig options
casual

THE LITTLE FLEET
food trucks, full bar
beachy atmosphere
great for kids
very casual

LATE

**ALL OPEN UNTIL
AT LEAST MIDNIGHT,
MANY UNTIL 2 AM**

7 MONKS
stylish bar food

LOW BAR
meat & cheese boards

BREW
local ingredients
sandwiches, wraps, salads
breakfast all day

**KILKENNY'S IRISH
PUBLIC HOUSE**
cheddar ale soup

U&I LOUNGE
gyros, perch dinner

J&S HAMBURGER
breakfast all day
milk shakes

BRADY'S
pizza, burgers
pool tables

MODE'S BUM STEER
steaks, salad bar
70s atmosphere

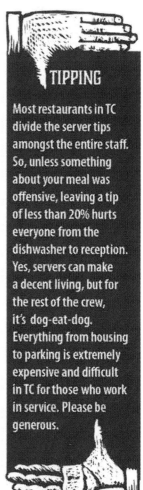

TIPPING

Most restaurants in TC divide the server tips amongst the entire staff. So, unless something about your meal was offensive, leaving a tip of less than 20% hurts everyone from the dishwasher to reception. Yes, servers can make a decent living, but for the rest of the crew, it's dog-eat-dog. Everything from housing to parking is extremely expensive and difficult in TC for those who work in service. Please be generous.

FUSTINI'S SCHOOL OF COOKING Demonstration classes are a different and delicious way to spend a night out. Watch, chat, taste.

like and covered with hair stood up on two legs and reportedly "sneered" at him before vanishing into the dark.

Let's Make Dinner

TC DOESN'T HAVE A TRADER JOE'S, BUT WE DO HAVE MANY LOCAL BUSINESSES THAT GO ALL OUT TO PROVIDE FRESH FOOD, OFTEN LOCALLY SOURCED.

GENERAL GROCERY SHOPPING

Home grown **ORYANA** stocks organic produce, meats, eggs and cheeses. Even in the winter, many items are locally sourced. Senior discounts (you must be at least 55) on Wednesdays. If you need a specialty item and you can stand the crowds, **MEIJER** has one of the largest produce sections in town. Brand-new **LUCKY'S** is a strong competitor and friendlier atmosphere. Both **TOM'S** and **OLESON'S** are local businesses. Some locations are better maintained than others. Oleson's has locally sourced and specialty meats in their freezer section.
FAMILY FARE is the go-to spot for quick townie shopping.

SPECIALTY GROCERY SHOPPING

TC LATINO GROCERY stocks Mexican cheeses, chorizo and dried chiles. Crazy huge meat section from their own farm. Delicious tamales, good hot or cold.
MAXBAUER MARKET has the best butcher shop in town, followed closely by **BURRITT'S FRESH MARKETS**. Burritt's also carries fresh fish and seafood, some produce and lots of wine.
BAYSIDE MARKET specializes in steaks and home-made sausage. **DEERING'S** also carries local sausage and jerky.
FOLGARELLI'S has many European specialty items, plus lots of cheeses and wine and a full deli.
THE CHEESE LADY has great cheese, expert staff, and you can taste before you buy.

BEER & WINE & SPIRITS

THE BEVERAGE COMPANY is #1 with its large selection, friendly staff and convenient parking.
TILLEY'S PARTY STORE is conveniently located near the West End beaches. **ALLEY'S MARKET** is behind BREW.
BON VIN has wonderful service and selection.
GRAND TRAVERSE DISTILLERY won 8 medals in 2017. Try their pure gold Islay Rye Whiskey. And sommelier Amanda Danielson of Trattoria Stella and The Franklin brings her expertise to the cellars of **BLUE GOAT WINE AND PROVISIONS**.

46

FARMERS MARKETS

SARA HARDY FARMERS MARKET
located across from Clinch Park every Wednesday & Saturday, May to October

THE VILLAGE FARMERS MARKET
located at The Commons outside May to October Mondays, 12 – 4 PM inside the rest of the year Saturdays, 10 – 2 PM

LOCALLY MADE

GREAT LAKES POTATO CHIPS superior skin-on chips

HARWOOD GOLD for maple syrup

SLEEPING BEAR FARMS for honey

AMERICAN SPOON for small-batch jams, jellies, relishes

LEELANAU CHEESE for award-winning raclette and spreads

IDYLL FARMS for goat cheese

ERG makes energy bars

ESCH ROAD and **FOOD FOR THOUGHT** for all natural jams, jellies, salsa

FRESH COAST for chocolate

¶ And so the legend goes. Back at the campfire, after we righted the rods and canoe, bagged what remained of

HOW TO
harvest leeks

WHEN TIMOTHY YOUNG SEES A BRIGHT GREEN FOREST FLOOR, HE KNOWS LEEK SEASON IS IMMINENT. THE YOUNG SHOOTS GIVE THE FOREST A "VERY SLIGHT GREEN HAZE," HE SAID.

Young, founder and president of Food For Thought, says leeks — or ramps — are the first food to spring up each spring. They're found exclusively in deciduous (hardwood) forests and especially like old-growth woods.

Allium tricoccum is known as wild leeks, leeks, ramps, wild onions, ransom (probably the source of the word "ramps") and wild garlic.

Wild leeks are edible from the sprout stage into late fall, but are typically harvested in early spring. Over-harvesting is a problem and many places ban leek-gathering altogether. It's illegal in national parks, including Sleeping Bear Dunes National Lakeshore. Young said it's OK to harvest ramps on state-owned land in Michigan as well as private property, but he strongly encourages asking permission first — and harvesting responsibly.

"The worst thing is to go out in the woods with a wheelbarrow and a shovel," Young said. The shovel destroys the leek's root system.

The bulb is fully formed when the leaves — which resemble tulip leaves — start to turn brown and drop. Slide your fingers down into the ground, feel for the build and snap it off at the base.

The window for the browning leaves/leaf drop stage is fairly short, about a week or two, but the bulbs are edible through late fall — if you can find them without the leaves as a clue.

Young uses leeks the same way he uses onions — in soups, sautees, salads and pickled. Food For Thought sells a wild leek relish as well as a wild leek marinara sauce. **JT**

ON STATE-OWNED LAND IN MICHIGAN YOU CANNOT "DESTROY, DAMAGE, OR REMOVE A TREE, INCLUDING A DEAD AND DOWNED TREE AND WOODY DEBRIS, SHRUB, WILDFLOWER, GRASS, OR OTHER VEGETATION. EXCEPT IN A WILDLIFE FOOD PLOT, THIS SUBDIVISION DOES NOT APPLY TO PICKING AND REMOVING MUSHROOMS, BERRIES, AND EDIBLE FRUITS OR NUTS FOR PERSONAL USE."

THE HARVESTING OF AMERICAN GINSENG IS TOTALLY PROHIBITED.

Farmland & foodies, a perfect pairing

THE GRAND TRAVERSE REGION WAS AN EARLY ADOPTER OF THE FARM-TO-TABLE MOVEMENT. ITS BASE AS AN AGRICULTURAL COMMUNITY COUPLED WITH ITS BURGEONING REPUTATION AS A FOODIE DESTINATION TURNED INTO THE PERFECT PAIRING.

Patty Cantrell helped, too. She grew up in the Ozarks and eventually landed at the Michigan Land Use Institute, now called Groundwork Center for Resilient Communities. She and her fellow land-use activists were chagrined to see orchards being replaced by McMansions, farms turning into subdivisions. Local land conservancies were doing what they could, but they couldn't always keep up. Cantrell and colleagues approached it from an economics standpoint — make farming profitable and fewer people will sell their land.

It started with more farmers markets — there's one in practically every town and village now — and moved to restaurants, grocery stores and schools. The local food movement in this region is often used as a model for other communities.

LOCAL FOOD RULERS

Chefs Myles Anton, of **TRATTORIA STELLA** (Italian), supports local farms to such an extent that close to four dozen are listed as purveyors. It also has its own garden, grows its own herbs and kitchen staff regularly forages in the woods for mushrooms and other delicacies. They're big on using the whole animal (preferably a heritage breed), so try the sweetbreads. The farmers who provided the day's ingredients are usually listed on the chalkboard. Trattoria's Stella sister

black panthers, and UFOs. Up in Michigan, we have more than our fair share of those occurrences, too. While I

restaurant, **THE FRANKLIN**, in downtown Traverse City, is also dedicated to local foods, including local potatoes in its Disco Fingers, as close to poutine as you'll get in this town.

9 BEAN ROWS, named after a line in a William Butler Yeats poem ("Lake Isle of Innisfree") has it all — a farm, a CSA, a market, a presence at local farm markets, a bakery and a restaurant. Chef Paul Carlson, at the restaurant in downtown Suttons Bay, uses as much local food as possible from 9 Bean Rows' own farm as well as food from Bare Knuckle Farm, Bardenhagen Farms, Sweeter Song Farm, Clean Plate Farm, the Olds family (excellent sweet corn), Second Spring Farm, Boss Mouse Cheese, Leelanau Cheese, Idyll Farms and Carlson's Fish Market. 9 Bean Rows' croissants are exemplary and the bakery/market on M-204 between Suttons Bay and Lake Leelanau has seasonal produce, breads and fancier pastries including napoleons and eclairs. The restaurant is open 3:30 to 9 PM, Monday through Saturday.

THE COOKS' HOUSE, quickly becoming nationally known for its innovative from-scratch food (and one of the few places in the area to get curry), says 90 percent of its menu is made from local products. Even the artwork on the walls is made by local artists. The tasting menu (five or seven courses) is a good way to get lots of different food. The cheese board earns raves. Local walleye is sometimes served smoked; springtime offerings include morels and asparagus.

THE GRAND TRAVERSE RESORT'S multiple kitchens utilize as much local food as possible, from cherries in desserts to locally made beer. Look for the tallest building in the land, out in Acme.

In Glen Arbor at **BLU**, Chef Randy Chamberlain, a Traverse City kid who grew up in his dad's restaurant, has turned local ingredients into delicious dishes accompanied by a spectacular view of Sleeping Bear Bay. There's a prix fixe menu, $33 for three courses if seated by 5 p.m. Local offerings can include cherries, mushrooms and guinea fowl.

WANT TO VISIT A FARM?
See page 174.

For extra fun, **HILLSIDE HOMESTEAD**, near Suttons Bay, serves dinner from its farm, turn of the century-style.

LA BECASSE, on South Dunns Farm Road in Burdickville (near Glen Lake), is truly French, with nice local touches, including eggs from Dennis Mikses in Solon Township, pheasant from David Rinkey of Beulah and rabbit from Cedar's Bunny Hop Ranch. La Becasse is the only restaurant serving Leelanau Cheese's aged raclette (also made by a French expat). Chef-owner Guillaume Hazael-Massieux also runs **BISTRO FOU-FOU** in a former fire station in downtown Traverse City.

AMICAL, next to the State Theater in downtown Traverse City, was among the first restaurants to bring European flavor with local ingredients to the area. They use Zenner's hydroponic tomatoes (available year-round), Great Lakes fish and asparagus from Norconk Farms near Empire. Much of the meat comes from Rice Centennial Farm in Beulah, known for its hormone- and antibiotic-free beef. **JT**

A GOOD SOURCE FOR SOURCING YOUR LOCAL FOOD AND DRINK – WHETHER AT A STORE, RESTAURANT OR BAR – IS TASTE THE LOCAL DIFFERENCE, WWW. LOCALDIFFERENCE.ORG.

The Real Deal

A lot of Traverse Citians pine for a time when the National Cherry Festival was more of a small-town production. But really, all they need to do is wait a month until early August, when the quintessential county fair comes to town. It's your basic, though not inexpensive, carnival here.

The Northwest Michigan Fair (really just the Grand Traverse County fair, but a clever bit of marketing in the name, don't you think?) is true to the classic American summertime experience. It has all the sights, sounds and smells you expect: Elephant ears, Gibby's fries, a loud, flashing midway jam-packed with rides, games and carnival barkers. And, of course, horses, cows and pigs. While you will smell the animals, you won't smell their, um, well, animal byproducts. The kids who raise and show the livestock for 4-H and other clubs stay busy sweeping floors, mucking stalls and hosing the sweat and humidity of August off their prized wards.

It all comes together for one week a year at the well-kept and attractive fairgrounds, not quite 10 miles south of Traverse City. No dusty lot here. Shade trees give relief in the park and parking lot.

The fair has been around since 1908, the year the first Ford Model T struck out on roads built for horses. You can still get a taste for those times, like when a juggler on stilts performs in the shade of an old maple tree. **TC**

The fair moved from the Civic Center in TC to its current location in 1975.

Admission $3 for children and $5 for adults.

50

we nodded knowingly at others, and that before we knew it, dawn had come and it was time to go home where

BUCKLEY OLD ENGINE SHOW

As you drive around the area, you may notice that certain farmers have a hard time parting with their old machines. In 1967, a group of these fellows got together, revved their engines and made their own show. It was an immediate success and a few years later, they purchased 70 acres west of Buckley and began to build permanent exhibits, like a sawmill, an oil well demo, a foundry, a letter-press printer, a rock crusher and a tractor-driving school.

There really is something for everyone, including a children's play area and an enormous flea market.

The show is always the third weekend of August, Thursday through Sunday. Adult tickets cost $10 a day, kids under 15 get in free. No dogs allowed.

Oil & Gas in Northern Michigan

Not many people know it, but Michigan has been an important source of petroleum since 1870.

The state may be shaped like a mitten, but geologically, it's more like a kitchen sink. About 14,000 feet thick at its deepest point, the oldest rock was deposited about 500 million years ago and the newest a mere 150 million years ago. The entire basin was once covered in a shallow sea, then it was chewed up by the glaciers, which added the topography of moraines, drumlins, valleys, streams and lakes we see today.

The first oil well was dug in Port Huron in 1870. A couple of years later, drilling also began in Muskegon. The boom didn't begin until the '20s, when hundreds of wells were drilled from Dundee to TC. Only one "giant" oil field was ever discovered, however, and that was near Albion. A fortune teller disclosed that a "black river of oil" lay beneath Ferne Houseknecht's dairy farm, and Ferne convinced a neighbor to drill. Ferne's "Golden Gulch" eventually produced more than 100 million barrels of oil.

Everything went right for Ferne, but we Insiders have had a taste of what can go wrong. In 1973, a local ham radio operator overheard Amoco employees discussing problems at the wells in Williamsburg (just south of Acme). Inexperienced drillers had tapped into a pocket of gas under high pressure. The pressure was forcing the gas out any which way, creating mysterious giant, hissing cauldrons, geysers and bubbling mud holes. More than 450 people were evacuated for months and M-72 was virtually destroyed. Outside the township hall in Williamsburg is a green, capped pipe that still vents gas to this day.

we all could at last feel invincible once again. THE END

BREWTOWN

TC 52

TC HAS BEEN BREWING ITS
OWN BEER FOR ENOUGH YEARS
NOW THAT THEY'VE FIGURED IT OUT. CHECK OUT ZACH
VELCOFF'S GUIDE TO THE BEST TASTES IN TOWN.

For some of the best craft beers in town, fly down to **RARE BIRD BREWPUB**. They've got 34 taps, of which six typically pour their own concoctions, like Damn Coppers, made exclusively with Michigan hops; Tres Hundo, an even hoppier brew whose bitterness is balanced nicely with local honey; or Yo Hefe!, an easy-drinking wheat/barley session lager. The brewpub, which takes its name from brewer Tina Schuett and manager Nate Crane's shared loved of birding, also offers a delicious dinner menu, and serves up pub grub — like fried Michigan cheddar curds, garlic fries, and hot wings — until midnight!

If you keep gluten-free, or simply prefer a lighter beverage, try **TAPROOT**, which inherited the mantle of Traverse City's downtown cider house from Northern Naturals in 2016. Since then, they've been pouring a wide variety of crisp ciders and cider cocktails. Old Northern Naturals favorites like their organic Lavender Cider are on tap here, as are new house classics like Taproot's Madagascar Vanilla Bean Bourbon Barrel Aged Cider. While you drink, enjoy some cider-braised bratwurst, plus live music five nights a week!

For one of the finest flights this town has to offer, try a board of five beers at **FERMENT**. With flagship classics like their 45th Parallele pale ale and Union Street Stout, and unique specialty pours like Gruit To It and The Beet Gose On, they've got something for the craft novice and the more adventurous drinker alike. And for the true connoisseur, a bottle-conditioned Belgian Dubbel or Wild Rhythm and Ryem saison makes the perfect addition to a cellar. If you'd like to try your own hand at brewing, they also offer courses — the cost of which includes all the instruction and materials you'll need — on their website, www.breweryferment.com

COMING UP NEXT, A GREAT LAKES SURFING STORY BY MICHAEL DELP...

If you've spent your day studying at the library or strolling along the Boardman Lake, why not spend your evening sipping craft beer and eating wood-fired flatbread pizza at **THE FILLING STATION MICROBREWERY**? Brewer David Cannizzaro brings twenty years of homebrewing experience to the operation, brewing three and ten-barrel batches of thirst-quenching delights like the Rolling Stock IPL, the Kettle Black Rye Kolsch, or the Jacktown Mocha Stout, sure to go great with a rocket or wolverine pie, and — depending on the night — some live music by the old train tracks!

For brew with a view, drive up Old Mission Peninsula to **JOLLY PUMPKIN RESTAURANT & BREWERY**. In this rustic farmhouse-style eatery overlooking the West Bay, you can enjoy a plate of ribs or fish and chips with some of the most unique beers Northern Michigan has to offer—favorites like Bam di Castagna, a farmhouse ale brewed with a mash of malt and chestnuts; Cucurbitophobia (fear of pumpkins), a barrel-aged gose; or La Roja, an unfiltered, unpasteurized amber ale. If you're there in spring or summer, don't be surprised to see a wedding party going on at the **MISSION TABLE**, their upscale restaurant and event space next door.

Like beer? Like pork? Ever thought of combining them? Well you can, at **RIGHT BRAIN BREWERY**. Their Mangalitsa Pig Porter is brewed with the heads and bones of pigs, and goes great with their ham n' provolone sandwich on fresh sourdough! Alternatively, if you're not feeling the whole meat beer thing, play it safe with a Peanut Butter CEO Stout (not made with the heads and bones of CEOs) or a Concrete Dinosaur IPA.

Can't get enough cider? Then another must on your list has to be **LEFT FOOT CHARLEY** in The Village at Grand Traverse Commons. Wine is certainly their specialty (and we recommend their Traminette or Gitali sparkling Pinot Noir!), but their ciders and perries are also not to be missed! On a warm summer day, enjoy sipping a glass of Henry's Pippin, or the Neil Young-inspired Cinnamon Girl, on their wine garden patio.

MICHIGAN HOP ALLIANCE

Brian and Amy Tennis formed the Michigan Hop Alliance in 2010 to process their own hops. In addition to producing more than 20 varieties, several of which are being grown for the first time on a commercial scale in North America. Michigan Hop Alliance works with other farmers throughout the process to grow, pick, dry, and/or pelletize hops as well as market the final product.

The Michigan Hop Alliance works closely with breweries throughout the state, including Grand Rapids Brewing Company, Brewery Vivant, Short's and Stormcloud.

BEST BARS

54

OPEN MIC
Left Foot Charley / Hayloft /
Union Street Station

QUIETEST
Amical / Mode's Bum Steer

CRAZY LOUD
Union Street Station

COZIEST
U&I Lounge / Trattoria Stella

COOLEST
7 Monks / Rare Bird / Low Bar

DATE NIGHT
Low Bar / Trattoria Stella

AFTER WORK
7 Monks / The Parlor

FEEL OLD
Rare Bird / Double Wide

FEEL YOUNG
Mode's Bum Steer / North Peak

PEOPLE WATCHING
Red Ginger / The Franklin

VIEW
Top of the Park / Apache Trout Grill /
Indigo

DANCE
Sidetraxx

JAZZ
West Bay Beach Holiday Inn / Poppycocks

ON THE WATER
West End Tavern / Apache Trout Grill
/ West Bay Beach / Indigo

HIDE
Little Bo's / U&I Lounge

BE SEEN
Little Fleet / Red Ginger

TAKE YOUR PARENTS
Jolly Pumpkin / Mackinaw Brewing

TAKE YOUR KIDS
Bubba's / Little Fleet

TAKE YOUR DOG
Little Fleet

PLAY
Workshop / Double Wide

WORK
Brew / U&I Lounge

MIXOLOGY
The Parlor / Low Bar

A BUSHY, BUSHY BLOND HAIRDO ¶ I never rode the big sets outside Wiamea Bay, the waves rising like the

TC IS A PASSIONATE COFFEE TOWN—SO PASSIONATE, IN FACT, THAT YOU WON'T FIND A STARBUCKS WITHIN THE CITY LIMITS. WE'D BE HARD PRESSED (PUN INTENDED) TO PICK A FAVORITE CAFÉ, BUT FOR JAVA ON THE GO, AND THE BEST CUP OF COLD BREW YOU'LL EVER HAVE, CHECK OUT THE <u>PLANETARY COFFEE TRUCK</u> ON EIGHTH STREET. IF YOU'RE IN THE MOOD FOR A SIT-DOWN EXPERIENCE, HIGHER GROUNDS ROASTS THEIR BEANS ON SITE—THERE'S NOTHING LIKE WATCHING THE ROASTING PROCESS WHILE YOU SIP YOUR POUROVER!

Higher Grounds

Back in 2001, Chris Treter was just a kid doing post-grad work at a coffee-growers coop in Chiapas, Mexico. He saw the poverty, lack of access to education, power and water, and asked the farmers what he could do to help. "You could sell our coffee," was the answer.

Chris and his partner purchased a single bag of beans and shipped them home to Leland. The business of organic free-trade coffee began to take off, and soon they were able to purchase their own roaster. It still took years of hand-packaging and endless hand-selling at farmers markets before Higher Grounds found a market in stores.

Today, Treter's company is growing at a rate of 20% annually and buys coffee beans from Mexico and nine other countries, including Ethiopia, Palestine, Democratic Republic of Congo, and Nicaragua.

HIGHER GROUNDS is available in most local grocery stores.

LEELANAU COFFEE ROASTING has been in business since 1998, and is also available in stores locally. Their cafe is located in Glen Arbor on Western Ave.

In TC, there's more great coffee everywhere.

BREW, on Front Street, a great place to sit by yourself and work

BLK MRKT, in the Warehouse District for people-watching

GOOD HARBOR COFFEE AND BAKERY, also on Front. Not much seating, but a quick in-and-out. Great cookies.

CUPPA JO, at the Commons and a drive-through on Munson Avenue.

CAVALLINO CAFE on Lake Street in the Warehouse District.

MORSELS, on Front at River's End for a bite-sized sweet treat with your java.

ORYANA CAFE, inside the Oryana Food Coop for on-the-go or sip in.

walls of canyons, each breaker an avalanche of foam and sound. ¶ I never took the chance to drift up and down the

WALK, RUN, SKI, BIKE – IT'S ALL RIGHT IN TC

PELIZZARI NATURAL AREA

These 62 acres of old cherry orchards are the perfect go-to spot on the east side of town. Located on Center Road, just a mile out on Old Mission Peninsula, its combination of hills and meadows, forest and sky suit almost everyone, and is particularly favored by dog-walkers. The hardwood trail is beautiful in the fall, and good for all seasons when the weather's bad. Skiers will appreciate the long downhill slope in the middle of the park. There used to be a healthy fairy population in the hemlock forest, but that was eradicated a few months before the big storm of 2015 took out many of the trees.

Pelizzari Natural Area is protected by The Grand Traverse Regional Land Conservancy (GTRLC), owned by Peninsula Township, managed by the GTRLC.

HICKORY MEADOWS

Located at the end of Randolph Street on the west side of Traverse City, these 112, mostly open acres are heavily used by dog-walkers. There's a 2-mile loop for walking / biking, and in the winter, a .8-mile loop is maintained for cross-country skiing. Although it's not one of TC's greatest beauty-spots, the trail that heads north towards M-72 (no loop) passes through some lovely swampland.

Hickory Meadows is owned by the City of Traverse City and Charter Township of Garfield Recreation Authority and managed by the Grand Traverse Conservation District.

KIDS CREEK

This whole ridge was once home to the largest buffalo herd east of the Mississippi. Most of the land went to big box stores, but Garfield Township persuaded owners to donate a little pocket. Volunteers then arrived to clean up the stream, resulting in less sedimentation clogging up West Bay.

The 3/4 loop is perfect for a quick walk on a gravel path before or after shopping or a movie. Kids will like the little, stocked fish pond near Great Wolf Lodge.

Parking is in the shopping center lot, between Kohl's and Bed Bath & Beyond. The trailhead is right next to the "Exit" sign.

MILLER CREEK

Miller Creek is a little pocket of nature hidden behind Home Depot at the Crossings Mall. Use the mall's main entrance and head toward Faith Reformed Church on Crossing Circle Drive. Take the downward trail, it heads toward the creek. A shortish loop follows the creek through old hardwoods —including some spectacularly scarred ironwoods—over a bridge, through a couple of swamps, and back over a bridge to return. A great spot for a quick walk, and kids will delight in enormous trees and access to the creek. Be aware that hunting is allowed in this park with Charter Township approval.

Bonzai Pipeline. I never caught a wave on the North Shore of Oahu in November, pumped up for the winter

DEYOUNG NATURAL AREA

This preserve is actually in Leelanau County, but it's only a couple of miles outside TC. Follow West Bay around to West Bay Marina, then turn left on Cherry Bend. The sign is on the right.

The park is an old homestead, settled around the time of the Civil War, and the conservancy land is on both sides of the road. The Cherry Bend Road trailhead leads down to Cedar Lake (nice for a picnic or a little fishing) then winds its way through mature cedars. It's gloomy in there, so a good place for a walk on hot summer days or when the weather is rough: nothing gets through those trees.

If you're a runner — and particularly if it's color season — keep going past the Cherry Bend trailhead and take a left on Strand Road. A second trailhead there makes a mile and a half loop around an old field. The path is mown grass, and there's very little traffic, so you won't be dog-dodging. There are great views of the hardwood forests to the north and west. Be aware that hunting is allowed in this park from October 1 to January 1 with a permit from the Leelanau Conservancy.

The DeYoung Nature Area is one of Leelanau Conservancy's biggest projects and protects a full mile of Cedar Lake shoreline.

Grand Travers Commons
Cedar Cathedral Trail

GRAND TRAVERSE COMMONS

This amazingly large and diverse park borders the Munson Hospital complex and The Village at Grand Traverse Commons, and was originally a part of the former Traverse City State Psychiatric Hospital.

Unlike most area parks, the trails were established organically and criss-cross here and there all over the place. It's easy to get lost. Fortunately, there's always someone not far away and you can ask directions.

A good starter hike is to park at the trailhead near Greenspire School on 1026 Red Drive. Take the first right, across the stream. The trail runs up a hill: watch for the Hippy Tree on the left. Like the do-it-yourself trails, the park allows artistic expression in the form of paint. The old reservoir near the Cedar Cathedral trail is an eye-opener as well.

Directly across from the Hippy Tree is a little, puffing spring. Kids will love both of these attractions. Continued lefthand turns will take you back to the parking lot.

Taking a left off the Greenspire trail makes a longer loop. You'll need to make right-hand turns to get back to the parking lot.

The dark and mysterious Cedar Cathedral trail is accessed from within The Village. Enter off Division on West Eleventh and turn right after passing the Trattoria Stella. Park in the lot just past Pleasanton Bakery. Following the long edge of the parking lot, walk towards the hills. You'll pass ELF, on the left: they're responsible for the delightful fairy establishments. Then follow the green signs. Remember to take all left-hand turns to get back to where you started.

Grand Traverse Commons is a showcase of species and land diversity. If you let your dog run off the trail, be prepared to pick off any number of assorted burrs and to wash off the mud.

The park is a part of the Grand Traverse Commons Redevelopment District.

IF YOU PLAN ON WALKING SNOWY TRAILS, GET YOURSELF A PAIR OF TRACTION DEVICES FOR YOUR BOOTS. SLIP-ON CLEETS LIKE YAKTRAX AND STABELICERS WILL END WINTER MINCING AND PUT SOME SWING BACK IN YOUR STEP. THEY MAY ALSO SAVE YOU FROM A TRIP TO THE HOSPITAL ON THE BACK OF A SNOWMOBILE.

FAST FOOD NATURE

REFITT NATURE PRESERVE

One of TC's lesser known preserves, Refitt is situated right behind the Traverse City State Park, on the other side of the TART Trail. There are over 100 acres of white pine and blueberries, swamp and hardwood forest, with lots of funky boardwalks and bridges. Its completely level terrain and 1.5-mile loop make it a great spot for runners staying in one of the Miracle Mile hotels along highway.

Refitt is accessed off US-31 N on Four Mile Road. Take a quick right on Oak Drive and follow that to the end.

Hunting is not allowed.

Refitt Nature Preserve is owned and operated by The Grand Traverse Regional Land Conservancy.

60

Grand Traverse Regional Land Conservancy

WITH THE SUPPORT OF INDIVIDUAL DONORS, FOUNDATIONS AND VOLUNTEERS, AND THE PARTNERSHIP OF LOCAL, STATE AND FEDERAL AGENCIES, WE HAVE PROTECTED MORE THAN 39,000 ACRES OF LAND AND MORE THAN 121 MILES OF SHORELINE ALONG THE REGION'S EXCEPTIONAL RIVERS, LAKES AND STREAMS.

Leelanau Land Conservancy

THE CONSERVANCY WORKS WITH PRIVATE LANDOWNERS TO PERMANENTLY PROTECT THE NATURAL FEATURES OF THEIR LAND FOR FUTURE GENERATIONS BY CREATING INDIVIDUALIZED LEGAL AGREEMENTS THAT PLACE CERTAIN DEVELOPMENT RESTRICTIONS ON THE PROPERTY. WE HAVE PRESERVED OVER 11,500 ACRES AND CREATED 25 NATURAL AREAS FOR PUBLIC ENJOYMENT WITH MORE THAN 15 MILES OF HIKING TRAILS.

flush a big hen up into the sky but before I could bring the gun to my shoulder, my eyes would catch on the way

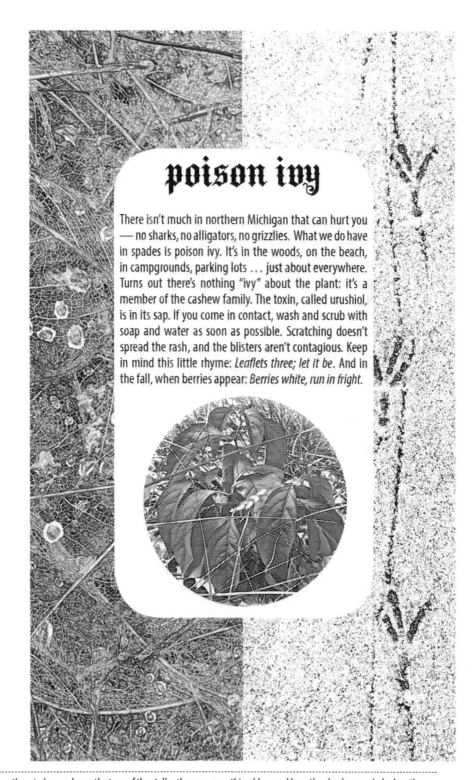

poison ivy

There isn't much in northern Michigan that can hurt you — no sharks, no alligators, no grizzlies. What we do have in spades is poison ivy. It's in the woods, on the beach, in campgrounds, parking lots ... just about everywhere. Turns out there's nothing "ivy" about the plant: it's a member of the cashew family. The toxin, called urushiol, is in its sap. If you come in contact, wash and scrub with soap and water as soon as possible. Scratching doesn't spread the rash, and the blisters aren't contagious. Keep in mind this little rhyme: *Leaflets three; let it be*. And in the fall, when berries appear: *Berries white, run in fright*.

WALK YOUR DOG

FIRST OF ALL, THE BAD NEWS: DOGS ARE NOT ALLOWED ON ANY OF THE BEACHES IN TC.

Not that you won't see dogs on downtown beaches, especially early in the morning or during off-season for tourists. But be aware that you may be stopped, ticketed and fined. Dog-snitchers have also been known to capture your license plate number and call the police. Just saying.

Now for the good news: dogs on leashes are welcome almost everywhere — even in stores (without food) and some restaurants with outdoor seating.

Sleeping Bear National Lakeshore in Leelanau County does allow dogs on some of its beaches, notably Otter Creek (see page 184). The campground at D.H. Day also allows dogs (page 109, as well as most of the beach surrounding Pyramid Point (page 196).

rustled against each other. Then the wind rolling away, rising and falling over the tops of the corn, like wave

BARK PARKS

If your dog is of a sociable disposition, there are a couple of off-leash bark parks.

In downtown TC, the park is located on the corner of Division and Bay streets, just across the Parkway from the West End Beach. There are two fenced areas, one for large dogs, one for small.

Fifteen minutes outside of town, the Silver Lake Recreation Area at 1785 N. East Silver Lake Road has two large fenced-in areas for small dogs and big dogs.

· · · · · · · · · · · · · · · · · · · ·

The **CIVIC CENTER**, while not at all a "bark park," is a fine place for leashed dogs who like to meet other leashed dogs. Lots of space in the middle of the park for a game of fetch.

POPULAR DOG WALKS

All of the TC parks allow dogs on leashes. Popular sites include:

- **THE TART TRAIL** from the Holiday Inn to the Open Space. Cross the Parkway safely by using the tunnels: one is just west of the Holiday Inn and the other is at Cass Street.

- **HICKORY MEADOWS** (page 55)

- **THE GRAND TRAVERSE COMMONS** (page 59)

- **PELIZZARI NATURAL AREA** (page 56)

- **BOARDMAN LAKE TRAIL**: a 3-mile boardwalk and paved trail that circles around the north and east shore of Boardman Lake. Park or walk to the Traverse Area District Library at 610 Woodmere Avenue to access the trail. There are lots of biking commuters here, so a short leash is required.

- You can take your dog hiking or skiing at the **VASA TRAIL** … and dogs can be off-leash there, too.

In Leelanau County, leashed pets are welcome on most trails during the summer. Winter is a different story.

Pets are prohibited at the following designated cross-country ski trails during the periods of December 1 through March 31:

- **SLEEPING BEAR HERITAGE TRAIL**

- **PLATTE PLAINS TRAIL SYSTEM** (including Bass Lake, Otter Creek, and Lasso Loop Trails)

- **WINDY MORAINE**   · **BAY VIEW**

- **SHAUGER HILL**   · **GOOD HARBOR BAY**

- **ALLIGATOR HILL**   · **OLD INDIAN**

Keeping dogs off the beaches helps protect Michigan's piping plover. Both threatened and endangered, the total population — here and on the Atlantic— is estimated at less than 7,000 individual birds. One third of the total population lives on National Lakeshore beaches.

FOLLOW CASS ST OUT OF TOWN TO ONE OF THE BEST WALKING PARKS IN THE AREA.

Just after the railroad tracks, there's a large parking lot on your left. Both the Boardman River Nature Center and the Grand Traverse Conservation District are located here.

1 FOX DEN: Walk down the paved hill towards Boardman Dam. The path goes left, just before the dam building. Keep left for a short, .6- mile loop over Jack's Creek, through a marsh bordered by birches, then back through a swamp with more snake grass than you can shake a stick at. This is a perfect walk for young children: not too long and plenty of different terrain.

2 SABIN POND: Reach this trail by heading out of the parking lot in the direction of the buildings. The gravel path leads to the trailhead. Sabin Pond Trail is about a mile long and involves a lot of stairs, some of them not in very good condition. There are also board walks and bridges, two viewing platforms and some muck. If your knees are healthy, don't be discouraged: this is a gorgeous trail at almost every time of year. (I'm sure it's beautiful on a snowy winter day as well, but the stairs are impossible.) If you've got kids, have them look out for the bear claw marks. They were made about eight years ago on an ironwood tree. They're located on the upside of the trail, near the school bus parking lot.

The Boardman River is one of Michigan's top ten fisheries, and the Boardman River Dams Ecosystem Restoration Project aims to keep it that way by removing the old, inefficient dams and reconnecting over 160 miles of stream. The project is one of the most comprehensive dam removal and restoration undertakings in Michigan's history.

EQUISETUM, AKA SNAKE GRASS OR HORSETAIL, ONCE COVERED THE FLOOR BENEATH THE GIANT FERN TREES OF THE PALEOZOIC. CALLED A "LIVING FOSSIL," IT IS VIRTUALLY UNCHANGED — EXCEPT THAT IT'S NO LONGER 100 FEET TALL. MOST OF OUR FOSSIL FUEL COMES FROM THESE EARLY FORESTS.

Boardman River Nature Center

The Nature Center is a wonderful top-off for your walk. There's an interpretive gallery with live animals and rotating exhibits, interactive displays and some crazy taxidermy.

If you stop by before the trip, pick up a Discovery Pack for the kids. Themes include:

Amazing Amphibians & Reptiles
Birding Bonanza
Budding Botanist
Fossil Frenzy
Insect Investigator
Nature Detective

Naturally Wild Birthday Parties are also available at the Center. Open Tuesday – Friday and some Saturdays.

JEWELWEED IS A NATIVE PLANT, AND NATIVE AMERICANS USED IT TO STOP THE ITCH FROM POISON IVY. IT MUST HAVE WORKED, BECAUSE TRAVELERS TOOK THE PLANT HOME WITH THEM, AND IT IS NOW FOUND ALL OVER NORTHERN EUROPE.

ON THE SABIN POND TRAIL, YOU'LL FIND THE PLANT GROWING ALONG THE BOARDWALKS IN THE AUTUMN. THE FLOWER IS ORANGE, WITH YELLOW SPOTS ON THE THROAT. PLEASE DON'T TAKE IT HOME WITH YOU.

Traverse City State Hospital

The Grand Traverse Commons is the old site of the Traverse City State Hospital, also known as the Northern Michigan Asylum. Perry Hannah secured the contract for the state-run asylum, hoping that it would bring professionals to the area to work, live and stay. Finished in 1885, the asylum opened with 43 patients. A decade later, nearly 1,000 patients were under the care of a staff of 250.

James Munson was the first superintendent of the facility, and a proponent of the "beauty is therapy" and "work is therapy" philosophy popular at the time. Munson's humane treatment of the mentally ill dovetailed nicely with the design of the buildings. Known as the Kirkbride style, for the psychiatrist who developed it, the wings are staggered to allow more light and fresh air. This asylum, like many other Kirkbrides built around the country, also had extensive farmlands and gardens, including a hot house for fresh flowers for the patients — "beauty is therapy!" Munson also prohibited straitjackets in the asylum, and put the inmates to work farming, canning and polishing floors — "work is therapy!"

Changes in health care law drained funding from state-run facilities, and the farms were shut down in the 1950s. Most of the out-buildings were demolished in the 1970s. The hospital was closed in 1989.

The buildings mouldered over the next decade while the city and its citizens argued over what to do with them. In 2000, the Minervini Group won the contract to renovate. G.T. Commons is one the largest historic renovation projects in the U.S.

of California on the inland side of the peninsula. I wanted my feet on a board, my back tanned and my hair

BACK WHEN WE INSIDERS WERE KIDS, RAVENS WERE UNCOMMON TO THE POINT OF INVISIBILITY.

But about a decade ago, they began to show up in wooded areas where crows congregated. Today they can even be found within the city limits.

Ravens and crows are both highly intelligent birds — they can solve problems, imitate and judge. While ravens have traditionally preferred isolated open spaces, climate change and loss of habitat have forced them to adapt to a more crowded, crow-like existence.

Ravens are larger than crows, with a bigger beak and shaggy feathers around the beak and throat. Their tails are distinctly wedge-shaped.

Their most distinctive quality, however, is their voice. They can sound like a crying baby, a frog or two pieces of wood knocking together. They croak and creak. Up to 30 different raven sounds have been recorded, each one specific to an alarm or an action.

Crows and ravens are omnivorous: They'll eat carrion, seeds and human food. Ravens take it a bit further, though, snatching up small mammals and birds as well.

Ravens are also fiercely territorial and will attack owls and eagles to defend their nests. Be careful in the spring when the youngsters are leaving the nest. A raven family in the forest at Pelizzari Natural Area on Old Mission Peninsula has sent this Insider running for cover, toy poodle in arms.

**A FLOCK OF CROWS IS CALLED A MURDER.
A FLOCK OF RAVENS IS CALLED A CONSPIRACY.**

perfectly blond. A bushy bushy blond hair do, made even bushier and more blond by the salt spray and the sun.

Tour the Asylum

Guided Historic Tour:
A two-hour guided walk of the Village (Building 50), including the campus, historical buildings, renovation projects and the steam tunnel. No children under age 11.

Photography Tour:
A three-hour guided tour with access to unrenovated buildings and tunnel.

Architectural Tour:
A 90-minute guided tour that examines the Kirkbride design, philosophy and construction history.

How Thin the Veil is a memoir of 45 days spent in the Traverse City State Hospital. Originally published in 1952, it opens a window into mental health treatment and patient conditions of the time. It's a love story, too. Available at local stores and Amazon.

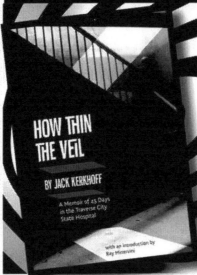

HOW THIN THE VEIL
BY JACK KERKHOFF
A Memoir of 45 Days in the Traverse City State Hospital
with an introduction by Ray Minervini

• THE • VILLAGE

Ray Minervini's mantra for his restoration project at Building 50 — now The Village — was "lights in the windows, art on the walls and music in the halls." Now, 17 years from the start of the project, we can only say, "amen."

The Village is made up of everything it takes to, well, make a village, like schools, businesses, food, salons, health clubs, auditoriums and gardens. Much of the shopping is concentrated in The Mercado, a long, winding, tunnel-like series of shops and eateries. When the weather is awful, this is a great place to hang out and browse. You can even bring your dog.

The Village also has condos and offices for sale and rent.

Cordia at the G.T. Commons is an innovative residential establishment for seniors, both those who are independent as well as those who require assistance.

There are many businesses located in the buildings surrounding The Village. Walk around and explore.

The G.T. Commons are a State Historical Site and on the National Registry of Historical Places.

Concerts on the Lawn

Weekly concerts run from June through August on the **GRAND LAWN OF THE GRAND TRAVERSE PAVILIONS CAMPUS**. Bring your own chairs or blankets, and a picnic, too.. Concessions are also available, starting at 5:30 PM, with a picnic-style menu and Moomer's ice cream. The concerts are every Thursday at 7 PM and last about an hour.

Historic Barns Park

THIS 54-ACRE PROPERTY WAS PURCHASED WITH MILLAGE FUNDING APPROVED BY GARFIELD TOWNSHIP AND TRAVERSE CITY VOTERS IN 2004.

Once used by State Hospital patients for food and therapy, the Historic Barns Park aims to be a regional gathering place for public recreation, community events, agriculture, horticulture and environmental design.

The Cathedral Barn is a newly restored event venue with 3,535 square feet of event space.

The Botanic Garden

The grand plan is that the Botanic Garden will cover half of the space at the Park. With an emphasis on plant species native to northwest Michigan, the gardens will create and enhance habitats for various forms of wildlife.

There is also an indoor community classroom, shop and meeting room.

of ticket sales, making sure that one of those times I had my dad's 8mm Kodak hidden under my parka. The

CREAKS IN THE ATTIC, FOOTSTEPS ON THE STAIRS, HUMAN APPARITIONS THAT COME AND LEAVE AT THE TURN OF A HEAD. THE SPIRITS OF THE TRAVERSE CITY AREA ARE SAID TO BE BUSY.

There are long-standing legends and enough new reports to have sparked at least a couple of paranormal groups that investigate places where people believe they've seen, heard or felt a ghost. Some are in private homes, but there are enough in public places to create a little tour of sites where some say you can be alone without really being alone.

Here's a spine-chilling list of some of the area's non-flesh residents:

BOWERS HARBOR INN

A bitter and jealous ghost is said to turn lights off and on at the Bowers Harbor Inn, now called the Mission Table and Tasting Room. The inn overlooks the picturesque harbor of the same name on the east side of Old Mission Peninsula. It's believed to be the spirit of Genevive Stickney. She and her husband Charles Stickney, a Chicago lumber baron, had it built in 1928 as a summer home. Genevive, also known as Jennie, was obese and her husband had an elevator installed to help her navigate the inn's two stories. He also hired a nurse to look after his wife's health. It turns out he also had the nurse tending to some of his own needs, so to speak, behind Jennie's back. After her husband died and left the inn to his wife, but his money to his mistress, Genevive is said to have hanged herself in the elevator shaft.

Some say a faint but chilling figure of a woman has appeared on their vacation photos from the inn, or in a mirror behind them. Some have reported faucets being turned on and the clanging of pots and pans when nobody's in the kitchen. TV crews for mystery and haunting shows have also done segments on Jennie's reputed posthumous antics.

copy I'd made was dark, and grainy and you could barely hear any sound, but could see those two kids looking

GT COMMONS

The grand, Victorian buildings of Grand Traverse Commons off Division Street in Traverse City are a source of pride in how they were renovated in recent decades and turned into a bustling center of life and commerce. But there's a darker past. It was built in 1885 as a state mental institution, set against a wooded slope on the western edge of town, with eerie tunnels connecting some of the buildings. Many Traverse Citians worked there in its century as a mental institution, but some of Michigan's saddest stories played out and even ended beneath the spires. The idyllic setting was part of the therapy, but on the dark side, so were shock treatment and lobotomies.

The linchpin is the imposing Building 50, now home to trendy shops, fine dining and sought-after offices. Yet through the years have come stories about voices and closing doors, shadows moving in the halls and a portal to Hell in one of the tunnels. There's also an eerie tale of a tape recording made in one of the buildings that included a voice — unheard during the actual recording — moaning that it wanted to leave.

OAKWOOD CEMETERY

This sprawling final resting place on E. 8th Street between Garfield and Munson avenues is believed to be overseen by the friendly spirit of its first sexton, Roderick Gray. The short, bearded Scotsman appears to a local clairvoyant on occasion, giving him messages to pass along. He's even smoking a pipe, like he did in life back in the 1800s.

CENTRAL GRADE SCHOOL

Now an elementary school, the school at 301 7th Street in Traverse City, has been the subject of haunting rumors for generations. Some students say they've seen a ghost come down from the third floor. The school's Lars Hockstad Auditorium now hosts many community events and is one of several venues for movies during the Traverse City Film Festival. There's a statue of Abraham Lincoln standing to the left of the stage. Some have said they've seen the statue shake or even turn its head. —**TC**

OLD MISSION

Old Mission Peninsula

THERE'S NOTHING QUITE LIKE THIS JEWEL BOX OF ORCHARDS, VINEYARDS AND BAY VIEWS. OLD MISSION WAS ALSO THE FIRST HOME OF THE FIRST EUROPEANS IN THE TC AREA.

Rev. Peter Dougherty sailed into the little harbor near Haserot Beach for the second time in the spring of 1839. He'd been looking around for a favorable spot to start a missionary, and had originally elected to build a log church in Elk Rapids. Local Native leader Chief Aghosa convinced him to relocate, church and all — to Old Mission. One lone native was there to meet the reverend, but with the help of some smoke signals, the rest of the band returned from its hunting expedition on the other side of the peninsula.

Chief Aghosa, the leader of the band, was an affable young fellow who took the Christian name of Addison Potts. Aghosa's band built a bark hut for the missionary, which became the school when Doughtery's more substantial post and beam home was finished. Under the terms of the Treaty of 1836, the federal government was required to provide for the Ottawa and Chippewa, and paid Dougherty $3,000 per year to maintain the "reservation," which was also on US government property.

By 1850, there were more than 40 log homes, wigwams, cabins, stores, mechanic shops, a church and a school at the end of Old Mission. The church bell was cast from British pennies collected by the natives. Forests had been cleared and replaced with corn and potatoes. A post office was established by 1851, the only one north of Muskegon and south of Mackinac. But treaty rights changed in 1850, and the various native groups consolidated to purchase property across West Bay in Omena. Dougherty went with them. (See page 224.)

In 1861, Solon Rushmore bought Dougherty's house, and it remained with the family for about 100 years. The Rushmores later turned the home into an inn that catered to resorters arriving by steamship — big business beginning around 1870. The *Illinois*, a steamship with upscale accommodations for 250 passengers, published a schedule in 1904 providing a Friday departure from Chicago at 7 PM, with arrival in Old Mission two days later. Round trip fare was $13, and an overnight in Old Mission an additional $1.50. The Old Mission Beach Resort Association located on the north side of Haserot Bay (now the Leffingwell Association) was described in 1891 as "a diversified woodland with nearly three quarters of a mile of hard sandy beach with southerly exposure upon a land-locked harbor ... confessedly the most attractive and healthful locality on Michigan waters."

Dougherty's home was acquired by Peninsula Township in 2006, and today it is administered by the Peter Dougherty Society.

A replica of the church is on Mission Road.

unloading boxcars of dry milk for a guy who owned a dairy and an ice cream factory. Fifty pound bags stacked

MISSION POINT LIGHTHOUSE

Built in 1870 and standing just off the 45th parallel, the lighthouse is the most popular destination on Old Mission. Climb to the top of the tower, tour the museum and visit the Hessler Log Cabin exhibit nearby.

Don't forget your bathing suit! The water is very shallow here, and good fun for little kids.

Want to live in the lighthouse? See more about that on page 217.

The lighthouse is surrounded by hundreds of acres of parkland, criss-crossed with trails for hikers, horses, biking, skiing and walking with your dog. Access directly from the lighthouse parking lot, or from the old Murray Farm at the end of Ridgewood Road. There's also seasonal access on Murray Road with dramatic old forests and ridges. Beach access is difficult, and even if you get there, you might not get back.

thirty high, forty deep, one kid to a car and the whole day to kill yourself. At night I'd hop on my Schwinn

Bowers Harbor

This is the place to park if you want to paddle to the island. There's a boat launch and restroom facilities. There isn't really a beach, but next door at The Boathouse restaurant, you can get an excellent meal and sit on its deck.

Once upon a time, in the winter of 1851, the captain and crew of the *Madeline*, a 56-foot, twin-masted schooner, docked here for the winter. On board were five young men who the captain thought would benefit from a bit of schooling. He hired a 17-year-old teacher and they spent the frozen season learning reading, writing and arithmetic, making the *Madeline* the first school for non-natives in the area.

The captain of the ship was named Fitzgerald. Many years later, his grandson, who owned an insurance company, named a freighter after himself, the *SS Edmund Fitzgerald*. It didn't end well. The ship went down on Lake Superior on November 10, 1975. All hands perished. The *Fitzgerald* also goes down in history as being the largest ship on the Great Lakes when she launched in 1958, and the largest ever to sink.

Meanwhile, the *Madeline* is still around today. In the 1980s, 165 Maritime Heritage Alliance volunteers gave 40,000 hours to build a replica of the ship. Her mission is to serve as she did once before, as a floating school for the interpretation of Great Lakes maritime history. The *Madeline* is open to visitors in her home port of Traverse City and travels to other Great Lakes ports under local sponsorship. More information at maritimeheritagealliance.org.

For lots more about Old Mission, visit the Old Mission Historical Society's website at omphistoricalsociety.org.

Corvette and take the High Street hill route so I could feel the wind in my face then ride around Baldwin Lake for

Power Island

Marion Island, Ford Island, Rennie Island… the 200-acre island in West Bay has had its share of monikers over the last 100 years. We don't know what the Native Americans called it, but they said it was haunted. Henry Ford saw the island during a company picnic at Bowers Harbor and thought it would make a fine resort and bought it in 1917. In fact, there was already a pavilion on the smaller isle, Bassett, infamous as an unsupervised party destination.

Ford never did build the resort, but he did hold parties there, and supposedly tossed a drunken Babe Ruth in the drink when he was here as a guest of the National Cherry Festival.

Developers targeted the island in the 1970s for private homes, but Eugene and Sayde Power stepped up with a major contribution and the island was acquired by the Nature Conservancy. It is now a public park owned by Grand Traverse County.

Power Island has 3 miles of waterfront and over 5 miles of hiking trails. An isthmus connects Power Island to Bassett. There are a few rustic campsites on both. Call 231-922-4818 for reservations.

It's a 6.5 mile boat ride from Clinch Park Marina and 3.5 mile ride from Bower's Harbor Marina. There's also a shuttle that runs during the summer, leaving from the dock at Bowers Harbor.

Drinking water is available only on Power Island. Good dogs are welcome. You must take out whatever you bring in as there is no trash pick-up on the islands.

PYATT LAKE

For a short walk through a strange place, stop off at the Pyatt Lake reserve. More than 250 different species of plants reside in this postage-stamp of a park, making it one of the most diverse in the TC area. In the autumn, the mushroom variety is incredible.

Get to the reserve from Bowers Harbor on Peninsula Drive. Take Neah Ta Wanta Road, then a right on Pyatt Road.

Red-winged blackbird (male)

YOU CAN'T GET LOST

Old Mission Peninsula is 22 miles long and, in some places, less than a mile wide. M-37 — locally known as Center Road — is the main drag, and terminates at the Mission Point Lighthouse. Center Road has big hills and views of both bays, plus the island. Traffic can be heavy as far as Mapleton (where there's a grocery store) but drops dramatically north of there. There are three points of public access. In order of appearance: East Bay Boat Launch, Archie Park and Lighthouse Park.

On the west side runs Peninsula Drive, a mostly sleepy, winding road with paved shoulders. The only public access to the water is at Bowers Harbor. From there on back to TC, it's mansions all the way.

On the east side, there are two roads that hug the shore: Bayshore Drive and Bluff Road. Both of these are also quiet and excellent for biking. No public access to the shore.

Dozens of roads run east–west on the peninsula, through farms and forests. Take a tour; you can't get lost.

a quick swim, hoping for a ski boat to come close enough to shore to send even the smallest wake my way.

Quilt Barns

There are about 100 historic barns on Old Mission Peninsula, most of which no longer serve agricultural operations. In 2001, a woman from Ohio came up with the idea of painting a quilt section on the side of her barn to honor her mother. The idea spread, and more than 2,000 barns across the country are now decorated, including 10 on Old Mission. Visit nowbarnsofoldmission.com for information on the trail and details.

THE OLD MISSION GENERAL STORE is busting at its old-timey seams with everything you might want to take on your picnic at the Point. You can also eat your ice cream in a rocking chair on the porch.

This is not the original location of the general store and post office: it was moved here during the Civil War.

LIQUOR
BAIT
ICE
BLUEBERRIES
ICE CREAM

BUCHAN'S BLUEBERRY HILL Ben and Lori Buchan are the fifth generation to own and operate the 100-year-old farm. Pick your own blueberries, apples and peaches. Homemade ice cream is served in the summer and cider in the fall.

BEACHES

HASEROT BEACH & BOAT LAUNCH || Deep and cold. A play structure for the kiddies.
Brand new **KELLEY PARK**, just down the beach from Haserot, is shallower and you can bring your dog.
MISSION POINT LIGHTHOUSE & PARK || Very shallow, often rocky or impassable when water levels are high.

ANTIQUES

OLD BARN ANTIQUES SHOP || Since 1910.

GROCERIES

PENINSULA MARKET
OLD MISSION GENERAL STORE

RESTAURANTS

PENINSULA GRILL || Local bar food.
MISSION TABLE || Dinner only with Chef Paul Olsen.
JOLLY PUMPKIN || Lunch and dinner, a brewery and distillery.
THE BOATHOUSE || Fine dining on West Bay.
OLD MISSION TAVERN || Lunch and dinner in a combined dining room and gallery.

The Ghosts of Old Mission

Bicyclists who ride Old Mission Peninsula's rolling hills sometimes experience sudden drops in temperature. These cold spots can be explained in terms of geophysical factors. However, a little imagination provides another explanation. These places might well be the gathering spots for the ghosts of murder victims from years past, unable to rest peacefully because their violent ends were in such dramatic contrast to the pristine beauty of the Peninsula.

In 1895, the body of Julia Curtis, Woodruff Parmelee's young mistress, was found in what locals called the hemlock swamp along the eastern edge of the Peninsula, a couple of miles north of Traverse City. In his 40s, Parmelee was not only more than twice Julia's age, but twice married and recently divorced from his second wife. It was also discovered that at the time of her death, Julia was pregnant, a fact that the prosecution insisted gave Parmelee motive. Taken together, all these details bear a striking resemblance to those of the 1906 trial that formed the basis for Theodore Dreiser's *An American Tragedy,* since in both cases the victim was a pregnant young woman whom the lover did not want to marry.

The Curtis house still stands on the intersection of Center Road and Wakalut Road. A few miles north is Island View Road on which now sits the building that houses the Old Mission Peninsula School and the Peninsula Community Library. On this road, known in the 1920s as Swede Road, was the farm of Stephen Carroll and his wife Mame, a divorcee who came to the marriage with her son Braddock. One morning in 1921, Carroll was found dead near a stall in his barn, the back of his skull crushed. Family and neighbors split on whether this was a terrible accident or a murder, some insisting that Carroll had been kicked by one of his horses, others contending that stepson Braddock, who frequently quarreled with Carroll, had killed his stepfather after an argument over the use of the family car.

Braddock was found not guilty, a verdict that to this day is not well accepted by some of Carroll's descendants. To add a little spice to the story, there is the reputation of Mame as a witch, and the perhaps apocryphal claim that on nearby Nelson Road, beneath an elm tree, was found a blood-stained handkerchief around a stone that some claim was the murder weapon.

Still further north, across from the intersection of Center Road and Smokey Hollow, was another barn on another farm where on another morning, this time in 1937, Chester Colerick was found shot dead by Ralph Helferich. The two had been friends and owners of neighboring farms, but Ralph came to believe his wife was involved with Joe, and so on that morning, Ralph drove the short distance to his neighbor's farm, found Chester in the barn attending to his morning chores and shot him with his 12 gauge shotgun. He then returned home, told his wife, "Well, I've done for Joe," then kissed their daughter, went outside and with the same shotgun literally blew the top of his head off.

The ghosts of four victims, the pregnant young woman, and three farmers. Three violent acts upsetting the rural peacefulness of the Peninsula. Their ghosts now reminding us that hot blooded passion leaves cold dead bodies. —*Stephen Lewis writes about murder in his two historical mysteries,* Murder on Old Mission *and* Murder Undone, *available in local book stores or at Amazon.*

intro to "409" to shake the house and drive my sister crazy. She preferred Del Shannon or the Platters, but it

78

The Cherry Industry

PERHAPS NO ONE WOULD BE MORE SURPRISED BY
TRAVERSE CITY'S CLAIM TO FAME THAN THE MAN WHO
STARTED IT ALL MORE THAN TWO-HUNDRED YEARS AGO.
A PRESBYTERIAN MISSIONARY BY THE NAME OF PETER
DOUGHERTY PLANTED A CHERRY ORCHARD FOR REASONS
THAT EVEN HE WOULD BE UNLIKELY TO EXPLAIN.

Whatever his motives were — merely playful experimentation or a taste for pies and preserves — to both the surprise of his fellow settlers and the local Native Americans the orchard thrived. Millions of pounds of cherries later, the Traverse Bay area continues to keep the tradition alive.

The National Cherry Festival that serves as an attraction for 500,000 tourists every year had its humble beginnings as the Blessing of the Blossoms Festival in 1925. What was once a two-day celebration of the explosion of blooms in mid-June has since been moved to accommodate the July 4th holiday. Although this no doubt proved a shrewd choice for attracting more tourists, it also had the unceremonious consequence of missing the blooming white flowers for which the event was originally known. A fact that Festival tourists are unlikely to discover while indulging in the near bottomless cherry-fueled inventions, is that the bulk of the produce sold in the Traverse Bay area during this time is not from the region—or even from Michigan. Instead, Washington state supplies most of the fruit that the Cherry Festival is known for. Northern Michigan cherries aren't usually ready for harvest until mid-July, which leaves the National Cherry Festival in the unusual place of celebrating a fruit that is grown thousands of miles away.

In 2004 the non-denominational ceremony that took place at the inception of the first festival was revived and a clergyman blessed the coming growing season for both grapes and cherries. Only one-half of those prayers have been answered; today hundreds of acres of cherries continue to be knocked down to make way for more grapes, in no small part due to the exploding demand of wine and wineries. Also, sweet cherry harvests have been less than exceptional due to several years of early frosts. The devastating season in 2002 was repeated in 2012, and two once-in-a-lifetime events occurring so near to each other has likely spooked many in the industry. In addition to fickle weather having the ultimate say in producers' harvests, the Cherry Industry Administrative Board operating under the Department of Agriculture restricts the processing of tart cherries, leading to infamous instances of "dumping," like the 30 million pounds mostly from Michigan that had to be tossed in 2009. Tens of thousands of pounds were dumped again in 2016. Although this may procure images of tyrannical bureaucracies in Washington D.C., passing judgment on fruits and vegetables, without any restrictions the value of cherries would likely drop and, in turn, hurt the farmers. —**HC**

was surf music all the time for us: Jan and Dean, two girls for every boy in Surf City, or the Markets helping

MIGRANT WORKERS

Migrant workers are a fact of life on farms that produce labor-intensive produce like asparagus, peaches, apples and strawberries. When cherry farming first became intensive back in the 1940s, workers were trucked in from the New Deal work programs. Then, WWII got in the way, and the cherry-pickers came from Jamaica. After the war, it was mostly Mexico. Area cherry farmers were so grateful for the thousands of Mexicans who showed up for the harvest in 1951 that they built them a float for the Cherry Royale Parade.

Mechanization changed everything in the cherry industry in the 1970s, reducing drastically the amount of laborers needed to harvest. But apples and peaches still need a pair of human hands, and according to the Farm Bureau, Michigan farms demand 49,000 laborers each and every year.

Increasingly, the migrants aren't coming anymore. Tighter legislation in 1996, plus the increasingly heated arguments for building a wall, have forced some farmers to give up on delicate crops. In Leelanau County, apple orchards are at only 60% of what they were even five years ago.

What's taking their place? Grapes, for the most part. While grapes require hand-labor for pruning and maintaining vines, machinery does exist that can eventually replace the humans.

Some day soon, labor-intensive Michigan apples, blueberries, asparagus and peaches may be just a sweet, summer memory.

Attending an event with a lot of local young people, it's hard to miss the fact that there are

SO MANY BLONDES.

Rural road names are an excellent way to gauge the ethnicity of the immigrant population. Take Leelanau County, for example. Suttons Bay immigrants tended to be German. The same in Lake Leelanau. The French preferred Leland, while the Swedes and Norwegians headed to Northport. The Polish population is centered in Cedar; Gill's Pier was mostly Bohemian.

The short answer to the astounding amount of natural UpNorth blondes is that many Central Europeans chose to settle here, perhaps because it reminded them of home.

us through the Surfer Stomp. Then we'd hop around the room and make ourselves look like we were surfing,

OLD MISSION

THE GRAND TRAVERSE REGION HAS TWO OF MICHIGAN'S FOUR FEDERALLY RECOGNIZED WINE GROWING AREAS.

OLD MISSION IS ONE OF THEM.

holding our hands out from our sides, or dancing out to the end of the board to hang ten, do a curl, then dip

The Wineries of Old Mission Peninsula

OLD MISSION IS THAT PENINSULA BETWEEN MICHIGAN'S PINKY AND THE REST OF THE HAND, WHICH CAN'T QUITE BE EXPLAINED IN ANATOMICAL TERMS. THAT 22-MILE-LONG STRETCH OF NATURAL BEAUTY AND PRIME REAL ESTATE IS FAMOUS FOR ITS RED, WHITE AND SPARKLING WINES.

Grape (much like cherry) growers talk about the microclimates created by the surrounding East and West Grand Traverse Bays and rises and dips in land.

Ed O'Keefe was the first winemaker to harness those elements and condense them down to the wine glass on a commercial level, back in 1974.

Since then, nine other wineries have planted vines and set up shop on Old Mission, making for at least a full day's worth of seeing and tasting this unique peninsula.

down into the pipeline for a long shot out of the living groom. Some nights it was the Ventures or the Waiki-kis

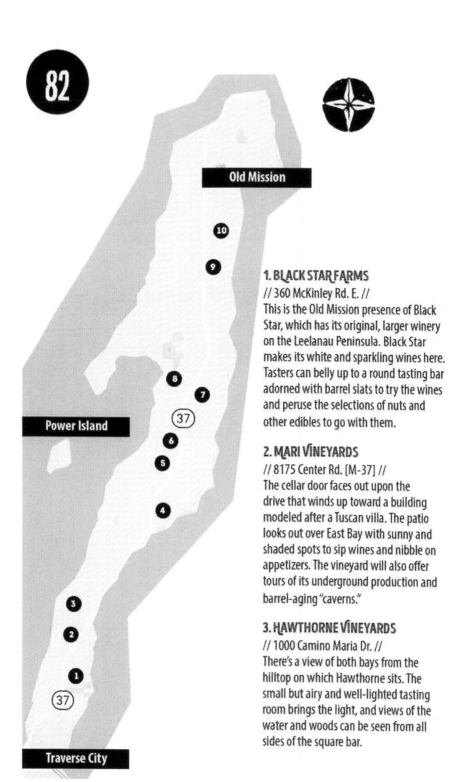

Old Mission

Power Island

Traverse City

1. BLACK STAR FARMS
// 360 McKinley Rd. E. //
This is the Old Mission presence of Black Star, which has its original, larger winery on the Leelanau Peninsula. Black Star makes its white and sparkling wines here. Tasters can belly up to a round tasting bar adorned with barrel slats to try the wines and peruse the selections of nuts and other edibles to go with them.

2. MARI VINEYARDS
// 8175 Center Rd. [M-37] //
The cellar door faces out upon the drive that winds up toward a building modeled after a Tuscan villa. The patio looks out over East Bay with sunny and shaded spots to sip wines and nibble on appetizers. The vineyard will also offer tours of its underground production and barrel-aging "caverns."

3. HAWTHORNE VINEYARDS
// 1000 Camino Maria Dr. //
There's a view of both bays from the hilltop on which Hawthorne sits. The small but airy and well-lighted tasting room brings the light, and views of the water and woods can be seen from all sides of the square bar.

4. PENINSULA CELLARS

// 11480 Center Rd. [M-37] //
This cozy tasting room is in a repurposed one-room schoolhouse. The quaint setting shows up in the names of the wines themselves; names like Detention and Homework. A patio with a fence decorated by grapevines provides a place to recess with a glass.

5. BONOBO

// 12011 Center Rd. [M-37] //
Behind the unassuming front door of Bonobo Winery lies a tasting room with living room-like alcoves and a patio view of West Grand Traverse Bay. There are bays in the room surrounding the tasting bar with indoor-outdoor fireplaces. Sharing the crackling warmth is a patio with a sweeping vista and outdoor space heaters to keep the chill off. There's star power here, too. Basic cable home-improvement hunk and TC native Carter Oosterhouse and his family are owners. Their friend, TV celebrity chef Mario Batali, who has a home in Northport, has designed a menu of appetizers to complement the Bonobo wine list.

6. CHATEAU GRAND TRAVERSE

// 12239 Center Rd. [M-37] //
The spacious and shady porch, with Adirondack chairs and end tables, is a pleasant respite on a hot, sunny day. The extensive gift shop here goes beyond the usual polo shirts and corkscrews. In addition to the tasting bar is a relaxing outdoor serving area muffled from the world by the very vines from which their bottles are filled.

7. BRYS ESTATE VINEYARD AND WINERY

// 3309 Blue Water Rd. //
A memorable touch in Brys' homey, country winery is the barrel room, beckoning with the aroma of wine-soaked wood. The stainless steel fermentation tanks are just on the other side. Outside, you may sip from a glass on the lower deck, on an upper deck overlooking vines, hills, and East Bay, or a shady garden with a bocce ball court and bucket of balls for a laid-back competition. There's also a sun-drenched "secret garden" down the hill with lavender, berries and herbs.

8. BOWERS HARBOR VINEYARDS

// 2896 Bowers Harbor Rd. //
Grapevines twist their way through the arbor that greets visitors to this vineyard and shades the walkway to the rustic tasting room. In European fashion, tables and chairs are set between vine rows on the rolling vineyard that faces Bowers Harbor, a small inlet of West Bay near some of the older, luxurious homes of Peninsula Drive. Heated pavilions are available for colder days. There's a 1-mile nature walk through the vineyards: good views both winter and summer.

9. CHATEAU CHANTAL

// 15900 Rue de Vin. //
When it comes to grand Old Mission vistas, Chantal appears to be king of the hill. The woods and vines of the peninsula itself are in full splendor here, as are both bays. The shop and tasting room are spacious, and there's a roomy deck on the East Bay side that has a gazebo-serving room when it's open.

10. 2 LADS WINERY

// 16985 Smokey Hollow Rd. //
Enter the curving, climbing drive past old fruit trees up to the modern winery. The tasting room is one of sharp angles and stainless steel, with a commanding view of East Bay from the bar. The winery produces small lots of red, white and sparkling wines. **TC**

NOT A DRINKER? CHATEAU CHANTAL AND BLACK STAR FARMS BOTH OFFER SPARKLING GRAPE JUICE.

---

music and always loud, an ocean of sound rolling through the neighborhood. ¶ I was landlocked until I was

ONE WAY OR ANOTHER, ALL ROADS LEAD TO ACME. SURELY IT WAS ON THE OLD MACKINAC TRAIL, AND IT'S STILL THE FASTEST WAY TO GET TO THE INTERSTATE.

There was industry here in the 1930s: The Milliken family manufactured hand-held insecticide sprayers before they became politicians and doctors. But for most of its history it was just a crossroads on the way to somewhere else.

The Grand Traverse Resort & Spa was the first to put Acme on the map, buying up orchards, a trailer park and beach property in the early 1980s — just about the time the cherry industry was losing ground to foreign imports. The Grand Traverse Band of Ottawa and Chippewa Indians bought the resort in 2003.

The loudest hoopla came from the Meijer complex just south of town. For 14 years, locals, environmentalists and developers fought over the details. At one point, Meijer, which already had a store in TC, withdrew its advertising support from the *Record-Eagle*. The economically diminished newspaper was sold shortly afterwards. The whole long, sad story was covered nationally in *Harper's Magazine*.

PARKS & MORE

DEEPWATER POINT NATURAL AREA is a sweet spot for a short walk. Wander around through the woods, or hang out with the frogs and birds on its wetland beach.

SAND LAKES QUIET AREA, east of town on Broomhead Road, is an enormous place with 12 lakes and 12.5 miles of trails. It's popular in the summer with mountain bikers and campers. In the winter, it's a great place for skiing and snow-shoeing. Snowmobilers also like the area.

The **VASA** trailhead is in Acme, on Bartlett Road. More about the VASA on pages 95 and 153.

WILSON ANTIQUES has an annex in Acme. Cool salvage from Detroit.

THE MUSIC HOUSE MUSEUM focuses on automated instruments, like music boxes and player-pianos. You can take a self-guided tour, or docents are available.

THE G.T. BUTTERFLY AND BUG ZOO is also located in Acme. Take a class or just walk around and look.

HOXIE'S FARM MARKET on M-72 has you-pick apples and pumpkins, haystacks, a corn maze in the fall and wagon rides.

Flintfields Horse Park

Just south of Acme, off M-72 on Bates Road is **FLINTFIELDS**, a world-class equestrian show ground. There are over 80 acres of gardens, show and practice rings, concessions and covered event spaces. Even if you aren't "horse-people," this is an amazing place to spend an afternoon. Sit on the lawn and watch the show, or get up-close-and-personable with the noblest of beasts.

The Flint Fields Horse Park has a notable economic impact on the area, bringing in between $15-$20 million of spending in the Traverse City community over the summer.

Great Lakes Equestrian Festival

JULY 5 – 30 AND AUGUST 2 – 13

These nationally rated hunter/jumper competitions at Flintfields feature classes and classics for children, juniors, adult and amateur-owner riders. During operation weeks, the festival also has classes for young horses, the professional hunter derby and open jumpers.

The premier Grand Prix is held each Sunday during July and August.

WEAR THE RIGHT SHOES. FLIP-FLOPS AND SANDALS ARE NOT APPROPRIATE AROUND HORSES. YOU KNOW WHY.

LEARN TO RIDE

RANCH RUDOLPH, south of TC, offers classses, summer camps and trail rides. Operates seven days a week during the summer. Call for reservations.

OUTRIDER HORSEBACK RIDING in Lake Ann has Western-style horseback camping and trail rides. Pony rides, too. Call for reservations.

BLUE OXER RIDING ACADEMY in Maple city specializes in English riding lessons. Call for reservations.

NORTHERN PINES FARM offers the basics of horsemanship as well as the finer points of the hunter / jumper show ring. Call for reservations.

H&H STABLES in Empire features therapeutic riding programs. Good reviews from first-timers. Stop in any time for pony rides.

desire to always be in the passing lane. Once in a w e we'd drive to Lake Michigan during thunderstorms and

YUBA

Farm foreman Jim Scott with John Shaw, early 50s.

I GREW UP ON A CHERRY FARM IN YUBA.
MY GRANDPARENTS BOUGHT THE PROPERTY
AFTER THE GREAT DEPRESSION AND MOVED
HERE FROM KANSAS CITY.

By the time I was born, there were 300 acres of fruit trees and a processing plant in Elk Rapids that my grandfather built. An army of Mexican-Americans arrived every summer for the harvest: the Reyna family from Florida, and others from Brownsville, Texas. They lived in tiny "picker shacks" across the highway, cooking and bathing in communal facilities. I was not allowed over there, and had to stand on the side of the road and yell for my friends to come and play. We didn't share a language, but we taught each other songs and games.

There were six of us kids, including cousins, and as soon as we could count we went to work in the cherry stand: "60 cents a quart, two for a dollar" was the going rate. When I reached sixth grade, I began working at the Elk Rapids plant, sitting on the line and discarding the rotten fruit, among other things. The line was so loud that I could sing at the top of my lungs without anyone hearing me.

It wasn't all work during the summers. We had a couple of ponies that we could ride for miles up and down Yuba Creek, taking down and putting back up the barbed-wire fences along the way. My mother sent us to the Yuba Bible Camp — along with every other kid in the neighborhood — where a ventriloquist dressed all in black taught us about Jesus.

Mechanization in the '70s changed everything. Instead of a hundred hands, we only needed a crew of six for harvesting. The farm was sold in the '90s and most of it is now the Yuba Creek Natural Area. —**HS**

body surf off the coast off the Muskegon State Park, the beach littered with alewives and empty bottles. We'd

Yuba Creek Natural Area

There are two entrances to this 413-acre park. The first one, off US-31, has a short, .4-mile loop with big views and lots of wildflowers. Russian olive bushes were threatening to overwhelm the place, and drastic measures were taken in 2016 to stop their invasion.

The other parking spot is down the hill off US-31 on Yuba Road. There's a long, straight trail down the middle of the valley. Eagles nest here and are often seen circling overhead.

Near the south side of the park, two record-breaking beeches are tucked into a hill.

Hunting is allowed in this park.

Yuba

Now considered a ghost town, Yuba used to boast three churches, a sawmill, a cheese factory, a woolen mill and a post office. All that's left is the school, built in 1860, and the out-of-business Yuba Trading Post across the road.

On the other side of the highway, in that little triangle of ditch, there's a staircase leading down to what some consider the oldest known Caucasian grave in the northwestern region of Michigan's Lower Peninsula. The grave belongs to two-year-old William Leith, who died in February 1859.

Sayler Park

This park was hit hard by the storm of 2015. There's a boat launch and decent beach with good swimming. Lots of picnic spots, plus three covered areas available for events. Blueberries grow wild under the pine trees.

Maple Bay Natural Area

There aren't enough nice things to say about this park with the biggest, wildest beach outside of Sleeping Bear. Look for the field of sunflowers on US-31, heading towards Elk Rapids. The farmhouse is part of the park, and you can walk around it and look in the windows. Kiteboarders love this area, and on a windy day, there can be a whole flock of them performing on the bay. It's a bit of a walk down to the beach, so you might want to travel light. The downed trees and general disarray of the trail is also the result of the wind storm of 2015.

Hike (or wade) north to the point to look for Petoskey stones. Some of this property is private, so you must stay on the beach. Petobego Pond is on the other side of the point and it's full of birds. Kids may like to search for the old duck blind.

Hunting is allowed in this park.

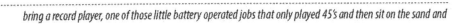

bring a record player, one of those little battery operated jobs that only played 45's and then sit on the sand and

ELK RAPIDS

MUCH LIKE TRAVERSE CITY, ELK RAPIDS WAS A DIRTY, INDUSTRIAL TOWN IN THE 1800S, WITH CHEMICAL AND CEMENT FACTORIES, AN IRON SMELTING FACILITY AND, OF COURSE, A SAWMILL.

Also like its neighbor to the west, the trees ran out —— many of them going to Chicago for rebuilding after the 1871 fire —— and the Great Depression killed everything else.

Elk Rapids has struggled over the years to make itself a tourist destination, and it deserves attention for the finest beach for kids ever conceived. Not only is it long and wide, but kids can float up and down the Elk River, where there's a fun little dam to jump over. Dogs like it too, and are allowed on the beach on leashes.

It's easy to spend the day in Elk Rapids. Explore the marina, and there's a charming little library perched on a hill between the harbor and the beach.

Get a picnic at **CELLAR 152**, or eat on the patio across the street at **SIREN HALL**. Great breakfast at the **HARBOR CAFE**. **PEARL'S NEW ORLEANS KITCHEN** is down the road a bit, on Ames Street, as is the brand new **ETHANOLOGY DISTILLATION**.

SHORT'S BREWING COMPANY

Short's, one of the best breweries in Michigan, has its production facility in Elk Rapids. Their new outdoor pub-space will operate Monday-Friday from 3 to 10 PM and Saturday and Sunday from 12 to 10 PM. Tours available Saturday and Sunday afternoons at 3 PM. Short's is available locally in most bars and grocery stores.

watch the surf, waiting for what we thought was a set, something rideable. There on the beach it was always

GUNTZVILLER TAXIDERMY & SPIRIT OF THE WOODS MUSEUM

Is that a two-headed cow? Yes, it is.

Don't miss this spot — watch for the giant mastodon tangled in hollyhocks along US-31 heading north to Elk Rapids. Inside are some serious collections of arrowheads and other artifacts that George Guntzviller collected 100 years ago while plowing his land. Even more compelling are the dioramas of local fauna. Kids will LOVE exploring this charming, truly UpNorth treasure.

Elk Lake

It might not look like it from the highway — all those stumps! — but Elk Lake is deep: 192 feet to be precise. Only about 12 miles square, it's protected from the sea lamprey that wreaked such havoc on Lake Michigan fish during the '30s and '40s.

In 2016, DNA fish researcher Jory Jonas was on a sampling trip on the lake and pulled up something she'd never seen before. Turns out, she and her team had discovered a small population of native lake trout, long gone from the big lake, but protected in the deep, waters of Elk Lake.

Elk Lake is part of the Chain of Lakes, a series of 14 lakes and interconnecting rivers that cover 75 miles and include Elk Lake, Lake Skegemog and Torch Lake. Navigable by small boat, except for the dam in Bellaire.

DRIVE THE CHAIN OF LAKES

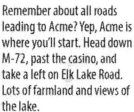

Remember about all roads leading to Acme? Yep, Acme is where you'll start. Head down M-72, past the casino, and take a left on Elk Lake Road. Lots of farmland and views of the lake.

At the traffic light, turn right on Ames Street and head through Kewadin. Keep left — you're now on Cairn Highway. That little pyramid is made of rocks collected all over the county.

You'll end up back on US-31, and follow that to Eastport. Turn right on M-88. This road takes you through Central Lake, Bellaire and Mancelona.

As an alternative, you can drive County Road 593 (East Torch Lake Road) along the shore of Torch Lake.

Keep going. You'll cross Clam River then pass through the little towns of Alden (The Adorable) and Rapid City (less adorable), where you can catch M-72 back to TC.

Lots of places to eat along the way, particularly in Bellaire.

Gold Finch

Quail

Nuthatch

Cardinal

Song Thrush

Pheasant

Ford came back from his senior trip to California, his new long blond hair making him look like Brian Wilson, a

THE SANDHILL CRANE IS ANOTHER UPNORTH BIRD THAT WAS SELDOM SEEN 50 YEARS AGO.

Sandhill cranes nest on the ground, which was part of the problem when industrialization, then development disturbed their breeding grounds. Hunters took out many of the rest. In 1944, there were only 27 breeding pairs left in the Lower Peninsula. Legislation has helped them rebound, and they've done spectacularly well, with numbers reaching 25,000 in 2012.

Sandhill cranes are big birds. Really big: like 4 feet tall. They eat frogs, fish and insects, but you'll often find them in corn and grain fields as well. Yes, the farmers complain, but Dave Luukkonen, avian research specialist for the Michigan Department of Natural Resources, says Michigan isn't quite ready for a hunting season yet.

Sandhills make solitary nests on the ground or over shallow water and typically lay two eggs. The colts are ready to fly in about 70 days and remain with their parents for a year. It takes up to seven years for a sandhill to reach maturity. They live an average of 20 years.

Sandhills are migratory, nesting in the northern states and Canada, then traveling to Texas, Florida and Mexico for the winter. As a point of interest, cranes have the longest fossil history of any known bird: a ten-million-year-old fossil was found in Nebraska.

You can often spot the cranes across the highway from the Maple Bay Natural Area and in Leelanau County.

battered up Hobie tied to his van with clothesline. I offer him twenty bucks at his garage sale and he took it, just

LAKE ANN

The Quintessential Northern Michigan Small-Town Store

THE TOWN OF LAKE ANN (WHICH IS TECHNICALLY A "VILLAGE" ACCORDING TO THE SIGNS COMING INTO THE PLACE) IS A TINY ONE WITH ONE LITTLE BANK, A POST OFFICE, A NEWLY OPENED BREWPUB, COFFEE SHOP AND —IF YOU LIKE A PLACE THAT HAS EVERYTHING— ONE SUPER-COOL GENERAL STORE.

With one main street cutting through the place, you can't miss it. The saloon-style building looks straight out of a Hollywood western. On the marquee out front, there's always an advertisement for some new item or exciting bargain: Delmonico steaks, pork tenderloins, homegrown cucumbers, rhubarb, blueberries and cherries in summertime.

More than just some rinky-dink spot to get perishable odds and ends when you're loathe to drive 20 minutes into Traverse City, this real-deal general store stocks everything from fennel seeds to fish hooks, brake fluid to Bordeaux. "If We Don't Have It, You Don't Need It" is the Lake Ann Grocery motto. And that goes for your crazy hardware needs, too: a full stock of nails, screws, hinges, hasps, compression and flare fittings, grommets, toilet seat hinge bolts, gasket shellac compound and six sizes of nipple pipes. Nipple pipes!

During the summer, Lake Ann Grocery is usually buzzing with a mix of locals, rental property visitors and campers buying stuff like firewood, ice and beer. (There's a state forest campground located on the lake just down the road in addition to a newly created public beach.) In fall and winter, the place opens at 6 AM making it a favorite donut and coffee stop for early morning bird and deer hunters. If you're out this way and don't have a clue where you're going, owners John and Sandy Nuske have owned the place for something like a *bazillion* years and can point you in the right direction. **BB**

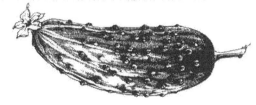

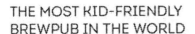

THE MOST KID-FRIENDLY BREWPUB IN THE WORLD

Having children is a blessing, right? They infuse meaning and enrich our everyday lives and blah, blah, blah. Kids are wonderful, that is, until at the end of the day when all you want to do is get a bite to eat and sip on a cold craft beer unfettered by their constant bickering and complaining about being bored.

Fifteen minutes west of Traverse City, Lake Ann Brewery is situated right across the hardly-traveled street from the shady and recently remodeled Lake Ann Village Park (with swing set, climbing structure, slides and basketball hoops). Helicopter parents will rejoice in the fact that you can clearly monitor the goings-on at the park right from a window seat at the pub.

Right next to the pub, there's a soft-serve ice cream shop (Cory's Cones), while on the other side sits the Stone Oven, which provides unexpectedly creative and delicious menu items such as the adult Mac n' Cheese and Greek quesadillas for hungry pub customers. There's a kid's menu, too, which offers more than just the standard hot dog and chicken fingers fare.

Restaurant staff will bring your food to your seat at the pub after your order. But a lot of local parents — Lake Ann is a family-friendly village with over 3,000 full-time residents living within 3 miles of the pub — like to keep their kids busy by having them run next door to do the ordering and pickup. After dinner, give them a five-spot and send them next door for a cone or down to Lake Ann Grocery to pick out a DVD to round out the night. **BB**

IF WE DON'T HAVE IT YOU DON'T NEED IT

top of my dad's 67' jeep, a red leftover from some local fire department and drove around town all summer, the

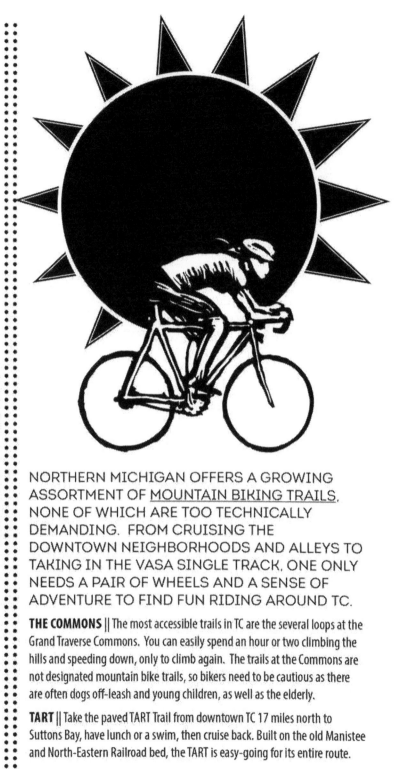

BIKE

NORTHERN MICHIGAN OFFERS A GROWING ASSORTMENT OF <u>MOUNTAIN BIKING TRAILS</u>, NONE OF WHICH ARE TOO TECHNICALLY DEMANDING. FROM CRUISING THE DOWNTOWN NEIGHBORHOODS AND ALLEYS TO TAKING IN THE VASA SINGLE TRACK, ONE ONLY NEEDS A PAIR OF WHEELS AND A SENSE OF ADVENTURE TO FIND FUN RIDING AROUND TC.

THE COMMONS || The most accessible trails in TC are the several loops at the Grand Traverse Commons. You can easily spend an hour or two climbing the hills and speeding down, only to climb again. The trails at the Commons are not designated mountain bike trails, so bikers need to be cautious as there are often dogs off-leash and young children, as well as the elderly.

TART || Take the paved TART Trail from downtown TC 17 miles north to Suttons Bay, have lunch or a swim, then cruise back. Built on the old Manistee and North-Eastern Railroad bed, the TART is easy-going for its entire route.

the Beach Boys blasting from the one speaker I had tied to the windshield frame. We hung our feet out over the

There's a gradual, low-grade climb for several miles before descending to Suttons Bay. Be ready for runners, walkers of all ages and darting children.

VASA || Just outside Traverse City, the 14-mile Vasa Single track winds through both established forest and scrubby new growth. The trail is accessed from Supply Road, 10 miles east of town. The VASA is best in May and June when the wildflowers are blooming, and then in October when the woods blaze with color. The first two thirds of the trail are relatively easy, while the last third requires some muscle to climb four significant hills.

HICKORY MEADOWS || Right on the edge of TC and very flat. If you ride up from town, though, it's a big climb.

ARCADIA BLUFFS || Forty-five miles southwest of TC, Arcadia Bluffs provides a moderately vigorous ride. The course is approximately 12 miles long and the first half is a superb roller coaster ride as you glide the shoulder of a bluff above Upper Herring Lake. Access the mountain bike trail at the junction of Metzger and St. Pierre Roads. The easiest way to Arcadia is US-31 to Joyfield Road. Head west on Joyfield, then a quick left on M-22, which will take you to St. Pierre.

GLACIAL HILLS || The extensive trail and road system of Glacial Hills Pathway and Natural Area lies 40 miles northeast of Traverse. There are several different sections of mountain bike trails to choose from, some of which are the most technically demanding trails in the area. Be prepared to climb the many wooded hills. Also, be aware that the trail systems are used by walkers and dogs, so caution is required. The easiest access is off Eckhardt Road. Head to Bellaire for refreshments.

LAKE ANN || Closer to Traverse City is a 6-mile loop on the Lake Ann Pathway off of Reynolds Road. The trails are really hilly. If you're not into hills, take the trail on the east side of the road. Watch out for walkers.

NORTH COUNTRY TRAIL || Big hills and views of the river valley on this out and back trail. Park at the Marilla Road trailhead near Mesick, 28 miles south of TC. **DM**

READY, SET, GO

IF YOU'RE HERE ON VACATION OR ARE LIVING IN DOWNTOWN TC, TOURING AROUND COULDN'T BE EASIER.

Head down Sixth Street and bump along the cobblestones in TC's oldest neighborhood. Turn left on Wadsworth and ride south to Tenth Street. Take another left and follow Tenth to the Oryana Food Coop. You can pick up the paved Boardman Lake Trail behind the Coop. The trail doesn't go all the way around the lake yet, but it's getting there.

For a longer ride, head east (left, across the bridge) on the Boardman Lake Trail and get on the TART Trail on the other side of the TC Public Library. The TART is smooth sailing all the way to Acme. However, if the wind is blowing from the west, expect a struggle returning to town.

FYI: the TART ends on Bunker Hill Road in Acme, and from there you can get on the VASA.

Road Biking the Peninsulas

ROAD CYCLING IN LEELANAU COUNTY AND ON OLD MISSION PENINSULA OFFERS THE BIKER A WIDE RANGE OF DISTANCES, TERRAINS AND VISTAS. BECAUSE SO MANY BIKERS TAKE TO THE BACK ROADS THROUGHOUT THE SEASON, LOCAL DRIVERS EXPECT TO SEE RIDERS ON THE ROAD AND ARE GENERALLY RESPECTFUL. HOWEVER, AS A CYCLIST IT IS IMPORTANT TO REMEMBER THAT WHAT GOES AROUND COMES AROUND, SO IF YOU RIDE, RIDE CAUTIOUSLY AND RESPECTFULLY AS WELL.

LEELANAU

LEELANAU COUNTY provides the biker many choices: If you want the thrill of hills, the roads south of M-204 can be configured into different loops that maximize the climb. If you're looking for more gentle terrain, the roads in the north of the county tend to be less strenuous.

THE 17-MILE RIDE AROUND BIG AND LITTLE GLEN LAKES provide great views of the water and the dunes, plus two hills to climb. But circumnavigating both lobes of Lake Leelanau is a strenuous 50-mile ride. The west side of Lake Leelanau is scenic and hilly, while the southern, 10-mile section tends to be a bit monotonous with few view vistas. There are three stops for refreshment: Leland, Lake Leelanau and Cedar.

THE 14-MILE RIDE AROUND THE NORTH LOBE OF LAKE LEELANAU is relatively level, with great views of the blue waters. SCHOMBERG ROAD, in the west of the county, is a great roller coaster of a road, as are SWEDE and PETERSON roads in the east. North of Northport the road is flat and rather uninspiring, but it does take you to Cathead Bay (a beautiful hike to the beach) and the Leelanau State Park. While most rides force you onto M-22 or M-204 for a mile or two, the best rides tend to be in the county's interior where there are more views and less cars.

THE NEW HERITAGE TRAIL in the Sleeping Bear National Lakeshore is an ideal, moderate, 28-mile trip from Good Harbor (north of Cedar) to Manning Road (2 miles south of Empire). The trail is paved and primarily free of cars, though their are a few places where the trail is routed onto the road. The only substantial hills are south of Glen Arbor. South of Manning Road, the trail is still incomplete, but when finished it will provide bikers with a 40-mile trail through forests and along dunes.

THE TART TRAIL is a great 17-mile ride from Suttons Bay to Traverse City (or vice versa). The entire trail is paved and free of cars, though you must cross roads frequently. Take caution at these crossings, as the vehicle traffic travels at (at least) 55 mph. The TART Trail, a rails-to-trails project, climbs the hills at a gentle grade, and takes the rider through orchards and farmland. As the trail is used by pedestrians and in-line skaters, be prepared to share the road.

OLD MISSION

THE OLD MISSION PENINSULA is a go-to destination for bikers in the area. While only 22 miles in length, the P, as locals call it, provides over 100 miles of riding possibility. Many bikers park at Central High School and ride north from there. Center Road (M-37) is heavily trafficked for the first 10 miles, but has wide shoulders and is frequently ridden, particularly north of Mapleton, as it is the only way to reach the lighthouse.

EAST SHORE ROAD AND BLUFF ROAD, hugging the P's eastern shore, are windy and relatively flat, and provide endless views of East Bay, but have no paved shoulders, making for a sometimes scary ride.

PENINSULA DRIVE, on the western shore, winds 8 miles from TC to Bower's Harbor, two thirds of the way up the P. There can be a lot of traffic, but traffic speeds are low.

IF YOU WANT HILLS, you can map out many rides criss-crossing the peninsula's spine, going from bay to bay and back. SEVEN HILLS ROAD, running from Bowers Harbor north, is, as its name suggests, hilly.

If you need refreshments, you can find restaurants in Mapleton and Bowers Harbor, while the Old Mission General Store furnishes drinks, snacks and ice cream. And always, throughout the P you will find wineries and fruit stands. **DM**

> **Check out *Biking Northern Michigan* by Bob Downes and *The Trails of M-22* by Jim DuFresne for the nitty-gritty.**

CLUBS

CHERRY CAPITAL CYCLING CLUB || With about 400 members, CCCC is one of the oldest clubs in town and sponsors the annual tours, Ride Around Torch and the Leelanau Harvest Tour (see next page). The club also sponsors the Ride of Silence for those who have been injured or killed while riding a bike. The event is held annually on the third Wednesday in May.

NORTE! || NORTE! is a non-profit with the mission of building a bike-friendly community. On Wednesdays, during the summer, the group hosts TC Rides, a 5-mile event for all ages. The tour starts at F&M Park and ends at Little Fleet.

AU JUS CYCLING CLUB || This is an informal group of "50 somethings" who ride the Leelanau Trail section of the TART once a week. Burgers and beer in Suttons Bay follow.

SHORELINE CYCLING || For Manistee and Benzie residents, this club maintains trails and strives to increase access to cycling opportunities. Check their calendar for events.

RIDE AROUND TORCH

July 16, 2017

Torch Lake, with its eye-popping turquoise waters, is also the longest lake in Michigan. For this annual, one-day event, choose between several routes of varying lengths and difficulty — up to 100 miles.

The most popular is the 26-mile out and back along the north shore of Elk Lake to the village of Torch River, then a food stop at Crystal Beach Park.

The 100-mile route contains extreme hills and has been called Michigan's most challenging century.

All routes start at the Elk Rapids High School.

LEELANAU HARVEST TOUR

September 16, 2017

Grab friends and family for this all-ages and abilities tour of beautiful Leelanau county.

The tour begins at Suttons Bay High School, and riders can choose between paved routes of 20, 40, 65 and 100 miles that wind pass farms, orchards, vineyards and villages. All routes begin on the recently completed Leelanau Trail, northern Michigan's premier rails-to-trail. Test your strength on the challenging hills of the longer routes.

FOR BOTH TOURS, REGISTER EARLY FOR BETTER RATES.

Ride Around Torch and The Leelanau Harvest Tour are both recreational and social tours, not races. They are sponsored by the Cherry Capital Cycling Club and benefit the TART (Traverse Area Recreation and Transportation Trails, Inc.) in support of ongoing trail network expansion and improvements.

the neon lights we'd eat as slowly as possible waiting for the other kids to cruise past, all of them gaping

RENTALS

TC

Brick Wheels

City Bike Shop

Einstein Cycles

GT Cycle

McLain Cycle

Paddle TC

The River Outfitters

SUTTONS BAY

Body Balance

Suttons Bay Bikes

GLEN ARBOR

The Cyclery

REPAIRS

Brick Wheels

Einstein Cycle

McLain Cycle

2017-18 COMPETITION

July 21 ||| Tour de TART: Starts in TC and follows the TART 17 miles to Suttons Bay. All ages welcome. Two food stops plus a bus ride back.

August 5 ||| Cherry Roubaix: Downtown TC to Suttons Bay with an after- party at Hop Lot. Includes 80-, 51- and 20-mile courses. Proceeds benefit the TART Trails.

November 4 ||| Bell's Beer Iceman Cometh Challenge: A 30-mile point to point from Kalkaska to TC. The race got started in 1990 with 35 competitors. Expect up to 6,000 these days. The combined prize purse for the 2016 race totaled over $63,000 in cash for the professional and amateur riders.

January 21||| Fat Chance! at Crystal Mountain: a fat bike race sponsored by Short's Brewing Company.

February 11–12 ||| North American VASA Festival of Races: 42K and 10K races for fat bikes. Event at Timber Ridge Resort, 4050 Hammond Road East.

February 19 ||| The Vineyard Race at Forty-Five North: A fat bike race sponsored by Short's Brewing Company.

March 4 ||| Beard of Zeus at Timber Ridge: A fat bike race sponsored by Short's Brewing company.

STATE IS GREAT

WHEN IT COMES TO THE WEB OF TRAILS AROUND TRAVERSE CITY – BOTH PUBLIC AND PRIVATE – MOST OFF-ROADERS AGREE THE STATE-MAINTAINED PATHS ARE THE BEST.

They come at a cost, of course. Each vehicle needs a $26.25 annual ORV license, whether dirt bike or Jeep, and a $10 annual trail permit. Money raised goes to help maintain the trails and yes, the Department of Natural Resources checks to make sure permits are in place.

A new option for bikes, ATVs, snowmobiles and other vehicles opened up recently, too. Seasonal roads, typically two-tracks, are fair game for riding. Off-roaders say there are some gems out there, but several are "flat and boring."

But back to those state-owned routes. Trails aren't that crowded, says Dave Karczewski, a dirt bike rider, and they stretch for miles. He likes the Grand Traverse Cycle Trail, a 63-mile series of loops near the Boardman River south of Traverse City. Park in the lot off Supply Road (near Forks Campground and Martuch Road) and try a new route each time. "It's quite a workout," Karczewski admits, with lots of upper-body action that leaves his clothes "wringing wet" with sweat after a 20-mile ride. "Bring a total change of clothes," he laughs. The trail can take a rider from the Brown Bridge area to south of Kingsley (near the former Pugsley Correctional Facility) to as far east as Kalkaska.

Trails are categorized by width, says Todd Niess, a recreational specialist with the DNR based in Cadillac. The Grand Traverse Cycle Trail — Karczewski's jam — is the skinniest, but still wide enough for two-way traffic or side-by-side bikes. A 50-inch trail is designed for quads and ATVs and the widest state-built trail is 72 inches, designed for Jeeps and snowmobiles and two-way traffic.

Neiss (pronounced "Neece") is quick to point out the benefits of a state-run trail, namely that it's maintained. It's smoother in the right places but still fun. And it's safer. You won't ride over a wetland (a "sink" in off-roader language), trees are cleared and there are signs warning of sharp curves. On private property, Neiss points out, there's no heads-up about creeks or fences.

State trails also get you close to towns, where the fuel that propels off-roaders (gas, food and drinks) comes in handy.

That said, "The 80s," two 80-acre parcels of private land that you can access near the end of Holiday Road, has a lot of power lines (a definite legal no-no for anything other than snowmobiles, but a hella of a lot of fun to ride), a lot of hills, and some "really steep, really deep two-tracks," said a local rider. The Bendon swamp, near Interlochen, has good mud.

Joe Young, who takes his family out trail riding frequently using their four-wheeled Razrs, points out that snowmobile trails — of which there are plenty — are also open to ORV'ers, but he recommends only using them when there's no snow. He thinks most private property owners are cool with off-roaders, "unless you see signs." Many of the state trails are bordered by "private property" signs — and they need to be heeded. Often, just off the side of a state trail, there's a cool hill climb or mud hole, but "you better ask," Young says.

Young's advice to newcomers or visitors is to contact a local club — Mudbusters in Benzie County or Northwoods Wheelers in Grand Traverse — and ask for tips or to ride along. "One of the funnest things is to show someone your spots," he says.

Twisted Trails, near Manistee, is devoted to off-roading and has hills, rocks, mud bogs and onsite camping. It's open year-round and has trails for beginners up to extreme. **JT**

OTHER TIPS:

- The hottest part of the summer is too dusty for most people to go off-roading.

- Spring, fall and winter are great, but stay off groomed snowmobile trails in the winter.

- Buy the permits. The DNR is out there.

- Ride at dusk so you can see headlights coming at you.

- Don't drink and ride. Most of the deadly accidents (mainly snowmobiles) are thanks to drinking. The second leading cause is speeding.

- "No Wheeled Vehicles" signs are for real; snowmobiles can still use those bits, but ATV and bike-riders will get ticketed.

- Wear appropriate clothing. Safe dirt-bikers wear a type of "soft armor," a neck brace, proper undergarments (to ward off "monkey butt"), good boots and a helmet.

- Slower riders should pull over but faster riders shouldn't push someone they want to pass.

- Stay on the marked trail. It's better for the woods and for your vehicle.

Hangouts & Rentals on the next page.

OFF-ROAD / BMX

HANGOUTS

Loon's Nest, downtown Fife Lake — breakfast, lunch and bakery. Snowmobilers welcome but park in back, 231-879-3711.

Fife Lake Inn, downtown Fife Lake — dinner specials, full bar, plenty of parking, 231-879-4441.

Gordy's Place, 108 State St., downtown Fife Lake — beloved by snowmobilers, great olive burgers and "garbage burger," 231-879-4423

Fife Lakeside Resort and Party Store, 229 E. State St., Fife Lake — lodging, deli, some parts, licenses, 231-879-3341.

Mayfield Store, 4044 S. Garfield, about 3 miles south of Kingsley — lots of parking, closest business to snowmobile, horse and off-road trails, beer, wine, liquor, tables, groceries, deli, 231-263-1000.

The Hideaway, 211 E. Main (M-113), Kingsley — lots of parking, great burgers and specials, 231-263-4059.

Kingsley Motel, on Garfield about 2 miles north of Kingsley — close to trails, room for your trailers, some rooms have kitchenettes, 231-633-5464.

Ranch Rudolf, 6841 Brown Bridge Road — this is a perfect place to start your trail ride. There's parking (if you're a guest), lodging, drinks, food and a fireplace. Leave for your ride from your room, 231-947-9529.

Peegeo's, 525 High Lake Road — very accommodating to snowmobilers and off-roaders. Pretty popular with just about everyone, so there may be a line, 231-941-0313.

Courtade's Trading Post, 233 High Lake Road — gas (including rec gas), beer, cabins. 231-947-8945.

Swanny's, 9051 E. M-72, Williamsburg — this is close to the Diamond Trail/ Sand Lakes. You can park your trailer and leave from Swanny's. There's also liquor, beer, gas and pizza, 231-267-5651.

RENTALS

Blue Sky Rentals (at Peegeo's on High Lake Road) — snowmobile rentals and guided tours, 231-633-2583, 231-645-2628.

Snowblitz — based near Ranch Rudolf, so they can deliver your rental snowmobile right to you, 231-932-1800.

NORTH AMERICAN SNOWMOBILE FESTIVAL

FEBRUARY 2 – 4, 2018

Rev your winter engines at the Snowfest in the downtown Cadillac Commons. The three-day event includes drag races, timed races, snow drone demos, a chili cook-off, ice fishing, a snow sculpture competition and live evening entertainment.

The Snowfest is a family event for all ages. Kids will like the arcade games and glow bowling. Check out the antique snowmobile show.

NASFCADILLAC.COM

SHOW US YOUR BUNNYHOPS

TC has two sanctioned areas for BMX activities. The Grand Traverse County BMX Raceway, located at 3265 Nimrod Road, is an NBL (National Bicycle League) accredited track. During the summer, they host races and clinics for all ages. Bike and helmet rentals are also available.

For showing off your tricks, there's no better place than the TC Skate Park at the Civic Center. Lots of shade for watching the fun.

---

in limbo between Korea and Vietnam, swooning at every line to "Don't Worry Baby". ¶Once, on a whim, we

GET YOUR MOTOR TRAVERSIN'

"SONS OF ANARCHY" IN THE TRAVERSE AREA? IT'S MORE LIKE "SONS OF PHILANTHROPY."

One of the biggest, baddest events of the year for two-wheelers is the "Ride for Father Fred" in late June. It's a benefit for the Father Fred Foundation, which helps low-income people in the area. It's named after the late Catholic priest who started the event and had a special place in his heart for bikers.

The Blessing of the Bikes in May takes place down in Baldwin, nearly 70 miles south of Traverse City on M-37. That event brings bikers from all over to St. Ann Catholic Church to be blessed for a safe riding season, and spills over, even this far north.

As for touring groups, there's the Sleeping Bear Riders out of Sleeping Bear Motor Sports on US-31 in Interlochen (sleepingbearmotorsports.com) or the brand-exclusive Northern Chapter Harley Owners Group (northernchapter. com). They service and repair all brands, have a free antique motorcycle museum, and a campground for cyclists. They offer showers and wifi for bikers and they host the Great Lakes Harley Roundup in early June.

The Father Fred ride takes in the vineyards and vistas of Old Mission Peninsula, a popular ride for two (or four) wheels, popping with cherry blossoms in the spring and a full palette of colors in the fall. But scenic drives are everywhere around here, and bike riders are that much closer to the elements, whether it's dunes, woods, water, or attractive towns you're looking for.

DESTINATIONS

Top destinations or rides include following M-22 up one side of Michigan's pinky, aka the Leelanau Peninsula, and down the other. You'll pass golden Lake Michigan beaches; miles of dunes including the vast, broad-shouldered sandbox that is the dune climb, and five unique, lakeshore towns.

Another county favorite is to ring Lake Leelanau. It's a 55-mile loop, great for motorcycling and bicycles. From TC, head out of town on M-22. Take a left on Cherry Bend and follow that until you get to 641. That will take you up the eastern side of the lake. You'll need to cross Highway 204 at the Lake Leelanau narrows, but 641 goes all the way to the top of the lake, ending at M-22.

put contact paper that looked like wood all over the side of the jeep..a woodie for sure, than parked it at the

To return, take a left on M-22. Follow that through Leland, then take another left on 204. Back at Lake Leelanau, Highway 643 heads down the western side of the lake, then skirts off towards Cedar. Highway 651 will get you to M-72, and a left there will return you to TC.

There are three towns for catching lunch: Cedar, Lake Leelanau and Leland. **TC**

Find five different tour maps at **traversecity.com.**

Michigan repealed its helmet law in 2012. In a study done by Spectrum Health Butterworth Hospital in Grand Rapids covering the years 2012 – 2015, 10% of riders who were not wearing helmets died, compared with 3% of riders who wore helmets. Riders not wearing helmets also had more severe head injuries, spent more days in intensive care and more time on a ventilator.

According to Michigan State Police data, 138 persons were killed in 2015 motorcycle crashes – higher than any year dating back to 1985.

The average hospital cost for non-helmeted riders was $27,760 – 32% higher than for those wearing helmets.

For shopping and/or information, stop in at **Classic Motorsports** (classictc.com) along US-31/M-37, south of Traverse City.

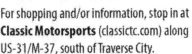

Cycle-Moore, a little farther down the road at 11075 US-31 South, Interlochen, has been around for 40 years. They have retail, a repair shop, campground and a free antique motorcycle museum. For more information about rides and rallies, see www.cycle-moore.com.

IF YOU LIKE TO RUN, YOU'RE IN GOOD COMPANY UPNORTH. JUST PUT ON A PAIR OF SHOES AND HEAD OUT THE DOOR.

Take your pick of the many area parks and beaches, or do as the Central High School cross country teams and run the sidewalks, then stop for a dip in the Bay at Bryant Park. If you prefer a track, there's a paved, 1-mile course at the Civic Center.

RACES

The Traverse City Track Club began with a weekly gathering of enthusiasts pushing themselves far and fast. More than 50 years later, this non-profit organization has grown into northern Michigan's largest, oldest running club. Check them out at TCTrackClub.com.

TC TRAIL RUNNING FESTIVAL
April 22, 2017 || 50K, 25K, 10K trail run

35TH ANNUAL BAYSHORE MARATHON
May 27 || 50K, 25K, 10K

NORTH MITTEN HALF MARATHON
May 28 || 10K, 5K

M22 CHALLENGE
June 10 || Run, bike, paddle event at Sleeping Bear Dunes National Lakeshore

CARTER'S KIDS FESTIVAL FUN RUN & CHERRY MILE
July 6 || 1M

MEIJER FESTIVAL OF RACES
July 8 || 13.1M, 5K, 10K, 15K

INTER'ROCKIN TRIATHLONS
July 9 || Olympic triathlon, sprint triathlon/duathlon

TRAVERSE CITY TRIATHLON
August 20 || half, Olympic, sprint triathlon/duathlon

HARVEST STOMPEDE
September 8–9 || 7M, 5K

SLEEPING BEAR MARATHON
October 7 || 26.2M, 13.1M, 5K

ZOMBIE RUN
October 28 || 5K

GET THE WHOLE LIST AT
RUNNINGINTHEUSA.COM

and calm, a hundred degrees in July. No surf anywhere for a hundred miles. ¶ When we saw Harley Marquardt

HOW TO
pee in the woods
BY JODEE TAYLOR

THE NATIONAL PARK SERVICE HAS A TIP FOR ALL OF US: "FRIENDS DON'T LET FRIENDS GO TO THE BATHROOM NEAR WATER SOURCES. JUST THINK, YOU MIGHT BE DRINKING FROM THAT WATER SOURCE THE NEXT DAY!"

Good advice. And, if you have to go No. 2, bring a bag, like you do for your dog.

Besides location, location, location, the rest of this advice is for girls.

Try to be uphill. In other words, you want your pee to flow away from you. Face downhill, or find/make a hole or absorbent terrain — sand is great.

Mind the objects, especially things like leaves or rocks that might cause rebound. Keep wind direction in mind, too.

Don't pull your pants and underwear down to past your knees. You want your pants to be about in the middle of your thighs when you squat. Then, before you start to pee, reach in front and pull your pants and underwear out of the way.

As for the squat, go for a wide base, feet about shoulder-width apart. Squat as low as you can, like you're sitting on a low chair, and use the hand that's not holding your pants to help out, if needed. You can even aim — really! Tip your pelvis to go higher or lower. If your thighs scream in the squat, you can try bracing your back against a tree with your thighs parallel to the ground.

Then, of course, "no matter how much you shake and dance, there's always a few drops left in your pants." Wave your tush and hips around to get those lingering drops, take a few seconds to air dry and, if you're using paper, please take it with you when you leave. **JT**

IF YOU CAME HERE TO CAMP, THEN YOU PROBABLY ALREADY KNOW WHERE YOU'RE GOING.

BUT HERE ARE A FEW FACTS TO TAKE INTO YOUR TENT.

KEITH J. CHARTERS TRAVERSE CITY STATE PARK . . . .

This 47-acre park first opened in 1920 and was part of the grand plan to bring tourism to TC following the lumber era. Squashed between US-31, the train tracks and the airport, it can be crowded and noisy . . . but then everywhere in TC is crowded and noisy in the summer. That said, there's a big beach across the highway and an overpass to get yourself there safely. In the southeast corner of the campground you'll find an opening in the fence that will get you onto the TART Trail. (See page 94.) It's a 4-mile ride to downtown TC. The Traverse City State Park is open year-around and has heated bathrooms.

INTERLOCHEN STATE PARK . . . .

Michigan's very first state park, it was established in 1917. It's also one of the largest, with 490 campsites. Fish and swim in two lakes, Duck and Green — but be aware that swimmer's itch is common in the summer. Ask for itch protection cream at a drugstore and save yourself the pain. The park hosts the John Griffin Memorial Car Show annually in August.

PLATTE RIVER CAMPGROUND . . . .

This campgound, located in the southern section of Sleeping Bear Dunes National Lakeshore, gets high marks for tranquility. Lots of room (privacy) and shade, and the river is right there for a paddle or a swim. Book well in advance, like six months, at least.

the sky. If you could hook up a trailer to such a thing, then you could rig up a surf board. ¶ We welded a frame

LEELANAU STATE PARK . . . .

Definitely one of the most beautiful locations for isolated camping with amenities. Located right at the very end of Leelanau Peninsula, this 1,740-acre park encompasses the entire tip of the peninsula, including the Grand Traverse Lighthouse. (See page 219.) There's lots of beach, but very marshy and/or rocky. A spectacular spot for sunsets. Take the Blue Trail to Cathead Bay and look for Petoskey stones. This campground can be very, very buggy.

D.H. DAY CAMPGROUND . . . .

Open from the first Friday in April to the last Sunday in November, there are 88 private sites and easy access to a gorgeous sandy beach. However, poison ivy is absolutely everywhere and the amenities are rustic, as in pit toilets. D.H.Day does not take reservations, but the daily turn-over is high. Line up early. It's a short bike ride from the park to Glen Haven (see page 190) and the Dune Climb. The trail also takes you to Glen Arbor.

SAND LAKES QUIET AREA . . . .

Three thousand acres, five lakes and 10 miles of no-motor trails, just south of Traverse City off M-72 on Broomhead Road. Campers are welcome, but hike-in only and bring a water filter. You'll need TP, too, for the vault toilets. The southside of Lake 1 is good for swimming. There's an 8.7 loop for walking or biking. This is a great place to ski if the VASA is too crazy for you.

CHAIN O'LAKES CAMPGROUND . . . .

This campground has cabins, full hook-ups and big rig sites. It's also right down the road from Short's Brewery. While there's no beach and no bathroom, there is something special about the place: it's the home of the Grove of the Midnight Sun. That's right. Druids live here. The non-profit religious organization offers public rituals and festivals, plus workshops and roundtable discussions.

together and mounted it on a plate that had what Christensen called both pitch and yaw capabilities and then

"Shooting the Rapids," Frances Anne Hopkins

NATIVE AMERICANS, THE FIRST PEOPLE OF MICHIGAN, LIVED PRIMARILY ALONG WATER ROUTES AND LAKE SHORES.

Most settlements were temporary — used during the summer, for example, and abandoned in the winter when natives would move to more temperate areas. Transport of people and supplies was by branch-framed, birch bark-covered canoe. The typical length was 14 feet and the canoes weighed about 50 pounds.

Keep that weight in mind if you're thinking about heading out onto the Big Lake, as we call Lake Michigan in the UpNorth. Problems seldom arise when paddlers keep to the shore, but the farther you stray, the greater your chances of disaster. Lake Michigan is huge — about the size of the state of West Virginia — and because of its long shape, big waves and strong currents are common. Light-weight watercraft can take a real beating when the wind comes up. Also, despite its turquoise color, Lake Michigan is not the Caribbean. In 2014, five kayakers were rescued near South Manitou, suffering from hypothermia. Even when air temps are hot, the water in the Manitou Passage never exceeds 60 degrees. That's cold enough to kill.

Not to worry, though. There are plenty of other exciting lakes and rivers to test your skills. Check out our list on the next page.

LOCAL AUTHOR JERRY DENNIS PERSONALLY PADDLED 1,500 MILES OF MICHIGAN RIVERS. READ ABOUT IT IN *Canoeing Michigan Rivers*, AVAILABLE IN AREA BOOKSTORES.

bolted some ski boots onto a mock-up board we'd managed to hack out of fiberglass resin and chunks of old

BOARDMAN LAKE

It's right in TC, and great for evening paddling. Watch for the cormorant tree on the west shore: when they roost, they grunt like pigs. Launch sites at Hull Park, Boardman Trail and Medalie Park.

WEST BAY

Paddle 3.6 miles to Power Island from the launch at Bowers Harbor. The west side of the island is wild and full of birds. Big winds can come up fast on the Bay, so keep your eye on the weather.

BROWN BRIDGE QUIET AREA

Located 11 miles south of TC, these 1,300 acres of city-owned land are lush with native flora and wild critters. The Boardman River, released from the dam in 2012, once again flows through its historic channel. A nice paddle for a windy day.

SPIDER LAKE & ARBUTUS LAKE

Part of the Forest Lakes system, these little lakes are full of coves and islands. The Spider Lake Boat Ramp is off E. Arbutus Road. For Arbutus Lake, use the launch at the State Forest Campground off N. Arbutus Road.

CEDAR RIVER PRESERVE

440 acres of peaceful paddling in the Solon Swamp. Look out for sandhill cranes and, perhaps, a glimpse of the rare carnivorous yellow pitcher plant. Access from the launches at Victoria Creek in Cedar village, or in Lake Leelanau.

CRYSTAL RIVER

Shallow and sparkling, this is the place for first-timers and families with kids. Start at Crystal River Outfitters in Glen Arbor, where they'll hook you up with a boat, then transport you 7 miles up the river. The paddle back will take two to three hours, depending on how much you dilly-dally. Just so you know, there are a couple of portages (pick up your boat and carry it) plus three culverts (big metal tubes under bridges) that you'll have to "shoot." Don't worry: folks have been shooting the culverts for 50 years and nothing worse has happened than a spider in the hair.

BETSIE RIVER

The upper and middle 30 miles of this state-designated Wild and Scenic River are truly wild and scenic, and some of the best paddling for nature lovers. This river can be difficult for beginners during high water with its narrow turns and fast drops. Talk to Mark Magee of Betsie River Canoe and Campgrounds for outfitting and reports.

MANISTEE RIVER

Considered the best trout stream east of the Rockies, this 190-mile waterway is a paddler's paradise. Lots of sandy little beaches, cliffs and wildlife. Great for kids and newbies. Outfitters include: Chippewa Landing, Wilderness Canoe, Smithville Landing and Manistee Paddlesports.

CHAIN OF LAKES

Fourteen connected lakes and rivers covering 50 miles. In September, join the Paddle Antrim Festival for a two-day kayak of the entire system with lots of company.

styrofoam from the refrigerator plant where my dad worked. We'd whittled it down to roughly the shape of the

Paddleboarding

Standup paddleboarding (SUP) got its start in the surf of Hawaii. Around here, they're most often seen gliding quietly on quiet lakes. According to the folks at Wet Mitten Surf Shop, just about anyone who can stand up can ride.

SUPs come in a variety of styles, from a real surf board to tandems. In TC, outfitters are everywhere, so take your pick. Suttons Bay Bikes rents in Suttons Bay; Sleeping Bear Surf and Kayak in Empire; and Crystal River Outfitters in Glen Arbor.

As the #1 biggest sporting trend in 2013, the SUP has slipped into some pretty unusual fitness programs. Yoga, for one. Both Yen Yoga and The River in TC offer classes.

On August 31, 2013, an historic gathering of canoes and kayaks formed a flotilla and held together for 30 seconds. The 2,099 boats are now a Guiness Record and the event raised $50,000 for Suttons Bay Public Schools.

Hobie, but from a distance it looked like some kind of deep sea fish, a Marlin, maybe, scuttled in mid-Michigan,

Surfing the Great Lakes

YOU WON'T BELIEVE THIS, BUT ÉTIENNE BRÛLÉ, THE FIRST WHITE EXPLORER TO GET BEYOND THE ST. LAWERENCE RIVER, SURFED LAKE HURON BACK IN 1610.

Brulé is famous for taking on the traditions of the Huron Indians, so he may have gotten the idea from his hosts.

It took several hundred years for surfing to resurface. While stationed in Hawaii during WWII, a Grand Haven native started fooling around with surfboard construction, using Navy surplus life rafts. He brought one home with him in 1955, and paddled out into Lake Michigan. Not long afterwards, surfing became a national obsession when California culture gave us "Gidget" and the Beach Boys. Read about Michigan's pioneering surf culture in *Some Like It Cold: Surfing the Malibu of the West* by William Povletich.

The southside of Grand Haven pier continues to be a favorite spot for Great Lakes surfers, but we've got a couple of UpNorth beaches of our own.

FRANKFORT
With its angled shoreline and full-on exposure to the weather, Frankfort is on top. Surfing in Michigan is best when it's cold, as weather patterns from spring to winter are more likely to produce the big winds necessary for big waves. How big are the waves? Well, only about 6- to 7-feet high, and that only happens a few times a year. Don't forget, though, that the waves that brought down the Edmund Fitzgerald were 30 feet high! For surfing info in Frankfort, stop by the BEACHNUT SURF SHOP.

EMPIRE
Great Lakes waves are shorter and less powerful than those on oceans. The interval between waves is also shorter. But what's really different is how windy it can be. On the ocean, very often the wind has stopped blowing even though the waves are still rolling in. Smaller waves are good for learning the craft. Stop in at SLEEPING BEAR SURF & KAYAK for more info.

run aground on the back of a Ford pick-up, with a bunch of kids driving it around as if they were part of a

THE MYERS BROTHERS DIDN'T INVENT KITEBOARDING, BUT THEY HAVE CERTAINLY SHINED A SPOTLIGHT ON IT.

Keegan and Matt Myers, founders of Broneah Kiteboarding and the M22 retail line, got hooked on kiteboarding while backpacking in Europe in 2002. They returned to Michigan ——pretty broke —— and started selling kites and lessons out of their van as a way to refill the coffers.

"Kiteboarding connected us to Michigan in a unique way," Matt said in a 2016 interview. "We studied the weather like sailors, understood the waves and currents like surfers and then put ourselves out there, miles offshore in Lake Michigan with nothing more than a board under our feet using the water to ground ourselves and a kite in the sky to pull us, powered by nothing but the wind. We truly respected nature for this simple phenomenon that was our bliss."

In the process of following their bliss, they turned the region into a kiteboarding destination. Now, amid M22 business growth, health scares and burgeoning families, they've cut back on the kiting.

Happily the sport already had gathered, uh, speed before Broneah and continues to thrive. Johnny Babka, 53, an adventurous sportster, discovered kiteboarding as a windsurfer and took his first falls around 2000.

His inaugural attempt was off Esch Road in the Sleeping Bear Dunes National Lakeshore. "My kite got picked up and landed about 30 yards away, right near a lady walking her dog," he laughed. "I said, 'I'm going back to windsurfing. This is a stupid sport.'"

But he'd already spent money on a kite, so he persisted. His second attempt, on Crystal Lake, wound up with his head stuck in the arm hole of his life jacket and his kite dragging him for 2 miles. "Everyone was laughing the whole time," he said.

He eventually took some lessons, something he strongly recommends to all beginners.

"It's good to have a windsurfing background or at least knowledge of the wind," he said. "You can't see the wind, you can only feel it."

Many kiteboarders came from a windsurfing or wakeboarding background —— and many were raised on ski slopes.

Babka is an advocate for learning to kiteboard on snow. He suggests starting with a smallish kite, about 4 feet wide by 2 feet tall, and a large field or frozen lake. You can use a pair of skis (they don't even have to be good skis), a kid's saucer or a snowboard. "The trick is keeping the kite in the air," he said. "On snow, it's easy to ski to the wind window."

Learning on snow also makes the inevitable falls easier, Babka said. When you fall in water, your kite gets wet and ends up feeling like you're "dragging a wet sleeping bag." Plus, if you're wearing skis, they'll pop off when you fall, something a snowboard doesn't do.

The equipment used on snow transfers easily to the water, Kuban said, but it's helpful to take a lesson on water after learning on snow. He uses a waverunner to stay close to his students in the water and provides all the gear (except a wetsuit) that a kiteboarder needs.

Launching and landing are the key parts of learning to kiteboard. Babka said he practiced for a year before he felt confident. Now he zips across ice and water, sometimes up to 60 mph and sometimes more than 150 miles in a day.

AS FOR WHERE HE GOES, HE TRIES TO BE SECRETIVE ... BUT HAS A FEW TIPS ABOUT WHERE <u>NOT</u> TO GO:

- Any inland lake in the summer. "There are too many boats, docks and hoists."
- Be careful near Sleeping Bear. If officials fear an accident — to the kiteboarder or anyone else — they'll restrict all kiting.
- Ditto Frankfort. Officials are quick to ban kiting if there's any hint of danger.
- West or East Bay close to town in the summer: too crowded, busy and dangerous.
- Lake Michigan's winds are typically too strong and the water too deep for beginners.
- Petobego Pond, on East Bay, is a great spot for beginners, Babka said. East Bay in Acme is shallow, which helps with falls.

Numerous area spots are ranked, both online and in real life, using criteria ranging from skill level to water temperature to wind direction to crowds.

Among the safety tips he disperses, Babka says everyone should kiteboard with a buddy, a rule that he doesn't always follow himself. "But I don't go 'whale-watching,'" slang for heading far out in the water, outside the zone you can safely swim to shore. Babka recalls having to swim for an hour near Point Betsie after his kite fell apart.

Organized tournaments are sparse, but pickup competitions are frequent, area kiters say. In 2016, close to 80 kiters gathered on a frozen Lake Leelanau for one of the organized events, Kite Jam. They competed for highest jump, fastest down the length of the lake, on a slalom course (around cones) and a "free for all."

For Babka and others, kiteboarding is a way to get out on the water and ice without the expense of a boat or lift fees. "I get a kick out of riding the waves," he says. "And once you ride on a frozen lake, you'll never ski again."

the truck, cantilevered, Christensen said. Land surfing is what we called it. Christensen would drive and I'd be

SAIL

Mike Johnson, Dave Irish, Bill Babel, Cam Shaw and Brian Hutchinson aboard *Traveller*.

Grand Traverse Yacht Club

SPORT SAILING STARTED ON WEST BAY IN 1960 WITH A DANCE AT DARROW'S MARINA (NOW WEST BAY MARINA), FOLLOWED BY SOME LIBATED PLANNING AT SLEDER'S TAVERN.

Lightnings, a sloop-rigged dinghy, were the racing boat of choice. A few years later, Ernie Isaacsen sailed into the Bay in his 28-foot sloop, "Escape." Ben Taylor, Ken Lindsay, Ned Lockwood and others soon added their own big boats, and the big races were on — first overnights to Charlevoix, then Leland, Mackinac Island, Beaver Island, as well as buoy races in the Bay. While many TC sailors have gone on to professional racing, only one GT Yacht Club boat ever hit the big time. *Traveller* — a one-ton sloop co-owned by Bob Shaw and Dave Irish — enjoyed a 6-year streak of big wins. The two men bought the stripped-down racing machine in Chicago, then sailed it single-handedly back to Harbor Springs in November 1975 — right through the storm that sent the *Edmund Fitzgerald* to the bottom of Lake Superior. They made it back all right, but *Traveller* sank in the harbor the next morning. After repairs, *Traveller* won the Port Huron to Mackinaw three times, the Harbor Springs Invitational twice, was first in class in the grand-daddy of all Great Lakes racing, the Chicago-Mac, as well as first overall in the 1-ton North American Races. Shaw retired from sailing long ago, but Dave Irish has sailed a Mac race every year since 1965.

With about 300 members, the GTYC hosts big boat buoy races on Wednesdays during the summer. Laser and Interlake races are on Tuesday and Thursday evenings. Occasionally, the club also hosts national and world-level "hard water," or ice boat competitions in the winter.

Discovery Pier

Located at the old TC Light and Power Coal Dock, Discovery Pier is a new addition to TC's boating culture. Purchased with a million dollar grant from TC's Rotary Charities, the Pier's mission is to secure a permanent home for tall ships, provide a space for maritime history and freshwater education, plus universal access to West Bay. You can find tall ships docked at the Pier from the following organizations:

Non-profit **Maritime Heritage Alliance** supports an active workshop for historic boat building, as well as a sailing mentoring program for at-risk youth and charter cruises aboard the cutter *Champion*.

Inland Seas, also a non-profit (see right), hosts educational cruises aboard the 65-foot schooner *Utopia*.

Traverse Tall Ships is a commercial outfit offering cruises on the *Manitou*, an 1800s cargo schooner replica, or the classic yacht *Scout*.

SAILING CHARTERS

Nauti-cat: Calling itself the largest commercial catamaran on the Great Lakes, the boat holds up to 40 passengers and hosts two-hour cruises of the Bay with microbrew selections.

Two Brothers Sailing: A private sailing charter, also on West Bay.

Traverse City Sail Charters: Group sails, weekend, overnight and charters are available on a Catalina 30.

LEARN TO SAIL

Traverse Area Community Sailing (TACS) offers programs for all ages and abilities. Endorsed by US Sailing, which awarded TACS the US Sailing Award for the Best Seasonal Community Sailing Program for Year in 2014.

INLAND SEAS

Inland Seas Education Association is dedicated to helping people of all ages experience the Great Lakes through hands-on, experiential learning activities aboard traditionally-rigged tall ship schooners. Now with two tall ship locations — in TC and Suttons Bay — the organization offers classes for all ages, including:

Discovery Sail: hands-on experience aboard the 77-foot schooner Inland Seas. Trawl for fish, collect plankton, and sample the lake bottom to uncover animals and conduct chemical tests on the water.

Microplastics Sail: Plastic is a problem in the Great Lakes, too. Participants on this two-hour sail collect plankton and observe under a microscope how microplastics enter and move through the food chain.

Astronomy Sail: Astronomer Dick Cookman shares his extensive knowledge of galaxies, stars, observational astronomy and history. A two-hour sail.

Check out their website at www.schoolship.org.

LET'S FACE IT, TRAVERSE CITY HAS BEEN DISCOVERED. THE NATURAL BEAUTY OF THE WATER, WOODS AND SAND HERE IS ABOUT AS GOOD AS IT GETS ANYWHERE.

If you're thinking of coming here for more than a visit, there are a few things you may want to know.

For one, real estate in post-recession TC is a seller's market, despite the fact that prices have not quite risen back to the levels of pre-recession TC. So if you see a house in your price range that you like, you may not have a lot of time to ponder it.

"If it's priced well, it sells almost immediately," says Bart Ford, manager/broker for Coldwell Banker Schmidt Realtors in Traverse City. But he says that working with an agent could open some doors that aren't already listed. Keeping their ears to the ground, they may be able to approach some homeowners who have been on the fence about listing. Knowing there's a buyer out there could influence them to sell.

Both upper- and lower-end buyers may want to have a check on file for a down-payment, ready to secure the right home when it comes along, Ford says.

THOSE MOVING IN WITH A FAMILY MAY BE INTERESTED IN THE SCHOOLS HERE.

Traverse City Area Public Schools, with two high schools, has a graduation rate of just over 80 percent, though many of the smaller schools in surrounding districts have higher rates. And while TCAPS (you'll often hear us talking about T-CAPS around here and it has nothing to do with head gear) has seen declining enrollment in recent years, it's been attributed to statewide population and birth-rate trends. Still, there are relatively numerous opportunities for kids with diverse interests here. The schools offer a strong slate of advance placement courses, occupational training, arts like drama and orchestra, and a wide range of sports. There are several Christian and charter schools in the area, as well.

A lot of people retire up here also, despite the fact that the weather makes this area pretty much the anti-Florida. Yet because it is a booming market for seniors, the median age here is 40, about a year higher than the rest of the state. Still, a lot of the seniors who live here choose to live in a warmer climate during our not-for-wimps winters.

One of the tonier addresses for seniors is Cordia, at Grand Traverse Commons. With the famous Kirkbride architecture of late 1800s "insane asylums", the former state hospital is now partitioned into 110 units. With rents beginning at $3,200 per month, it's not for the scrimping and saving senior. But that price tag does include housekeeping, one meal a day and valet parking. It's clearly for the active senior. Yet with a theater, gym, game rooms and spa, inhabitants may never have to leave the place.

While those who move here will want to meet the mostly friendly inhabitants who have lived here for years, they can also meet their co-Johnny- and Janey-come-latelies through the Newcomers Club of Grand Traverse. The group organizes picnics, fishing trips and a book club and volunteer efforts for local non-profits. All of that should serve to make any transplant feel at home here in no time. **TC**

----

a dolphin. I cold hear the music screaming from his speakers, my feet laced into an old pair of Kastle ski boots,

THE COMMON LOON IS UNCOMMON IN SO MANY WAYS:

- loons have red eyes — helpful for seeing underwater

- loons cannot walk on land or take off from land as their feet are situated too far back on their bodies

- loons can dive to depths of 200 feet and stay underwater for up to five minutes

- unlike most birds, loons do not have hollow bones and can move through the water with only their heads showing

- loons beat their wings more than 250 times per minute and can fly at speeds of 80 mph

- nothing, but nothing sounds like a loon

LOONS ARE GOOSE-SHAPED WATER BIRDS THAT LIVE IN THE NORTHERN PARTS OF AMERICA AND EUROPE. HERE IN THE UPNORTH, YOU CAN FIND THEM IN THE SPRING, AS SOON AS THE ICE MELTS OFF THE INLAND LAKES.

A loon nest is nothing special — a piled-up heap of vegetation and mud — but the nest is always a yard or less from deep water, so is often found on small islands and heavily forested shores. Within six weeks of hatching, a loon chick is as big as its parent and can fly. Unfortunately, only one of every four chicks make it to that age as they're often gobbled up by turtles, eagles, hawks and predatory fish.

Loon populations dropped steeply during the 1900s: in the late 1980s there were only 200 mating pairs and the loon was listed in Michigan as a threatened species. The numbers are slightly better now, but not by much. Loons require undisturbed habitat and are very sensitive to human activity. They may desert a nest just with the passing of a boat.

Nevertheless, loons are often seen around the area — even right out in front of Clinch Park — and their hauntingly eerie wail is a true call of UpNorth.

21% OF THE WORLD'S FRESH WATER

The Great Lakes began to form 14,000 years ago, at the end of the last glacial period. Retreating ice sheets carved basins into the land, which filled with meltwater.

In 2009, the lakes contained 84% of the surface freshwater of North America. If you spread that water evenly over the entire U.S. land area, it would reach a depth of 5 feet.

Historically, evaporation from the Great Lakes has been balanced by drainage, making the level of the lakes constant. But from 1986 to 2013, Lake Michigan and connected Lake Huron dropped more than 6 feet, reaching all-time record low levels. According to the US Army Corps of Engineers, water levels have recovered (about 7 inches) and are now consistent with long-term monthly averages.

The Saint Lawrence Seaway and Great Lakes Waterway make the Great Lakes accessible to ocean-going vessels. The Great Lakes are also connected by canal to the Gulf of Mexico by way of the Illinois River and the Mississippi River.

The word Michigan is from the Ojibwa *mishigami*, meaning great water or large lake.

The Great Lakes coast measures approximately 10,500 miles. Michigan has the longest shoreline of the United States.

The first U.S. Clean Water Act, vetoed by President Richard Nixon, passed by a congressional override in 1972. Pollution in the form of PCBs, phosphates and raw sewage has decreased in all the Great Lakes, with shallow Lake Erie seeing the greatest improvement. Mercury and plastic pollution continue to be of concern.

The Great Lakes supply drinking water to 30 million Americans and 10 million Canadians. This invaluable resource is collectively administered by state and provincial governments adjacent to the lakes. In 2008, legislatures of all eight states that border the Great Lakes, as well as the U.S. Congress, signed The Great Lakes Compact. It was passed into law by President George W. Bush.

Lake Champlain became the sixth Great Lake on March 6, 1998, when President Clinton signed Senate Bill 927. The Senate voted to revoke the designation 18 days later.

An estimated 160 new species have found their way into the Great Lakes ecosystem in the last 200 years, and many have become invasive. According to the Inland Seas Education Association (see page 117), a new species enters the Great Lakes every eight months. The zebra mussel, first discovered in 1988, is an ultra-efficient filter feeder originally from the Black and Caspian Seas. Zebra mussels are believed to be the source **of the avian botulism poisoning that has killed tens of thousands of birds in the Great Lakes. The U.S. Fish and Wildlife Service estimates that the economic impact of quagga and zebra mussels could be about $5 billion over the next decade.**

was part of the wind, that if I closed my eyes and crouched down, pretended like I was about to be washed

U.S. COAST GUARD

Established in 1946 as a single-plane search and rescue operation, the TC U.S. Coast Guard Air Station has grown to employ 29 officers and 112 enlisted personnel, making it one of the largest in the country. Its area of operations is also huge, including all of Lake Michigan and Lake Superior and most of Lake Huron.

The USCG TC Air Station currently deploys five MH-65 "Dolphin" Short Range Recovery Helicopters.

GREAT LAKES MARITIME ACADEMY

The Academy began in 1969, training men and women to be licensed mariners on ships of unlimited tonnage or horsepower. There are only seven maritime academies in the United States, and the TC school is the only freshwater maritime academy. In addition, it is the only maritime academy in the United States that offers graduates the opportunity to obtain licensing on both the Great Lakes and the oceans, as well as the additional credential of First Class Great Lakes Pilot.

Enbridge Pipeline 5

A major oil pipeline, capable of carrying over half a million barrels of oil a day, runs from western Canada to eastern Canada, then into the U.S. through the Straits of Mackinac. Pipeline 5 was completed in 1953. Before then, oil was shipped from Lake Superior to Lake Huron in tankers.

Although capacity was increased by 50,000 barrels in 2013, no improvements have been made to the pipeline. Enbridge denies any leaks in Pipeline 5 under the Straits, but the line is old, and spilled at Crystal Falls in 1999. Enbridge's Line 6 burst as well in 2010, polluting Talmadge Creek and the Kalamazoo River with more than a million gallons of heavy crude. It was the largest inland oil spill in the U.S. and one of the costliest in U.S. history. By the end of 2015, eight Michigan counties or municipalities called for the retirement of Line 5, including Cheboygan, Cheboygan County, Emmet County, Genesee County, Mackinaw City, Mentor Township, Munising Township and Wayne County.

LAKE MICHIGAN CAN BE DEADLY. In fact, there are more drownings and water rescues on Lake Michigan than on all the other big lakes combined. Part of the problem is its shape: at 307 miles long, there's nothing to stop the wind.

Mark Breederland, an educator with Michigan Sea Grant Extension, says that sandbars are a problem, too. Sandbars are clearly visible from many of the area beaches, and are a magnet for inexpert swimmers. Out and out the bathers wade until suddenly, the sandbar is gone and they're in over their heads, literally. Up comes a 3-foot wave, and then another, then another, and it's all over.

"BETWEEN MAY AND OCTOBER, THERE IS NO CONSISTENTLY BETTER PLACE TO BE FISHING IN AMERICA THAN TRAVERSE CITY... DIVERSITY IS THE KEY:

"LAKE MICHIGAN WITH SALMON AND STEELHEAD; GRAND TRAVERSE BAY WITH SOME OF THE BEST SMALLMOUTH POCKETS AND CARP FLATS IN AMERICA; AND MORE RIVERS AND NATURAL LAKES FILLED WITH TROUT, BASS, AND PANFISH THAN YOU CAN BEGIN TO TOUCH IN ONE SEASON. THE CALENDAR IN TRAVERSE CITY IS HONEST – SPECTACULAR YELLOW BIRCHES IN THE FALLS, FROSTY WHITE WINTERS, DAMP MISTY SPRINGS, AND RADIANT BLUE-GREEN SUMMERS. THE TRUE OUTDOOR AFICIONADO FINDS SOLACE (AND OPPORTUNITY) IN EVERY MONTH HERE."

– FIELD & STREAM'S 20 BEST FISHING TOWNS IN AMERICA, BY KIRK DEETER

Funicello would be squirming in her two piece to get her hands on me. ¶ Night surfing was best, We'd head out

Fish the Bays for Smallmouth Bass

Michigan is full of prime smallmouth bass waters, and one of the best is right out in front of TC, on either East or West Bay. Cast into dark spots in the water — usually a rock or vegetation — and you'll find the fish. In June, the smallmouth move to the shallows to spawn and you can fish by sight alone.

"LAKE TROUT FISHING IS A BLAST AND PROLLY THE EASIEST THING TO DO ON THE BAY. ALL YOU NEED IS A GRAPH AND SOME JIGGING SPOONS. LOOK IN 100 PLUS FT OF WATER, MARK A FISH DROP YOUR BAIT AND HANG ON. PRETTY MUCH THAT EASY."
– BASSBURNER, APR 17, 2013

MICHIGAN FISHING LICENSES ARE AVAILABLE ONLINE AT WWW.MDNR-ELICENSE.COM.

BOB GWIZDZ TALKS FISHING EVERY WEDNESDAY IN THE *RECORD-EAGLE.*

THE DNR POSTS A WEEKLY FISHING REPORT ON ITS WEBSITE, OR CALL 1-855-777-0908.

LOCAL AUTHOR JERRY DENNIS HAS QUITE THE COLLECTION OF BOOKS ABOUT FISHING. FIND HIS BOOKS AT LOCAL STORES OR ONLINE.

WALLEYE

SOME OF THE BEST WALLEYE FISHING IN THE REGION HAPPENS AT SOUTH LAKE LEELANAU AND LONG LAKE. BOTH LAKES RECIEVED MEGAPLANTS OF MILLIONS OF WALLEYE FRY IN THE 1980S, AND THE POPULATIONS ARE NOW SELF-SUSTAINING.

Use the Taylor Park launch for Long Lake. Lots of ice fishing opportunity here in the winter.

For Lake Leelanau, there's a paved ramp located off CR-643 on the lake's west side along The Narrows.

Lake Leelanau also has catfish, bluegills and rock bass.

For info, stop in at Leelanau Marina and Bait Shop on the Narrows.

FISH THE PIERS

NO BOAT? NO PROBLEM. THE FISHING IS GREAT
FROM SO MANY AREA PIERS.

**In downtown TC, there are three good spots
for casting your line:**

Clinch Park Marina

Great Lakes Maritime Pier: steelhead, lakers and brown in winter;
smallmouths in summer

Legion Park on the Boardman River: perch, bass. pike, rainbows, carp

In Leelanau, try:

Northport Marina Pier in Northport

The Narrows in Lake Leelanau

Suttons Bay Harbor for smallmouth and pike

These spots are also highly rated:

Arcadia Pier, Arcadia

Elk Rapids Pier, Elk Rapids

Elberta Fishing Platform, Elberta

Frankfort Pier, Frankfort, for trout and salmon

the corn, shocks and ears flying, imagining the sound of the tassels hitting the board to be the echo of heavy

The Right to Fish

Although fishing licenses were first issued in Michigan in 1865, they had nothing to do with protecting the resources and everything to do with state revenue. The lakes were swarming with fish and by 1929 they were swarming with fishermen as well. So many that the state enacted the first commercial fishing law of substance, establishing minimum size limits, season closures and legal types of commercial fishing gear. The number of licenses, however, was not restricted, and by the 1960s, the industry was in big trouble.

For one thing, the native lake trout, walleye, yellow perch, lake herring, lake sturgeon, bloater chubs and whitefish dropped 60% in a single decade, largely due to overfishing, but also because of the introduction of invasive species like sea lamprey, smelt, alewife and the common carp. A solution was found in the introduction of Pacific coho and Chinook salmon. It was something of an overnight success, with adult salmon returning immediately to coastal rivers and shore areas. In 1968, the Michigan DNR also capped the number of commercial licenses and reduced the legal amount of harvest. But it wasn't enough to bring back healthy populations and more changes followed quickly. In 1972, the DNR banned the use of small-mesh gill nets throughout the Great Lakes. Gill nets were cheap and easy to maintain. And cheap and easy was their downfall: gill nets don't discriminate between fish species — they snag everything within a given size, and undersized lake trout and salmon populations were suffering. So, two years later, the DNR banned large-mesh gill nets as well.

One unintended consequence of the ban was the splitting off of tribal commercial fishing from the state licensing system. Fishing had always been an important source of food for Native Americans as fish can be dried and stored, and the right to fish and hunt were reserved in the treaties negotiated between Michigan tribes and the federal government. After the gill nets bans, tribal fishermen began to assert their treaty right to fish in the Great Lakes without state interference. In 1985, the first Consent Decree was completed between the state, the tribes and the federal government, establishing that commercial resources would be shared between the state and tribes for the next 15 years. As a result, many state-licensed commercial fishers were either displaced or bought out by the state to accommodate treaty fishing in eastern Lake Superior, Northern Lake Huron and the majority of Lake Michigan. A new Consent Decree was signed in 2000.

The controversy over fishing rights was an ugly business during the '70s, with intense opposition and protests. But it did lead to local advocacy and federal recognition of the area's Native Americans. The Tribe in Peshawbestown applied for federal recognition in 1978, and two years later, was re-recognized by the federal government as the Grand Traverse Band of Ottawa and Chippewa Indians. The status change allowed the introduction of gaming, and the Tribe now operates two casinos in the area: Leelanau Sands in Peshawbestown and Turtle Creek in Williamsburg. Two percent of the casino's net-win is donated bi-annually to local governments and non-profits. Gaming revenue disbursement in February 2017 was $844,873.

Michigan wildlife officials ask people not to interfere with members of American Indian tribes who use spears or other traditional means of catching fish.

The Manistee

The Manistee River is renowned for its run of king salmon in late summer and early fall, and the steelhead run in late fall through spring. The river also has an excellent population of walleye, smallmouth bass and trout, making the river a true all-season fishery.

The salmon are the first to arrive. The runs usually start in late July or early August when the water temperatures in Lake Michigan warm up and river levels are high. However, if the rivers are warm and water levels low, the start will be delayed.

September brings on the chinooks and cohos. The steelhead will also begin to arrive, along with some browns.

One of the things anglers most like about the Manistee is its easy access. The river runs through millions of acres of public land and parking areas are abundant and marked. Lots of trails often lead to the river.

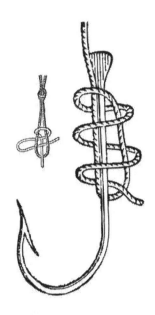

The Au Sable

THE AU SABLE IS LEGENDARY. AS ONE OF THE MOST STABLE FLOWING RIVERS IN THE COUNTRY, ITS STREAM-FED CONSISTENCY RESULTS IN SPECTACULAR HATCHES OF WILD BROWN, BROOK AND RAINBOW TROUT.

However, the Au Sable can be very crowded, particularly on the Mainstream. For less angler pressure, head to Au Sable's East Branch, which flows through Hartwick Pines State Forest.

The Mainstream is "no-kill, flies only" since 1988. All fish must be released immediately, unharmed.

The South Branch is good throughout the season for wading.

The North Branch is also good for wading and easy casting. Relatively free of canoe / kayak traffic, it's a good place for beginners. Flies-only regulations are in effect from the Sheep Ranch access to the North Branch's junction with the Mainstream.

Steelhead Water Foote Dam is the lightest fished, and the steelhead can be aggressive and unfussy.

TIE ONE ON

THE NORTHERN ANGLER on West Front Street in Traverse City is a friendly spot to check out gear, ogle their collection of over 300 flies, hire a guide or just ask questions.

ORVIS, also on Front Street, right downtown, operates a Fly Fishing School offering one- or two-day classes from May to September.

THE AU SABLE FLY SHOP in Grayling has a gear trade-in program and free gear inspection. They have everything else you'll need, too, including guides and clinics for beginners and intermediates.

to just a little over sixty. I had "Shutdown" coming from a guitar amp we had hooked up in the pick up bed and

FLY FISHING THE BOARDMAN

THERE'S ALWAYS GOOD FISHING ON THE BOARDMAN RIVER, WHERE TROUT, STEELHEAD AND SALMON CAN BE FOUND JUST ABOUT ANY DAY OF THE YEAR.

Both the North and South branches are good, particularly at the "Forks" where they merge to form the main stream. Access the upper portion of the river from Brown Bridge Road at the Forks, Trail Camp and Shecks Place.

Below Brown Bridge Pond, the river flows faster down to Keystone Pond, then on to Sabin Pond. The fish are bigger and the pools deeper. Most of the river flows through private land here, so access is very limited.

Below Sabin Dam the water is open all the way to the Bay. Here's where you'll find the salmon and steelhead migrations, but very few trout as the river gets too warm in the summer. Sometimes, there will be a fish weir in the stream: It's set there to prevent the salmon from moving upstream. Their eggs are taken for hatchery use.

The water flows slowly from here into Boardman Lake. And below the lake, there's yet another dam and a fish ladder. You can catch steelhead in this section during late fall, winter and early spring. The steelhead move into the river to spawn around the middle of March, and the season is open until the first of May.

Dam removal along the last 3 miles of the Boardman River is under way, and will ultimately open the river to its historical, free-flowing, 160 miles. The project is the largest river restoration in Michigan history. The Brown Bridge Dam was removed in 2013. The Boardman Dam is scheduled for demolition in 2017.

CARP

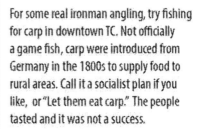

For some real ironman angling, try fishing for carp in downtown TC. Not officially a game fish, carp were introduced from Germany in the 1800s to supply food to rural areas. Call it a socialist plan if you like, or "Let them eat carp." The people tasted and it was not a success.

So, what makes carp fishing so much fun? The fact that they can grow to 50 pounds, for one. They also live long and grow wise, and getting one on a hook can be a real trial of wiliness and patience. You'll need to be invisible as well: don't wear white and don't cast a shadow.

Dough balls are the most common bait for carp, but according to local angler and writer Bob Butz, a can of sweet corn will do just as well, no cooking required.

The state record for the common carp is 61 ½ pounds, so use heavy rods and strong leaders. Butz recommends a reel that allows you to quickly adjust the drag tension. Set the drag as loose as possible, then, after you cast, reel up the slack and set the bail. If you get a strike, says Butz, "crank the drag up to a predetermined position or number, set the hook, and hold on."

Do not eat wild carp. They're bottom feeders, full of toxins, and carry a "black diamond" warning (never, ever eat) from the Michigan Department of Community Health.

Common carp and suckers can be also fished by spear or bow and arrow in the Great Lakes and non-trout inland waters.

Christensen was making the board buck like a horse. Up and down, up and down and then he ran head on into

I DON'T KNOW ANOTHER FISH IN THE RIVERS OF NORTHERN MICHIGAN HARDER TO CATCH THAN THE SALMON THAT BEGIN NOSING UPSTREAM FROM THE BIG LAKE EVERY FALL.

They are hard to catch because the farther they travel upstream, home to their dying places, the less they bite like ordinary fish if you can coax them to strike at all. But, oh, how people will tell you they do.

I call it "the great salmon lie" since, you see, to catch a salmon up in the headwaters of any river, you need to first find the ones willing (or in a surly enough mood, as is more often the case) to come hell-bent after your spinner, spoon, spawn sac, or fly. This is hard for an angler to do because of the multitude of fish that aren't remotely interested in anything you throw to them.

You might have to cover miles of river, casting over thousands of fish, before you find the one. Seeing the fish right there, so close you can sometimes poke them in the hoary eyes with the end of your pole, is a recipe for frustration unlike any in the angling world.

I hate the word "sporting" as it applies to hunting and fishing. Sports have rules to play by, rules concocted by men. But in hunting and fishing, out there away from the eyes of onlookers, the way by which you come about your quarry is largely your own. It's called "sporting ethics," but simply "ethics" would suffice.

THE GREAT SALMON LIE

So many salmon blacken the headwaters come fall (in some cases fish so thick that in jockeying for position they often shoulder one another up onto the banks.) It takes nothing less than "the courage of your convictions" not to simply drift your line through the gawping hooked jaws of one, and smartly raise your rod until the hook catches hold of his gnarled, toothy jaw on the other side.

The technique, called "lifting," sounds a tad better than "snagging," but the truth is that they both are the same. The only difference, as every bona fide "snagger" knows, is that with the latter method, anywhere you can fasten your hook onto the fish is okay.

Some river guides up here make their living this way, guiding their clients to foul-hooked fishes and, in essence, propagating the lie. I fished with enough of them to know that sometimes when guiding for salmon, the real art is not in the fishing but rather in the gyrations necessary to convince the uneducated tourists, who deep down want to believe that these giant fish are easily duped by their gentle touch and flawless presentation. So instead, this bit of treachery is involved.

---

one of Keith Kings Holsteins. Forty five stitches, broken jaw, flipped right out of the boots and skidded ten feet

In any case, I say better to use a pitchfork. Then perhaps when everybody goes home to their Budweiser, the riverbank bushes and trees wouldn't be spaghettied with so much monofilament — a lasting testament to sloppy fishermen and technique — left to tangle robins and ducklings come springtime.

Of course, then most would never experience the real power of salmon, which on a northern Michigan river is the stuff of dreams. Land a salmon up here and you've really accomplished something, since what passes for a river in these parts would more aptly be considered a stream in any other part of the world, or a "crick" where I come from. Tiny, crooked streams like these are perfect for tussling with trout, not 30-pound, demon-eyed salmon that would rather die than come to hand.

The best advice I ever heard on how to land a fish was to simply stay connected to it. One of those things easier said than done. Further, the salmon are so difficult to make bite that they cannot be relied upon to give you much of an education.

If you stay connected, your final dilemma rests in what to do with the fish once it's beached and in your clutches. Anything so difficult to catch and that fights as hard as a salmon — any animal that has it in its blood to fight itself so consistently to the brink of exhaustion and death — I think deserves the best of treatment once it has given its life to you. In the case of the salmon, this doesn't always mean throwing them back.

This sounds of the snagger's logic, that, "Well, they're just gonna die anyway." But as an upright hunter-gatherer type, I believe that sometimes the most respect you can show an animal once it has given itself over to capture is to prepare it for the table and share it with friends the best way one knows how.

I SUPPOSE THE UPSHOT OF ALL THIS IS RESPECT.

I'm not supposed to condone snagging because of the dishonor it transfers to the fish and riff-raff it brings to the river. Considering the alternative, a side of me can't help admire the utilitarian practicality of it.

Who is more ethical, I wonder? The quiet poacher who goes about his business, leaving no trace, and taking home only what he needs for a meal, or the so-called "sports" who play one fish after another to the point of waxy-eyed death (the fish's, unfortunately not theirs...pity, I know), only to turn them loose, and then later concoct stories about how the fish became connected to the line in the first place.

And so goes the lie. It's enough to make an honest fisherman take up a pitchfork.

Bob Butz, from *An Uncrowded Place: A Life Up North and a Young Man's Search for Home*

into a ditch. He was unconscious for two days. ¶ When I visited him the first time, I gave him the Hobie T-shirt

H**130**W TO
cast a fly rod

THE POINT OF FLY FISHING IS, OF COURSE, TO CATCH FISH. BUT THE BAIT, IN THIS CASE, IS AN ESSENTIALLY WEIGHTLESS "FLY" THAT LOOKS LIKE THE INSECTS FISH LIKE TO MUNCH.

The key is to cast the *line*, not the fly, according to Ted Kraimer, local fly fishing guide and Certified Casting Instructor. The forward cast and back cast are equal as far as force goes. The only difference is the direction they're moving.

With a good teacher, you can probably be on the water the first day, but other anglers can sense — as fish do — when a cast goes awry. Practice in a field or a lake, without a fly, to build muscle memory and control. Tie a piece of yarn to your line to simulate the fly and help avoid tangles or injuries.

Of course, casting is only a small part of fly fishing. Seasoned anglers know how to read the water, tie knots and choose flies. Really good fishermen will tell you they're still learning. Stay stealthy by not wearing bright colors. In the summer, lightweight breathable clothing with UV protection is great. In cooler temps, wear layers.

The sport is not cheap. A decent rod, reel and line setup starts at about $200. Then there are waders, leaders, tippet, accessories, flies, more flies … Taking a guided trip helps beginners not only learn the sport but guides often provide most of the equipment. It's a good way to decide if you want to pursue the sport. Most people are hooked. **JT**

---

the Beach Boys had signed when I joined their fan club. He wadded it up and threw it in the corner and said

ICE FISHING

Here's a sport with a lot of variables. You can sit on a bucket or in an armchair; watch the clouds or a TV; sip from a flask or a fully stocked fridge. It all depends on how much effort you want to put into your ice-man cave.

What you do need, no matter what, is a drill (auger) and a chisel (spud). You'll probably also want something to skim the ice off the hole you've created so you see what's happening. Only make the hole big enough to get a fish out. Anything bigger could catch a human. Something to keep in mind, though, is that winter-caught fish tend to be bigger than those hooked in the summer.

And lastly, pay attention to enormous variability of ice conditions. The Great Lakes Environmental Research Laboratory National Ice Center records showed only 9.7% of Michigan lakes were covered with ice as of February 2017. That's quite the drop from 34% in February 2016 and a whopping 88.3% the year before that.

Buy Local Fish

BURRITT'S FRESH MARKET in TC stocks local, fresh whitefish, lake trout, rainbow trout, perch and walleye. Smoked local whitefish and lake trout also available.

BAYSIDE MARKET on the east side of TC has local whitefish, walleye and perch.

TREATY FISH COMPANY, at the Tribal Marina in Peshawbestown, sells fresh lake trout, whitefish and, occasionally salmon, right off the boat. Call 231-620-5114 or find them at the Saturday Farmers Market at the Commons.

CARLSON'S FISH in Leland is a fifth generation operation out of Fishtown. Famous smoked whitefish paté and sausages, too.

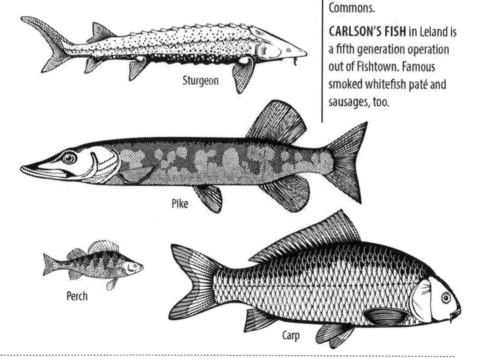

Sturgeon

Pike

Perch

Carp

H132W TO
build a canoe

BY JODEE TAYLOR

FIRST OF ALL, MAKE SURE YOUR SPACE IS BIG ENOUGH TO HOUSE THE CANOE – AND BIG ENOUGH TO GET THE FINISHED BOAT OUT OF.

Matt Martin, who built a 13-foot canoe, had a 40-by-50-foot pole barn to work in. It was big enough for his canoe, big enough to walk around in, but unheated, so he only worked during the warmer months. It took him more than two years to finish his canoe.

So make sure you have plenty of time, too.

Fifteen years ago, Martin was able to find knot-free Western Red Cedar boards that were 14 feet long. He says it's tougher to find those now and many canoe-makers have to splice lengths of cedar together. It still works fine and looks great, Martin says.

Start with a "form," which can be made out of plywood. It has to be very strong — "essentially a table," Martin says — perfectly straight and flat. He built an 8-inch-by-8-inch box (a "strongback") that was 16 feet long to house his future canoe. He tacked a string on each end, made the form, then shimmed the legs to make it flat.

Next come the cross-sections. "Say I want to build a canoe around a loaf of bread," Martin says. "Take a slice of bread, then another slice of bread a foot away." The cross-section forms have to be accurate to the shape of the boat and the forms have to be cut correctly and placed correctly, he says. He had a plan that included full-size halves of every form, so he was able to place those on the plywood, cut and sand them. "Canoecraft," by Ted Moores was Martin's bible.

Put tape on the cross-sections so the (upcoming) strips of cedar don't stick to them.

Now you can start with your cedar strips. Martin bought 1x6 boards (14 feet long) and cut ¼-inch strips from them using a table saw or bandsaw (less waste with a bandsaw). The resulting strips are pliable yet strong, soft yet light.

Canoe forms

Each strip gets a cove (concave edge) on one side and a bead (convex edge) on the other side. Use a router table to make those.

Start stapling the strips to your forms, fitting the bead into the cove and securing it with glue. (This is where the tape comes in, so the strips don't stick to the form.) Start at the gunwale edge and at the bottom and meet in the middle, with the canoe concave-side up. Some of the compound curves twist along the length of the canoe and will require heat guns and clamps, Martin says, but happily, cedar is pretty flexible.

Drape in fiberglass

When all the strips are in place, pull out the staples "and sand and sand and sand."

Next comes the fiberglass, which comes in sheets "like fabric," Martin says. Cut it to length, drape it over the boat and trim any extra. Smooth the fiberglass, then start pouring on the epoxy. The epoxy fills in the weave of the fiberglass; you'll probably need two to three coats.

Sand and sand and sand. You can use a power sander, but once you start working on the interior of the canoe, you may not have room to maneuver with power tools.

Flip the canoe over, hopefully onto a cradle-type structure on sawhorses. Repeat the fiberglass, epoxy and sanding routine on the interior of the canoe.

Now you can build the gunwales, which are made of solid hardwood. Cherry and ash work well; you want something that bends but it still has to be strong because it's going to be hitting things (trees, canoe racks, rocks). The gunwales don't need fiberglass. Put decks and caps in the bow and aft.

Finish (varnish) the entire canoe. Epoxy isn't UV-protected, so you need a varnish that is. Martin used a "captain's varnish" and applied three to four coats, then sanded, polished and buffed.

Now add the seats; make them removable if you want. Martin's dad wove a cane seat for his canoe.

You still need a paddle.

Martin's 13-foot canoe weighs about 30 pounds and holds everything he needs for three- to four-night trips on the Manistee River.

Photos by Matt Martin

FULL SWING

THERE ARE MORE THAN 50 COURSES IN THE AREA, WITH DESIGNS BOTH MODERN AND TRADITIONAL. NORTHERN MICHIGAN'S ROLLING TERRAIN, SANDY SCULPTABLE SOIL, BIG LAKES AND COOLER SUMMER TEMPERATURES MAKE FOR SOME OF THE BEST GOLFING CONDITIONS IN THE WORLD, AND MANY GOLF COURSE ARCHITECTS HAVE COME HERE TO MAKE THEIR MARK.

ARCADIA BLUFFS || Arcadia || A Warren Henderson design considered one of the best courses in the U.S. 18 seriously Scottish holes and GPS-equipped carts. Views of Lake Michigan. Public.

BAHLE FARMS || Suttons Bay || 18 holes through cherry orchards and forests designed by Gary Pulsipher. Watch out for the tree on par 4 fourteenth. Public.

BAY HARBOR || Petoskey || Arthur Hills and Boyne president Stephen Kircher worked together to make one of the most amazing routings you'll find anywhere in the area. Three 9-hole courses. Public.

BAY MEADOWS || TC || Great place for a quick game. Two 9-hole courses, an executive 9-hole course and a par 3 9-hole course. Public.

THE BEAR || Acme || 18 holes designed by Jack Nicklaus, The Bear is the home of the state's oldest and most prestigious tournament, the Michigan Open. Ranked 18th toughest course in the U.S. by *Golf Magazine*. Public.

BELVEDERE || Charlevoix || Designed by Scotsman Willie Watson in 1925, this beautifully maintained course is also on some of the highest terrain around. Public.

BLACK FOREST || Gaylord || Tom Doak's unique style favors knobs and hollows over undulations in the greens. A tough, interesting course. Public.

CEDAR RIVER || Bellaire || A big view course by Tom Weiskopf. Public.

CHAMPION HILL || Beulah || A rugged version of Arcadia Bluffs, and a lot cheaper. Deep bunkers and high-elevation views of Crystal Lake on these 18 holes. Public.

THE CROWN || TC || A fun 18 holes designed by Gary Pulsipher. Public.

CRYSTAL DOWNS || Frankfort || 18 holes designed by architects Alister MacKenzie and Perry Maxwell in 1929. Ranked 19 in the world by Golf.com. Views of Lake Michigan and Crystal Lake.

DUNMAGLAS || Charlevoix || A sprawling, Scottish-style 842-acre course through dunes and valleys. Not very busy. Public.

ELDORADO || Cadillac || A well designed, 18-hole course through hills and marshes. Public.

ELMBROOK || TC || 18 holes popular with locals. See the Bay from par 4 seventh. Public.

EMERALD VALE || Manton || A great course designed by Bruce Matthews. Excellent value. Public.

GRANDVIEW || Kalkaska || A surprisingly scenic18-hole course. Public.

HAWK'S EYE || Bellaire || Designed in 2004 by John Robinson. High terrain and great views. Public.

THE KINGSLEY CLUB || Kingsley || 18 holes. Voted 18th best modern course by *Golf Week Magazine*.

THE LEGEND || Bellaire || Mountain golf in an 18-hole Arnold Palmer design. Views of Lake Bellaire. Public.

LOCHENHEATH || Acme || 18 holes. Ranked Best in State in 2016 by *Golf Digest*. Nice views of East Bay. Public.

MANITOU PASSAGE || Cedar || An 18-hole Arnold Palmer design near Sleeping Bear Dunes National Lakeshore. Big make-over in 2010. Public.

MISTVIEW || Lake Ann || Two 18-hole courses. Fast greens and not too busy. Public.

NORTHPORT CREEK GOLF COURSE || the nation's first solar-powered golf course. Public.

PINECROFT || Bellaire || 18 holes of amazing views of Crystal Lake. Public.

SCHUSS MOUNTAIN || Bellaire || 18 holes, best on the back 9. Public.

SPRUCE RUN || Acme || Originally the Acme Public Golf Course, the 9 holes were redesigned to 18 by U of M Golf coach William Newcomb. An easier course than The Bear. Public.

SUGAR LOAF || Cedar || One of the best values near TC. Unchanged design from 1966 by C.D. Wagstaff. Can be windy and cold. Public.

SUNDANCE || Kewadin || A modern course designed in 2005 by Jerry Matthews. The ninth hole is one of the best par 5s in Michigan. Public.

TIMBERWOLF || Kalkaska || A modern Bruce Matthews design. Good price and quiet. Medium paced and well maintained. Public.

TORCH || Kewadin || The original A-Ga-ming was renamed the Torch in 2005. Water on 11 of the holes. Views of Torch Lake. Public.

WOLVERINE || Williamsburg || 18 holes designed by Gary Player right down the road from Turtle Creek Casino. Public.

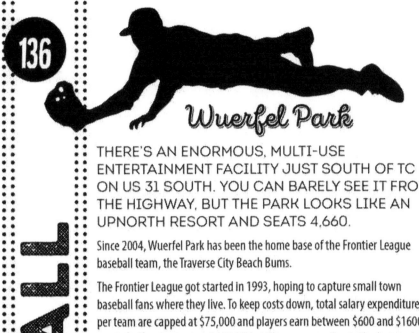

Wuerfel Park

THERE'S AN ENORMOUS, MULTI-USE ENTERTAINMENT FACILITY JUST SOUTH OF TC ON US 31 SOUTH. YOU CAN BARELY SEE IT FROM THE HIGHWAY, BUT THE PARK LOOKS LIKE AN UPNORTH RESORT AND SEATS 4,660.

Since 2004, Wuerfel Park has been the home base of the Frontier League baseball team, the Traverse City Beach Bums.

The Frontier League got started in 1993, hoping to capture small town baseball fans where they live. To keep costs down, total salary expenditures per team are capped at $75,000 and players earn between $600 and $1600 a month. There are currently 12 Midwest teams operating in the league. In 2016, the Evansville Otters were league champions. The year before, it was the TC Beach Bums.

Games start in May and run to the beginning of September, with the play-offs following. There are all kinds of seating options, from private suites to four-person tables to the Beach Bums Party Patio to a space on the lawn. There's a children's play area located right behind first base if the Beach Bums mascots, Suntan and Sunburn, aren't doing their jobs. Friday night fireworks when the homies are in town.

Pulled pork sandwiches, brats, burgers and sloppy joes are available at concessions, plus beer and wine. Short's Biergarten is conveniently located near the children's play area. All in all, a fun and affordable way for the whole family to spend a summer evening.

BASEBALL

WATCHING THE BIG LEAGUES — DOWNTOWN TC

How many TVs do you need to watch your favorite team? The following downtown bars have got you covered:

- U&I LOUNGE
- STATE STREET GRILL
- 7 MONK
- Also try SLEDER'S FAMILY TAVERN, just north of downtown on US-31 North

that was taped next to my bed. My dreams grew ever-specific: girls and beaches, then specific girls like Ginger

H**137**W TO

parallel park

BY JODEE TAYLOR

SUMMERS IN NORTHERN MICHIGAN CAN GET A BIT CONGESTED, AND MOST OF THE FUN SHOPS AND FESTIVALS ARE LOCATED IN PARKING-SPACE-CHALLENGED DOWNTOWNS..

Okay, you probably won't be able to avoid parallel parking your whole life anyway, so practice your skills now. Come on. It's fun.

There are as many parallel parking tips as there are drivers. Ours come from a longtime driver education teacher who has dealt with teenager flop sweat for two decades.

Find a spot that's big enough. Easier said than done, but don't try to pull your Yukon into a spot where a VW Beetle would barely fit. Tip: Look on the side streets or streets a block or two from the main drag and allow several feet more than the length of your car.

Pull alongside the car in front of the spot you want with about 2-3 feet in between the cars; the closer the better. Align your car with the other car as much as possible.

While stopped, turn your wheel all the way towards the curb. Stay stopped. Don't move while you're turning the wheel. Put your car in reverse.

Turn around and look out the back of your car at that wonderful spot you're aiming for. Start backing up with the steering wheel still turned all the way.

Back up until you see the front car's back bumper. Concentrate. Ignore everything else, like the cars waiting for you to pull into your spot.

(The next step is fraught with dissension. Some drivers skip it and go right to the following step.)

While stopped, turn your steering wheel back to the middle position. Start backing up again slowly until your car just clears the car in front. Stop again.

Turn your wheel all the way towards your desired spot — the opposite way you turned it originally. All the way. Don't move the car while you're turning the wheel. Imagine you're making an "S" with your car.

Now slowly keep backing into the spot with the steering wheel cranked all the way in the direction of the parking spot.

If at first you don't succeed, drive out and start over again from the beginning, when you pulled up beside the forward car. It's easier and faster than trying to adjust.

You've done it! Turn your steering wheel back to its normal position, inch forward or backward to adjust the car in its space, and step outside the car to bask in the applause of the onlookers. Then feed the meter.

Gibson on specific beaches, like Redondo and me riding the wild surf. In my fantasies they were all there, Carl

FALL & WINTER FESTIVALS CONCERTS FAIRS & SALES

TC 138 and area

SEPTEMBER

HARVEST STOMPEDE || Leelanau Peninsula || September 9 – 10
DOWNTOWN ART WALK || TC || September 8
ILUMINATE || Interlochen Center for the Arts || September 29
ACME FALL FESTIVAL || Acme || September 30
ANDY GROSS LIVE || TC Opera House || September 30
LEELANAU UNCAGED || Northport || September 30
OKTOBERFEST || TC || September 30

OCTOBER

HARVEST FESTIVUS || TC Commons || October 1
FIBER FESTIVAL || Leland || October 7 – 8
EMPIRE HOPS FESTIVAL || Empire || October 7
FALL FESTIVAL SALE & HAPPY APPLE DAYS || TC || October 7
LIV ON || TC Opera House || October 12
ADULT SHEL SILVERSTEIN || Studio Theatre TC || October 13 – 28
TERRY MCDONELL || National Writers Series TC || October 13
ZOMBIE RUN || TC || October 28
DOWNTOWN HALLOWEEN WALK || TC || October 28
TCHAIKOVSKY & VAUGHN WILLIAMS || Traverse Symphony Orchestra || October 29

NOVEMBER

ICEMAN COMETH CHALLENGE || TC || November 4
JEFF DANIELS AND THE BEN DANIELS BAND || TC Opera House || November 9
TRAVERSE CITY BEER WEEK || TC || November 10 – 17
MOZART & MENDELSSOHN || Traverse Symphony Orchestra || November 12
SEBASTIAN JUNGER & PHILIP CAPUTO || National Writers Series TC || November 15
"AN AMERICAN IN PARIS" || TC Opera House || November 18
"FORBIDDEN BORADWAY" || TC Opera House || November 19
"ANNIE" || Old Town Playhouse || November 24 – December 16

and Dennis, Mike Love and Al Jardine. I played them into a fantasy soundtrack for my life, sure that every move

DECEMBER

SANTA, TREE LIGHTING || TC || December 1
LADIES NIGHT SHOPPING || TC || Prizes, booze, specials || December 7
HOME FOR THE HOLIDAYS || Traverse Symphony Orchestra || December 9 – 10
MENS NIGHT SHOPPING || TC || More prizes, booze, specials || December 14
THE WIZARDS OF WINTER || TC Opera House || December 21
NEW YEAR'S EVE CHERRY BALL DROP || TC || December 31

JANUARY

SNOWSHOE HIKES AT SLEEPING BEAR || Empire || every Saturday through March
SQUIRREL NUT ZIPPERS AND DAVINA & THE VAGABONDS || TC Opera House || January 19

FEBRUARY

PICNIC AT THE OPERA HOUSE || TC || a variety show every Wednesday at noon
NORTH AMERICAN VASA 42ND ANNUAL FESTIVAL OF RACES || TC || February 10 – 11
MICROBREW AND MUSIC FESTIVAL || TC || February 10
NATALIE MACMASTER & DONNELL LEAHY || TC Opera House || February 10
WINTERLOCHEN || Interlochen Center for the Arts || February 17
ON YOUR FEET || TC Opera House || February 17
EMPIRE WINTERFEST || Empire || February 17
THE VINEYARD RACE AT 45-NORTH || Suttons Bay || February 18
THE BIRDLAND ALL-STARS FEATURING TOMMY IGOE || TC Opera House || February 25

MARCH

TC RESTAURANT WEEK || Three-courses for $30 || February 25 – March 3
12TH ANNUAL SUDS AND SNOW || TC || March 3
BEARD OF ZEUS FAT BIKE RACE || TC || March 3
THE MANHATTAN TRANSFER || TC Opera House || March 16
BEETHOVEN & SHOSTAKOVISH || Traverse Symphony Orchestra || March 18

APRIL

BENEDETTI ELSCHENBRIOCH GRYNYUK TRIO || TC Opera House || April 12
RODNEY CROWELL || TC Opera House || April 16
THE MOTH MAINSTAGE || TC Opera House || April 20
VIVALDI & HANDEL || Traverse Symphony Orchestra || April 22
TC CHOCOLATE FESTIVAL || TC || April 29

I made was punctuated by their intricate harmonies, or the driving sound of a couple guitars and a set of drums.

H**140**W TO
shovel your roof
BY JODEE TAYLOR

LEAKY ROOF? STAINED WALLS? EVEN IF THERE'S A LINGERING DRIP NEAR THE FLOOR, ICE ON THE ROOF COULD BE THE CULPRIT.

Tom Fabatz, of Creative Solutions Landscape and Tree in Grawn, has been shoveling roofs for more than 25 years. "Nine times out of 10" damage inside a house comes from water that freezes inside the roofline, causing the ice to create a barrier that gets under shingles and into nail holes.

Fabatz doesn't have a formula for when it's time to shovel the roof; he has customers who call when there's a foot of snow on the roof and others who wait too long — until there's 4 feet of mixed snow and ice.

That's when Fabatz recommends a sledgehammer. Usually, he likes to use a big blue scoop ("available at Ace") and suggests directing the snow to where you want it to end up, so it's not in the middle of the walkway or on top of a car. When there are layers of ice and snow, shovels can help break the layers into segments, then use the scoop to push the segments off.

Fabatz wears boots with metal studs and always moves deliberately. He said metal roofs are especially tricky. He knows of other roof shovelers who use hot water or ice melt, but he prefers the scoop/shovel method. Always shovel down, to protect the shingles, he says.

Protecting windows with plywood is also a good idea, Fabatz said, because ice can bounce or shatter.

Ignoring the snow or waiting too long are not options, he says. A 2-inch pile on one side of the roof might be a 6-foot drift on the other. A two-hour job quickly turns into a two-day job, he says. **JT**

I kept my frayed cut-offs and huarache sandals, let my hair stay long for awhile. Part of me stayed in the

HOW TO
plow your drive

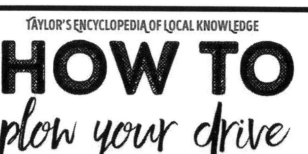

IF YOU WANT TO PLOW YOUR OWN DRIVEWAY, START WHILE THE SNOW IS STILL A GLEAM IN THE SKY.

Nick McAllister, a business owner and builder who plows a handful of driveways for clients every winter, likes to scope out a yard, decide where he's going to pile the snow, mark the edges of the driveway and be aware of other obstacles — long before the weather turns snowy.

"Put stakes in the ground, mark critical curves and the lawn, ask where the well is, know where the septic tank is," he advises. Then decide where to pile the snow.

"Plan for the worst," he says, and push the snow back as far as you can early on. "It takes more time but it's cheaper than having a front-end loader come in" partway through the winter.

As for technique, McAllister, who uses a straight plow, likes to lift the blade an inch or two once he hits the lawn so he doesn't rip up any grass. About a foot before you get to the pile, hit the lift button on the plow. Depending on the size of your vehicle, you can sometimes lift the snow as high as 6 or 7 feet.

If it's a gravel driveway, McAllister recommends driving around on it for awhile to pack the snow down before the first freeze, to set up a good snow pack.

If it's an asphalt driveway, go ahead and start when you want.

If you need to get snow away from a house or garage, try "back-blading," which means dropping the plow and driving in reverse so you're pulling the snow. **JT**

SKI / BOARD

LOCAL BOARDERS RATE THE PARKS ON PAGE 147.

OKAY, WE'RE NOT THE ROCKIES, BUT WE DO HAVE SOME BIG HILLS, AND ALL OF THEM ARE A SHORT DRIVE FROM DOWNTOWN TC.

PEOPLE HAVE BEEN SKIING FOR ABOUT 5,000 YEARS, BUT THE ORGANIZED SPORT DIDN'T START IN NORTHERN MICHIGAN UNTIL THE 1950S, WHEN MOST OF THE AREA'S RESORTS WERE FIRST CONCEIVED.

MICHIGAN WEATHER (ICE, SLUSH, ICE, SLUSH) CAN MAKE SKIING CHALLENGING, BUT POOR CONDITIONS CAN ALSO MAKE GRITTY RACERS. TED LOCKWOOD, A LOCAL REALTOR, SPENT FIVE YEARS ON THE U.S. DOWNHILL SKI TEAM.

TC IS ONE OF THE FEW AMERICAN TOWNS WITH A CITY-OWNED SKI AREA, HICKORY HILLS.

HICKORY HILLS

Traverse City opened this little resort in 1951 on 12 acres. The park is now a full 125 acres, with eight runs: one beginner, five intermediate and two advanced. There's also a terrain park on "Swede."

Lots of tow-ropes here, so wear appropriate gear. Rentals are available (but not gloves).

THE GRAND TRAVERSE SKI CLUB, located at Hickory Hills, also began in the 50s. At that time, qualification for national racing competitions required membership in a club.

TCSC continues to educate, offering a variety of clinics and training programs for skiers and coaches. Check out their website at GTSkiClub.org.

and my dad sold the jeep to buy a four door Corvair, a family car that looked like a rolling meat case.

MT. HOLIDAY
TRAVERSE CITY

MT. HOLIDAY PREDATED HICKORY HILLS BY A COUPLE OF YEARS. ORIGINALLY BUILT ON STATE LAND, THE AREA WAS CONSTRUCTED BY VOLUNTEERS AND PRISON LABOR.

In 1999, a non-profit was formed to save the resort from becoming just another hilly subdivision. It succeeded, and Mt. Holiday is alive and well and functioning as a four-seasons outdoor resort.

Mt. Holiday isn't very big — you can see almost everything right from the lodge — but it's a great place to get your ski legs on. There are three easy slopes, five intermediate, and three advanced. There's also a terrain park for boarders, and a slope just for tubing.

Mt. Holiday hosts the Kiwanis-Record Eagle Ski School for beginners. Private lessons are also available.

The T-Bar is a great spot for vicarious sport enjoyment, kid-watching and a couple of beers.

Visit Mt. Holiday in the summer to ride its zip lines.

CRYSTAL
THOMPSONVILLE

TWENTY-THREE MILES SOUTHWEST OF TC IS FAMILY-OWNED CRYSTAL MOUNTAIN.

Now in its 60th year, the resort claims all sorts of awards form Liftopia, Parent's Magazine and Conde Nast, including #2 best resort in U.S. and Canada, #2 for most challenging and #2 for best value. It's also #1 for snow quality and being beginner friendly.

Crystal Mountain has nine lifts and 58 downhill trails — a few of them long enough to make sitting on the lift welcome. There are also four terrain parks and four glade areas for skiing off-trail.

Crystal hosts the Snowsports Clinics for retirees and those who want to participate in NASTAR. NASTAR (National Standard Race) is a competitive racing program that allows racers of all ages from across the country to compare their scores. Private lessons and rentals are also available.

In 2017, Crystal plans an $11 million expansion to the Inn.

The Vista Lounge, on the upper level of the lodge, sometimes hosts live entertainment apres ski.

144

Leelanau used to have two major ski resorts: Timberlee and Sugar Loaf, both near Cedar. Sugar Loaf was by far the larger of the two, and once the biggest employer in the whole county. After 17 years of murky ownership issues, the abandoned resort was purchased by Jeff Katofsky from southern California. Plans are being made to restore Sugar Loaf to its former glory, and then some. Until that time, the only hills with running lifts are at The Homestead. The Homestead's Bay Mountain is a small, family-friendly ski park. Rentals and lessons available.

Now, I'm thirty years from that night, three decades from surfing cornfields and the ice waves of Sleeping Bear

SCHUSS
MANCELONA

HEAD 30 MILES NORTHEAST OF TC FOR A MORE LAID-BACK UPNORTH EXPERIENCE.

Schuss Mountain, part of Shanty Creek Resorts, is more affordable than Crystal or Boyne so the skiing population tends to be a bit more diverse. You'll also find area ski teams using the park for a slalom and giant slalom training ground, as well as for meets and invitationals, including both Division 1 and 2 State Finals. There are NASTAR races every Saturday and Sunday.

Schuss features four terrain parks and five quad-chair lifts. Private, group lessons and rentals are available.

The Shanty Creek resorts also offer dogsled rides for children and tubing for all ages.

CABERFAE
CADILLAC

CABERFAE SITS RIGHT IN THE LAKE-EFFECT SNOW BELT, SO IT GETS A LOT OF NATURAL WHITE STUFF.

A smaller park with some of the best deals around: $69 for one night's lodging and two ski days! 34 runs and lots of back-country for exploring. Best for intermediate and advanced skiers. Two terrain parks and new lifts. Rentals and lessons available.

NUB'S NOB
HARBOR SPRINGS

A REAL SKIER'S RESORT WITHOUT A LOT OF FRILLS.

Nub's has 53 runs, including 9 black diamonds, and *Outside Magazine* rated their terrain parks as best in the Midwest in 2013. One of the more affordable options as well, with rates well under Crystal and Boyne.

Private and group lessons for beginners and racers. A free learn-to-ski/board area with chairlift. Rentals available.

Live entertainment in Nub's Pub.

BOYNE
BOYNE CITY

THE BIGGEST RESORT IN NORTHERN MICHIGAN, WITH TWO PARKS: THE HIGHLANDS, WITH LONG TRAILS FOR BEGINNERS AND INTERMEDIATES, AND BOYNE MOUNTAIN FOR MORE EXPERIENCED SKIERS.

There are also six different terrain parks at the Mountain. And don't forget the indoor waterpark, Avalanche Mountain.

Boyne caters to an all-inclusive crowd (ski out the front door of your condo) and its prices reflect that high-roller population.

in November. Miles from being eighteen. Miles from Nancy Dolan the only girl I loved in all of high school, all of

H**146**W TO
fall when skiing

BY JODEE TAYLOR

NO ONE TEACHES SKIERS HOW TO FALL ANYMORE — OR, MORE EXACTLY, HOW TO GET UP AFTERWARDS.

Brad Miller, a professional ski instructor and director of racing at Shanty Creek, said a manual he uses for a professional organization he belongs to doesn't even mention falls or recovery.

Miller became a teacher and coach in 1979 and taught children and adults multiple ways to get back upright over the years, but nowadays, he laments, it's not a skill anyone learns.

But he still knows the tricks and recommends two methods:

If you're on a slant, the steeper the better, make sure your skis are downhill from your body and get them parallel to each other and perpendicular to the fall line of the hill. It helps, for the next part, to have good core and arm strength, but you should be able to push yourself up from this position, either by using your arms or by putting your poles under you and pushing up.

On a flatter surface — and Miller warns this might appear strange to onlookers, but it really works — lie on your belly, sprawled out and spread eagle, and put your skis in a "reverse wedge," with the tips apart and the tails together. Get onto your knees from this position, then stand up.

The second method is also one of the best for cross-country skiers, Miller said. Cross-country poles are so long they're harder to use for pushing up from a fall, plus they can break if you put too much weight on them. **JT**

STEEP FALL

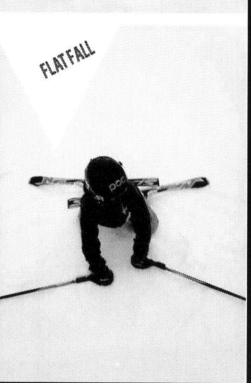

FLAT FALL

BOARDERS BEST

#1 **NUB'S NOB** · THE BEST PARK IN MICHIGAN. OUTSIDE OF THE U.P.'S MARQUETTE MOUNTAIN AND BOHEMIA.

#2 **BOYNE** · FOR ITS SHEER SIZE AND VARIETY.

#3 **SCHUSS** · $10 ON WEDNESDAYS AFTER 5 PM! A NICE PARK, SPONSORED BY MONSTER ENERGY.

#4 **CRYSTAL** · CRYSTAL CLIPPER LIFT IS SUPER FAST. $199 SEASON PASS FOR COLLEGE STUDENTS.

#5 **CABERFAE**· GREAT VALUE.

#6 **MT. HOLIDAY** · CONVENIENT FOR TC LOCALS AND NO TOW ROPES.

#7 **HICKORY HILLS** · CONVENIENT, CHEAP, AND THE PLACE WHERE MOST LOCALS GET THEIR START.

"SKI" COMES FROM THE OLD NORSE WORD "SKÍÐ," MEANING A "SPLIT PIECE OF WOOD OR FIREWOOD."

TUBE / SLED / SKATE

DO YOU LIKE YOUR SPORTS SITTING DOWN? TRY TUBING.

MT. HOLIDAY || TC

Tube with friends or host a party. Schedule starts at the top of the hour, and the run opens one hour after the slopes. Tubers must be able to ride independently. Express lift return.

TIMBERLEE HILLS || TC

Here's the biggest tubing hill around. Ride alone or on a tandem tube. While you warm-up inside Timberlee's Hilltop Hideaway, staff will deactivate your ticket so you won't lose a minute.

SKATE

In TC, there are three, public outdoor rinks.

- **THIRLBY FIELD**
- **TRAVERSE HEIGHTS ELEMENTARY SCHOOL**
- **F&M PARK** \\ sorry no warming house here

HOWE ARENA at the Civic Center and CENTRE ICE east of town both offer open skate sessions both day and night. Rentals available.

In SUTTONS BAY, there's a public outdoor rink at the corner of Broadway and Lincoln Streets.

THE HOMESTEAD in Glen Arbor also operates a free, outdoor rink. Rentals available from Mountain Flowers.

148

What happened last week came as a revelation. Like a bolt of light. I took the old Hobie down out of the garage

SLEDDING

IN TC

Downtown sledders head to the hill above the Boardman on SIXTH STREET. A short, gentle slope with the river for thrills. Fine for youngsters with adult supervision.

THE CIVIC CENTER has a great slope for kids — short and steep.

GRACE MCDONALD PARK on Arbutus Road has an easy slope with plenty of parking and a playground.

BRIMLEY ROAD near the observatory has a rugged hill used by rugged sledders.

LEELANAU

THE DUNE CLIMB at Sleeping Bear Dunes in Glen Arbor in the only place in the park where sledding is allowed. That big, 260-foot climb gets big rewards.

WILCO ROAD in Empire is closed in the winter, so perfect for sledding. Watch out, though, as it can be rough.

BAHLE PARK in Suttons Bay has an abandoned ski slope that's just right for a tobaggon.

In Leland, sled at the LELAND GOLF COURSE. Park at Leland Lodge.

BRAMEN PARK, near Northport, has a sledding hill, as does VERONICA VALLEY PARK, near Lake Leelanau.

HOCKEY

HOCKEY'S A BIG DEAL IN TC. GORDIE HOWE, WHO PLAYED 25 SEASONS WITH THE DETROIT RED WINGS, THE LONGEST TENURED PLAYER IN RED WING HISTORY, RETIRED HERE IN THE '80s AND WAS INSPIRATIONAL IN BRINGING THE SPORT HOME.

The Red Wings annually stage their Development Camp at Centre Ice Arena in the summer.

Centre ICE is home to the North Stars, a Tier III junior hockey team and member of the United States Premier Hockey League. Both area high schools have hockey programs, with West winning Big North Championships regularly since 2007. Games are played from November through February.

Curling and figure skating are also practiced here.

and set it out in the yard. Sprayed it with the hose a few times and then waxed it down with some old candle stubs. just like I used to do. Orange and blue in the last light. I took my tape deck out into the garage and drank

VASA

TC TRAILS

LAKE ANN

SLEEPING BEAR

LEELANAU

PERE MARQUETTE

THERE'S REALLY NOTHING BETTER THAN CROSS-COUNTRY SKIING. YOU CAN TAKE IT SLOW OR FAST; SKI IN SUNSHINE OR MOONLIGHT; TRAVEL UP, DOWN OR ON THE FLATS.

THE SPORT HAS A SHORT LEARNING CURVE, AFFORDABLE GEAR, AND IT'S ONE OF THE BEST WAYS TO GET OUTDOORS TO ENJOY WINTERTIME SIGHTS AND SOUNDS.

SKI TC 152

FOR THOSE X-COUNTRY SKI ENTHUSIASTS WHO DON'T WANT TO DRIVE TO THE LAKE SHORE OR THE VASA, TRAVERSE CITY OFFERS THREE IN-TOWN OR NEAR-TOWN OPTIONS.

On the west end of Randolph Street, HICKORY MEADOWS provides an easy, nearly two-mile loop. It isn't groomed, but it's always trafficked by pedestrians and dogs, and the meadows are fairly flat and easily accessible. Best to ski right after it snows and before the paths are trampled by dogs and walkers. If you are more daring, you can take to the woods and hills where the disk golf course is nestled. The hills are steep and you have to ski among trees, but the hills can be exhilarating — especially when there are trees at the bottom. You can also access Hickory Meadows from M-72, about a half-mile from Tom's West Bay. Right nearby is the cross-country oval at Hickory Hills.

For more varied terrain, head to the GRAND TRAVERSE COMMONS where several miles of loops take you through forest and fields. The trails are well-marked and give you many options. Be aware that the trails are used by walkers, snowshoers, fat-tire bikes, children and dogs. The best time to take to the trails is early morning, after an evening snowfall and before the snow is trampled down.

Two miles north of Front Street, on the east side of Center Road, the PELIZZARI NATURAL AREA offers two miles of ungroomed (often rough) trail opportunities. The terrain varies and, again, the paths are used by walkers and dogs. The trail straight east of the parking area leads to a wonderful gliding descent through the pines. And in the northeastern corner of the park there is a half-mile loop through a meadow with nice views of East Bay. **DM**

B was still sailing, that Mike Love's stingray had beaten the super stock dart for the ten thousandth time. I

Lake Ann
AN UNPRETENTIOUS SKI PATH

If your Nordic ski experience requires a pristinely groomed trail — if you hate winter dog walkers and snowshoers in denim and Carhartt® coveralls tramping about when you're trying to get your woodsy winter cardio on — then the first mile or so of the Lake Ann Pathway (just 15 minutes west of Traverse City off Reynold's Road) at times, can be frustrating.

Persevere, however, and a couple miles in the foot traffic usually stops and — if you're lucky enough to hit the thing at first light after a good winter storm — you get a glimpse of what a classic cross-country ski path should be.

The trail system is comprised of two main loops: one, small one that encircles the state forest campground, to the east side of Reynolds, along Lake Ann; the second — and the only one really worth talking about — to the west. With a lot of rolling terrain broken up with a handful of moderately challenging descents, the latter loop (under four miles) winds its way through hardwood maple forests, past three small, backwoods lakes and, finally, along a lazy stretch of the upper Platte River. The river in the dead of winter has cathedral-like beauty: picture a slow-moving run of gin-clear water hemmed in by snow-laden cedars.

Just as there are no signs to warn you of steep inclines, tight turns or keeping your unruly dog on a leash, there are no restrictions on taking off through the woods to break your own trail. With plenty of hills, deep woodsy bowls and — from January through Mid-March — lots of super deep snow, going off trail at the Lake Ann Pathway is definitely a lot of fun. **BB**

SKI VASA

THE VASA PATHWAY is popular with skate-skiers and features a series of loops (3K, 5K, 10K, 25K). Maintained and groomed under an agreement with the Michigan Department of Natural Resources and Grand Traverse County, the VASA Pathway is the home of the NORTH AMERICAN VASA cross-country ski race. The annual ICEMAN COMETH mountain bike race also uses a portion of the trail. Find the trailheads at 4450 Bartlett Road in Williamsburg, and also off Supply Road.

THE FOLLOWING AREAS ALSO OFFER GROOMED CROSS-COUNTY SKI TRAILS:

TART is a nonprofit formed in 1998 by four individual trail groups in the TC area. TART has two year-round trails, both groomed during the winter.

THE LEELANAU TRAIL runs between Traverse City and Suttons Bay and is 17 miles long. This flat, straight trail is groomed by volunteers from the Cherry Bend trailhead north to the 4th St. trailhead in Suttons Bay.

CRYSTAL MOUNTAIN has 40K of groomed trails.

SHANTY CREEK (Schuss and Summit) have 30K.

MOUNT HOLIDAY has 5K.

HICKORY HILLS has short oval.

Ski Sleeping Bear

SLEEPING BEAR HERITAGE TRAIL

This is the only trail in the park that's groomed. The trail currently runs 22 miles, from Empire to Bohemian Road. Trailheads are at Bar Lake Road, Pierce Stocking, Dune Climb, Glen Haven, Alligator Hill, Crystal River, Bay View and Port Oneida. Plans are in place to increase the run to 27 miles. No pets.

BAY VIEW

Three hilly loops totaling 8 miles with views of Olsen Farm and Lake Michigan. The easy 2.3-mile loop runs past Olsen Farm. The intermediate uses two trails: High Trail (1 mile) and Moosewood Trail (1.5 miles). Access easy and intermediate at Thoreson Road trailhead. The advanced loop uses Ridge Trail (.6 mile) and takes you to Lookout Point with big views of Lake Michigan. Access this off of Farms Trail at trail junction post 3. No pets.

around the garage. ¶ I went down inside to that place where the Beach boys live, where every car worth driving

ALLIGATOR HILL

Alligator Hill, just southwest of Glen Arbor in the Sleeping Bear National Lakeshore, provides the cross-country skier with some of the most challenging trails in Leelanau County. Because of the Alligator's bluff and dune geology, there are steep and curving trails on the south and east sides of the hills that will wind you as you climb and make your heart rush as you zoom down. From the west, however, the trail to the top is a simple, gradual climb. Since Alligator Hill was the epicenter of the 100-mile plus winds of the August 2015 storm, many of the trails will take you between piles of fallen timber.

The park contains nine miles of trails in three loops. There's an easy loop of 2.7 miles. The intermediate trail runs 2.4 miles with another 1.4 miles along Easy Trail and an optional 1.6 round trip to Big Glen Lookout. The advanced loop is 3.3 miles with access to the Advanced Trail. The trailhead for all trails is located off Stocking Road near the intersection of Day Farm Road. No pets.

GOOD HARBOR BAY

A flat 2.8-mile loop with access to Lake Michigan beach. The trailhead is just before the picnic area on Lake Michigan Road, off County Road 669.

OLD INDIAN

Two loops of about 2.5 miles through maple and beech forest with views of Lake Michigan. The easy trail is the Green Arrow Loop and Black Arrow Loop is advanced. Parking and the trailhead is off M-22 near the Sutter Road intersection. No pets.

PLATTE PLAINS

If you want flat and protected trails, the many former two tracks that wind through the Platte Plains, between Frankfort and Empire, are the perfect easy day's ski.

Platte Plains has three loops. Park at Esch Road for the easy loop, a 4.6-mile trail around Otter Creek and Otter Lake. The 1.1-mile intermediate loop runs from the Bass Lake Loop to the trailhead and parking lot off M-22 near Trail End Road. The advanced 6.6-mile Lasso Loop gives you a few short hills and three views of Lake Michigan. Access the trail from Platte River Campground. No pets.

SHAUGER HILL

2.4 hilly miles across Shauger Hill Road and Pierce Stocking Scenic Drive. There can be cars on this trail, but no pets allowed during the winter. Park off Pierce Stocking Scenic Drive in the access road before the kiosk.

WINDY MORAINE

This steep, hilly 1.5-mile loop gives big rewards with views of Glen Lake, Lake Michigan and the Sleeping Bear Dunes. The trailhead is located off Welch Road near the M-109 intersection. No pets.

Other Leelanau Trails

HOUDEK DUNES: North of Leland, Houdek Dunes, a Leelanau Conservancy preserve, offers the skier a moderate 3-mile loop that takes you through a fascinating inland dune ecology. The winding path takes you among some superb old birches and hidden glens tucked between oak-covered dunes.

LEELANAU STATE PARK: The 7 miles of loops in the Leelanau State Park, at the northern tip of Leelanau County, allow you to take the gentle trails that thread the beech and maple forest. The trail terrain is relatively gradual, yet the off the trail the captured dunes cast dappled shadow.

VERONICA VALLEY: On County Road 641, South Lake Leelanau Drive, you can ski the 2-mile loop at Veronica Valley County Park. The trails take you through the open fields of an former golf course as well as a series of small ponds hidden in the pines. **DM**

Ski Pere Marquette

LOST LAKE PATHWAY: The ski trail around Lake Dubonnet, or what locals call Mud Lake, is part of the Pere Marquette State Forest system. There are 3 loops offering 6.3 miles of ungroomed trails, just 12 miles southwest of Traverse City; to get there, take US-31 west past Interlochen Corners, turn north on onto Gonder Road just past Interlochen Golf Course. The trail head is about a mile down on the left. It's best to get there soon after a new snowfall, otherwise the trail becomes a hiking, snowshoe, dog-walking trail which ruins the ski tracks. In non-winter seasons, this trail is also good for hiking, mountain biking and birding. There are also primitive campsites throughout the first loop. This trail system also joins the shore-to-shore horse trail with a separate camping area off of loop 2. There are no fees but donations are welcome. No dogs.

MUNCIE LAKES PATHWAY, part of the Pere Marquette Forest, offers 11.5 miles of groomed trails. The terrain varies from novice to experienced skiers, with the first 2 loops fairly flat with just a few gentle slopes. The trails abut the snowmobile trails that begin at Ranch Rudolph so skiers must take extra caution at road crossings. The majority of the time, skiers can enjoy the peace and quiet of nature, but there also times when the drone of snowmobiles will drive you nuts. The outer loop eventually parallels the Boardman River for a short segment and provides a beautiful resting spot for a pack lunch or photo opportunities. This trail system is accessible off of Ranch Rudolph Road. Take Garfield south to Hobbs Hwy, Hobbs to Ranch Rudolph Road; the trail head is approximately 3 — 4 miles down on the L side. These trails are groomed by a volunteer member of the Traverse City Hiking Club. Donation envelopes are at the trailhead since donations are STRONGLY recommended. No dogs. **AK**

RACE

NORTH AMERICAN VASA NORDIC SKI RACES

FEBRUARY 10 – 11, 2018

Gustav Eriksson Vasa was the king of Sweden from 1523 – 1560 and is called the founder of modern Sweden because of his efforts to raise taxes, end feudalism and allow a Swedish Reformation. The Lutheran Church of Sweden was personally established by King Vasa. But before Vasa got his crown, he was running from the Danes who wanted to keep Sweden part of their post-Viking empire. Vasa spent two years raising an army and battling the foe — often on skies — before he achieved his goal of a sovereign Sweden. An 85-mile flight on skis from Mora, Sweden, to Norway was part of that adventure.

In 1922, Anders Pers, from Mora, had the idea of a race commemorating Vasa's epic trek . The race was called the Vasaloppet, and currently attracts up to 12,000 participants a year.

The North American VASA Nordic Ski Races brings that tradition to northern Michigan. Beginning in 1976, the event features freestyle and classic races for race distances of 6K, 12K, 27K, and 50K. Races start and finish at the Timber Ridge Resort.

The VASA is Michigan's premier cross-country ski trail, and uses the latest and greatest in grooming technology. The VASA Pathway is maintained by volunteers and operated by the Traverse Area Recreation and Transportation Trails (TART).

WHITE PINE STAMPEDE

This race has been held on the first Saturday of February every year since 1977 — except for 2012 when the event was canceled due to lack of snow. The 50K and 20K point-to-point begins at the Mancelona High School and runs to Shanty Creek Resorts in Bellaire. There's also a 10K non-competitive, timed event.

Five dollars from each entry is donated to the Children's Hospital of Michigan Foundation.

sits on the hoods of GTO's, Z-28's and Chevy Super Sports with 396's so frightening they could rip the tires right

FAT BIKES WERE SIMULTANEOUSLY DEVELOPED IN ALASKA AND NEW MEXICO. IT KIND OF MAKES SENSE, AS THE WIDE TIRES ARE GOOD FOR SOFT GROUND, LIKE SNOW AND SAND.

If you've never tried one before, you can test-drive in the snow any Friday night at Timber Ridge Resort, compliments of Einstein Cycles.

A good beginner track is the 15K WINTER SPORTS SINGLETRACK TRAIL, part of the VASA Pathway system. Lots to experiment with there — sand, hills, close trees — and the trail is groomed regularly, or maybe the word is "grooved." Access from the trailhead on Supply Road.

45-NORTH VINEYARD TRAIL in Lake Leelanau is fun, and more scenic. For three miles, the trail wanders around through vineyards. The trailhead is near the tasting room.

RACE

If you're already a pro, check out these 2018 winter races:

January 20 || **Fat Chance Fat Tire Bike Race** (Short's Brewing Fat Bike Series) || Thompsonville

February 3 || **Hanson Hills** (Michigan Fat Bike Racing Series) || Grayling

February 10 || **North American Vasa Fat Bike Race** (Short's Brewing Fat Bike Series) || TC

February 18 || **Forty-Five North Vineyard Race** (Short's Brewing Fat Bike Series) || Lake Leelanau

February 24 – 25 || **Michigan Fat Bike Racing Series Finals** || Bellaire

February 24 || **Dogman Challenge Fat Bike Race** || Charlevoix

March 3 || **Beard of Zeus Fat Bike Race** (Short's Brewing Fat Bike Series) || TC

off the rims. I wanted Nancy Dolan to come up into the light, her face flushed and perfect, and tell me one more

OWL

CROW

SANDPIPER

LYNX

FOX

BEAR

SQUIRREL

DOG

OTTER

DEER

RABBIT

WOLF

SKUNK

MOUSE

time that she loved the way Al Jardine could crawl up into her spine and turn her liquid in my arms.

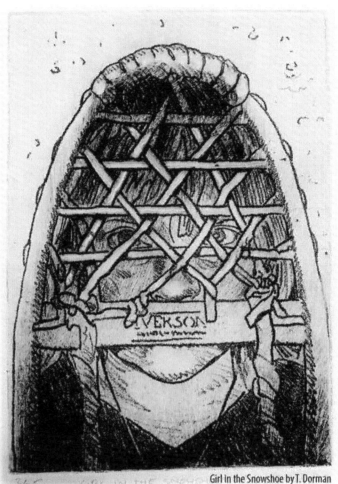

Girl in the Snowshoe by T. Dorman

INSIDERS CHUCKLE INTO THEIR COAT SLEEVES WHEN SHOWSHOE TRACKS APPEAR AFTER CHRISTMAS. CHUCKLE, THAT IS, IF THERE'S SNOW.

AND THERE'S THE CRUX OF THE MATTER: USING SNOWSHOES WHEN THERE'S LESS THAN 8 INCHES OF SNOW ON THE GROUND IS JUST SILLY.

I woke the wife and told her to call me in sick, then loaded up the woodie with my board inside and headed

HERE ARE A FEW MORE THINGS YOU SHOULD KNOW ABOUT SNOWSHOES:

Snowshoes are terrible on ice. They're also terrible on steep inclines: sure, you can probably get up the hill, but you'll have to take them off to get back down again. If you're determined to go up, try a kick step: kick the toes of your shoes into the slope, making a kind of staircase. The next guy to come along will thank you. If the snow's too hard, you'll have to herringbone (angle your shoes slightly outward) or sidestep.

DON'T BE A DUCK

Everyone will tell you that if you can walk, you can snowshoe. Hmmm. Snowshoes are (obviously) wider than a normal boot, and it's common to see folks waddling around, looking exhausted...and silly. The best method is to lift your shoes slightly as you walk, and slide those inner edges over each other. It's more of a swagger, and that always looks better than a waddle.

NO FAST TURNS

What's the best way to turn around? Walk in a semi-circle. If you're on a trail, slope, or otherwise hemmed in, you'll need to execute a "kick turn." Lift one foot high enough to place your entire snowshoe in the air, then put it back down at a right angle to the other (planted) shoe. Adjust the planted shoe to align and repeat as often as necessary. Try not to fall down. Poles are always helpful.

HUFF AND PUFF

No matter what you hear, snowshoeing is not for the faint of heart. Trail-breaking through those ideal 8 inches or more of snow uses 50 percent more energy than walking a groomed path. But why wear snow shoes on a groomed path?

So why wear snowshoes at all? The answer is that you can get to places that aren't normally accessible, like swamps, marshes, lake fronts or an animal stranded in a drifted meadow. Just hope that you can make a loop through those wild areas, though. Turning around in a cedar swamp is no walk in the park.

Guided walks

SLEEPING BEAR

On Saturdays during January and February, you can explore the trails with a National Park ranger. Guided hikes begin at 1 p.m. at the Philip A. Hart Visitor Center in Empire.

EMPIRE

Every winter Saturday until March 4, join the Empire group at 9922 Front Street.

OLD MISSION

Every winter Sunday, meet at 10:45 AM at the JOLLY PUMPKIN. A shuttle will take you to BRYS ESTATE, and from there you'll walk to BOWERS HARBOR VINEYARDS, then back to the Pumpkin. No tickets necessary.

Bring your own shoes or rent at Brick Wheels in downtown TC.

RACE

February X10, 2018

The LEELANAU OUTDOOR SNOW SHOE STAMPEDE in Maple City is good fun for all ages. Adults can race a 5K course, and kids can scramble through the one-mile Snowflake Race. Get a bowl of chili afterwards.

MICHIGAN RANKS THIRD IN THE COUNTRY FOR HUNTING REVENUE, AND THE NORTHWEST COUNTIES IN THE LOWER PENINSULA GET THE MOST HUNTERS.

Michigan has always had a lot of white tail deer, but before the age of the lumberjack, they were mostly in the south. The tall, dense, virgin forests UpNorth were more the stomping ground of elk and moose. By 1875 — the apex of lumbering — the elk were gone. Fifteen years later, so were the moose. For that matter, so were the deer of southern Michigan. Unregulated hunting and loss of habitat from clearing for farms sent the deer scrambling for cover, and the bushy, young forests of the lumbered UpNorth were perfect. The northern herd was estimated at 1 million deer in 1880. That's about the state population we have now.

About 90 percent of Michigan hunters hunt deer. Most of them are men, and the average age is 43. In 2015, 42 percent of hunters bagged their deer.

Despite the UpNorth appeal, most of the trophy deer these days are back in southern Michigan, where fields of corn and soybeans stretch from horizon to horizon. A couple of hard winters in the north (2014 – 15) decimated local populations, particularly in the Upper Peninsula.

Deer meat — venison — was the primary source of meat for settlers and lumberjacks. In the early days, hunters used dog packs and bright lights (shining) for massive slaughters. Many rural families still depend on venison for filling up their winter freezers, and a firearm is the weapon of choice.

Venison can be delicious, but a lot can go wrong, and there's nothing worse than gluey, gray deer meat. Letting your deer get away from you is one of the biggest no-nos. The longer you "push" a deer, the more adrenaline and lactic acid build up in the animal's system and muscles. That stuff doesn't taste good. The faster you get your deer down and field-dressed, the better the steaks.

Another problem can come from not cooling the meat fast enough. It used to be that hunters hung carcasses outside from a tree branch. That's a very bad idea unless the temps are in the 30s or lower. Internal bacteria takes over quickly after death, expelling gases and causing the animal to bloat. That's called decomposition. Best practice is to remove internal organs immediately, dress, skin and quarter the carcass, and get it on ice within an hour.

I felt that tinge of pain when you realize that time is right next to you in the passing lane, and you're already

The best cut of deer meat is the tenderloin. Don't over-cook — you want a rare or medium-rare interior or, guess what… That's right, it'll be gluey and gray.

Treat the rest of the meat as you would very lean beef. Venison can stand in for beef hamburger in just about everything.

More Red Meat

You won't believe what some people hunt in Michigan. House sparrows? Here's a schedule from the DNR:

COTTONTAIL RABBIT AND SNOWSHOE HARE: Sept. 15 – Mar. 31

OW: Aug. 1 – Sept. 30 and Feb. 1 – Mar. 31

DEER: Early Antlerless Firearm: Sept. 16 – 17
    Archery: Oct. 1 – Nov. 14 and Dec. 1 – Jan. 1
    Regular Firearm: Nov. 15 – 30
    Muzzleloading: Zone 1: Dec. 1 – 10 || Zone 2: Dec. 1-10 || Zone 3: Dec. 1 – 17
    Late Antlerless Firearm: Dec. 18 – Jan.1, 2018

PHEASANT (male only): Zone 1 (partial): Oct. 10 – 31
    Zone 2, 3: Oct. 20 – Nov. 14
    Zone 3 (partial): Dec. 1 – Jan. 1

QUAIL: Oct. 20 – Nov. 14

RUFFED GROUSE: Sept. 15 – Nov. 14 and Dec. 1 – Jan. 1

SHARP-TAILED GROUSE: Oct. 10 – 31

SQUIRREL - Fox and Gray: Sept. 15 – Mar. 1

WILD TURKEY: Spring Season: Apr. 17 – May 31

WOODCOCK: Sept. 23 – Nov. 6

OPOSSUM, PORCUPINE, WEASEL, RED SQUIRREL, SKUNK, GROUND SQUIRREL, WOODCHUCK, FERAL SWINE, FERAL PIGEONS, STARLING and HOUSE SPARROWS may be taken year-round with a valid Michigan hunting license.

Road Kill

In the fall, it's deer. In the spring, raccoons, opossums and skunks. Check that: it's skunks in spring, summer and fall. Ditto for squirrels, and in the greatest numbers, which either confirms their dashing derring-do or their lack of sense. Rabbits, on the other hand, although even more prolific than squirrels, rarely end up as food for crows. Neither do the self-same crows. And those herds of wild turkeys hobbling along the highways almost always make it to the other side unharmed.

One of the more dramatic extinctions on country roads can occur when frogs migrate in spring and autumn. Just imagine: the horror!

The saddest sight concerns raccoons, who rarely die alone. Most often it's the mother and all her little ones, or a mate who perishes beside his road kill companion.

As of 2014, motorists are allowed to keep (and eat) road kill deer by providing basic collision info to 911 dispatchers.

Animals that may not be picked up for any reason whatsoever include badgers, bobcats, crows, cub bears, ducks, elk, geese, moose, otters, spotted fawn deer, wild turkeys, wolves and woodcock.

---

redlined, the pistons almost molten, no honor in downshifting and swerving off to go home. Twenty minutes

LEELANAU COUNTY

OR SIMPLY "THE COUNTY," AS
IT IS CALLED BY LOCALS

164

HOW TO USE THE LEELANAU COUNTY GUIDE:

The Leelanau pages start just west of TC, on M-72, and head to Empire.

There are a couple of pages about sites south of Empire, then the guide makes a loop north, following M-22, all the way to Northport, then back south to TC.

Directions and village names always appear on the left side of the guide for easy reference.

full wet suit: looking more like a rubberized egg than a surfer. ¶ *I pulled into Platte Bay at five am. Early spring*

NORTHPORT

NORTH MANITOU

22

OMENA

LELAND

SOUTH MANITOU

PESHAWBESTOWN

204

SUTTONS BAY

LAKE LEELANAU

Sleeping Bear
Dunes National
Lakeshore

GLEN ARBOR

22

109

OLD MISSION

MAPLE CITY

CEDAR

EMPIRE

72

22

TRAVERSE CITY

LAKE ANN

TO FRANKFORT /
ELBERTA / BENZONIA /
ARCADIA

LEELANAU COUNTY IS A BIG PLACE, AND IT'S EASY TO GET LOST IN THE INTERIOR WHERE THE ROADS TWIST AROUND OLD FARM PROPERTIES, LAKES AND RIVERS.

SOMETHING TO REMEMBER, THOUGH, IS THAT M-22 GOES ALL THE WAY AROUND THE SHORELINE OF LEELANAU PENINSULA.

THE MAIN EAST-WEST ROADS ARE M-72 IN THE SOUTH AND 204 IN THE MIDDLE.

snow was still on the ground. Six steelhead fishermen gawked and howled when I walked past their fire, the

SLEEPING BEAR TOUR 1

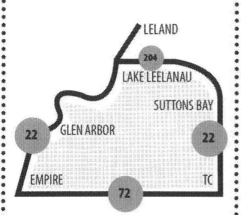

About 78 miles round-trip, less if you skip Leland.

There's no right or wrong way to take this tour, but heading west to Empire first will leave the wineries to the last.

For the wineries between Suttons Bay and TC, see page 234.

This tour features all the most breathtaking sites at Sleeping Bear. Return to TC along the shore of West Bay.

FOR KIDS:

Village Park in Empire, North Bar Lake (north of Empire) and Platte River (south of Empire) are all big favorites with kids. See pages 179, 186 and 184.

Visit the Dune Climb. See pages 186 – 187.

Kids love running down the dunes on the Pyramid Point Trail. See page 196.

A shipwreck rescue mission is re-enacted at Glen Haven every day at 3 PM. See page 190.

Glen Arbor is the most fun for kids. Plan ahead to kayak the Crystal River. See page 111.

If you're skipping the wineries, HOP LOT, outside of Suttons Bay, is perfect for a brew, some tacos, and table games with kids. See page 235.

If you're visiting in the fall, don't forget the corn mazes at JACOB'S. See pages 174 and 244.

FOR ADULTS:

The Pierce Stocking Drive is a nice way to get the views without a lot of walking. Page 186.

Visit the ghost town of Glen Haven and the Maritime Museum. See page 190.

Take a short, invigorating walk up Houdek Dunes for flowers, a view and appetite. Page 207.

Lots of shopping in Glen Arbor, Leland and Suttons Bay.

Wineries galore around Lake Leelanau and south of Suttons Bay.

bright orange of the Hobie just beginning to reflect the first light of the morning. I slipped into the big lake

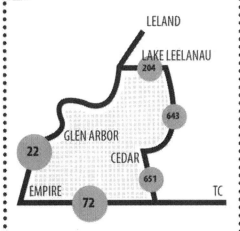

LELAND

LAKE LEELANAU
204

643

GLEN ARBOR

22

CEDAR

651

EMPIRE   TC

72

About 82 miles round trip, less if you skip Leland.

The best way to drive this tour is to head west to Empire first. You'll miss the traffic on M-22 south of Suttons Bay by returning along the interior lake and farmland roads.

This tour features gorgeous Sleeping Bear sites and a return through Leelanau's scenic interior.

FOR KIDS:

Village Park in Empire, North Bar (north of Empire) and Platte River (south of Empire) are all big favorites with kids. Pages 179, 186 and 184.

Visit the Dune Climb. See pages 186 – 187.

Kids love running down the dunes on the Pyramid Point Trail. See page 196.

A shipwreck rescue mission is re-enacted at Glen Haven every day at 3 PM. See page 190.

Glen Arbor is the most fun for kids. Plan ahead to kayak the Crystal River. See page 111.

If you're visiting in the fall, don't forget the corn mazes at JACOB'S, see pages 174 and 244. You can hit this on the way back to TC, and get some cider, too.

FOR ADULTS:

Get the views without a lot of walking at Pierce Stocking Drive. See page 186.

Visit the ghost town of Glen Haven and the Maritime Museum. See page 190.

Lots of shopping in Glen Arbor, Leland and Suttons Bay.

The wineries on this tour are both big award-winners. For a final glass and a big sunset view, stop at ROVE on the way back to TC. See page 174.

A famous murder mystery took place at Holy Rosary Church, north of Cedar on Schomberg Road. Read about it on the facing page.

through a band of shard ice, then dipped my hands and paddled out. ¶ Wind. Rain. Sleet. I could see waves

Cedar's Talking Skull

Sister Mary Janina came to the gentle hills and orchards of Isadore, a settlement north of Cedar, to teach the 200 or so children of farming families from Eastern Europe.

One August day in 1907, after she'd been there about a year, the parish priest left for an afternoon of fishing on Lake Leelanau with some friends. When Father Andrew Bieniawski and company returned with their catch that evening, Sister Janina was nowhere to be found. Her rosary hung from a doorknob and her Bible lay open on a windowsill. The priest, fellow sisters and neighbors called out to the churchyard and nearby farms, but nobody answered...

Then, 11 years later, as a new priest was planning to tear down the old wooden church and rebuild it in brick, he received a warning. Priests from nearby parishes whispered that a remodel would bring about a scandal to rock his unassuming little church. — Excerpted from *BLOOD ON THE MITTEN* by Tom Carr.

Mardi Link covers the full story in her book *ISADORE'S SECRET: Sin, Murder, and Confession in a Northern Michigan Town.*

BEST BEACHES FOR KIDS:

Platte River ...

Empire Beach / South Bar ...

North Bar ...

BEST BEACHES FOR ADULTS:

Otter Creek ...

Bobby's Beach ...

Good Harbor ...

BEST BEACHES FOR DOGS:

Otter Creek ...
(walk right when facing the water)

Good Harbor, County Road 669 ...
(walk left when facing the water)

Pets must be leashed.

BEST WALKS FOR MAN & BEAST:

Otter Creek ...

Pyramid Point ...

Good Harbor ...

Cathead Bay ...

Pets must be leashed.

breaking just off the sandbar, where the week before, I'd landed two huge steelhead. I could still hear my wife

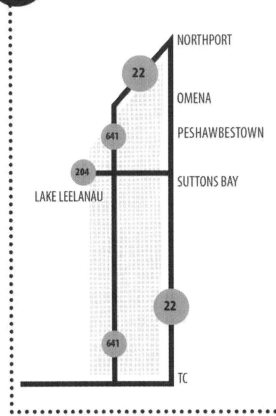

NORTHPORT

22

OMENA

641

PESHAWBESTOWN

204

SUTTONS BAY

LAKE LEELANAU

22

641

TC

About 60 miles roundtrip, plus all the ins and outs of the wineries.

We recommend you start this tour by heading west out of TC on M-72, then take County Road 641 north along the east shore of Lake Leelanau. When you cross 204 in Lake Leelanau, the road will also be called Eagle Highway.

That northern triangle is full of wineries, although most of them are clustered south of Omena. Get out your map and explore, or continue on to Northport and loop back on M-22 for spectacular bayside sunsets all the way to TC.

USE THE NORTHERN WINERIES GUIDE ON PAGE 228. AND DON'T FORGET TO PICK UP YOUR LEELANAU PENINSULA WINE TRAILS GUIDE AT ANY OF THE LOCAL WINERIES.

begging me to stay home, the dog howling in the yard when I pulled out. But I was here to surf not feel guilty I

FOR KIDS:

Well, if you're touring the wineries … good luck.

However, Lighthouse Point is a nice, family beach, and the lighthouse itself is full of stuff for kids to explore. Cathead Bay has great trails, dunes and beaches. See page 219.

GREEN BIRD ORGANIC CELLARS AND FARMS, near Northport (page 216), is very kid friendly, and BLACK STAR FARMS (south of Suttons Bay) has a petting zoo and other kiddie activities. See page 234.

There's a bowling alley and video arcade at TUCKER'S in Northport.

Kids like to shop at ENERDYNE in Suttons Bay.

FOR ADULTS:

There's a beautiful walk at Houdek Dunes Natural Area, just after Eagle Highway hooks up with M-22. See page 207.

ST. WENCESLAUS church is a jog off M-22 on E. Kolarik Road. The church is located at one of the most gorgeous spots in the county, and the churchyard is full of old Bohemian, metal-work grave markers. See page 273 for the Transylvania who's buried here.

TAMARACK GALLERY in Omena is best. Pick up some of D. Lory's wooden bowls for wedding presents.

told myself. I took the first wave that came my way. Five, maybe six feet and felt myself lift off like I was riding

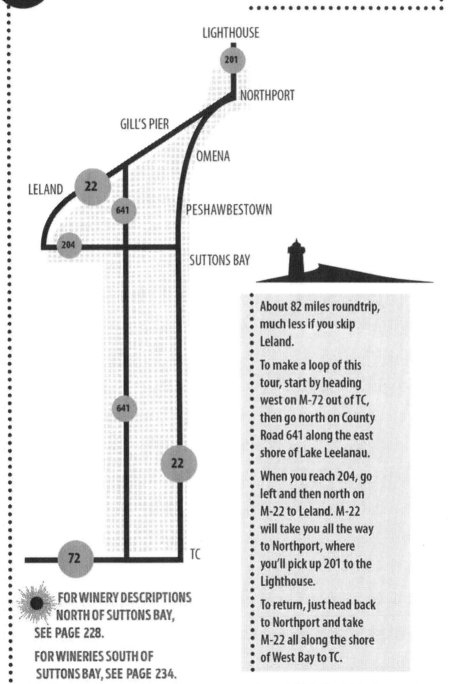

LIGHTHOUSE

201

NORTHPORT

GILL'S PIER

OMENA

LELAND   22

641

PESHAWBESTOWN

204

SUTTONS BAY

641

22

72   TC

About 82 miles roundtrip, much less if you skip Leland.

To make a loop of this tour, start by heading west on M-72 out of TC, then go north on County Road 641 along the east shore of Lake Leelanau.

When you reach 204, go left and then north on M-22 to Leland. M-22 will take you all the way to Northport, where you'll pick up 201 to the Lighthouse.

To return, just head back to Northport and take M-22 all along the shore of West Bay to TC.

FOR WINERY DESCRIPTIONS NORTH OF SUTTONS BAY, SEE PAGE 228.

FOR WINERIES SOUTH OF SUTTONS BAY, SEE PAGE 234.

some kind of wing. I rode for a mile, I thought, rode and pumped my legs, imagined that I walked to the end

FOR KIDS:

The beach in Leland goes on forever. There's a great walk along the Clay Cliffs, too. See page 206.

Kids will find food they like at both FISCHER'S HAPPY HOUR in Gill's Pier or at Northport's GARAGE BAR & GRILL. There's also that bowling alley at TUCKER'S in Northport.

The lighthouse at Lighthouse Point is the high spot, with fun stuff to look at and explore. See page 219.

Great walks through the woods and over the dunes to the beach at Cathead Bay. See page 219.

Kids might like the world's biggest pop bottle collection at CHRISTMAS COVE FARM on Kilcherman Road, north of Northport. There's cider, too, during apple season. See page 219.

GREEN BIRD ORGANIC CELLARS AND FARMS (page 216) is very kid friendly, and BLACK STAR FARMS has a petting zoo and other kiddie activities. See page 234.

If you're skipping the wineries, HOP LOT, just south of Suttons Bay, is perfect for a brew, some tacos and table games with kids. See page 235.

FOR ADULTS:

There's a nice walk at Houdek Dunes Natural Area. See page 207.

The St. Wenceslaus church is a jog off M-22 on E. Kolarik Road. The church is located at one of the loveliest spots in the county, and the churchyard is full of old Bohemian, metal-work grave markers. See right for the Transylvanian who's buried here.

TAMARACK GALLERY in Omena represents more than 60 artists.

Lots of shopping in Leland, Northport and Suttons Bay.

Wineries everywhere.

St. Wenceslaus

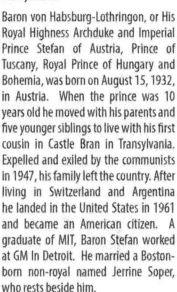

Who would have thought that the tiny Bohemian Church of Saint Wenceslaus in the Gills Pier community would be the final resting place of a real life Royal and refugee in exile from Castle Bran in Transylvania?

Baron von Habsburg-Lothringon, or His Royal Highness Archduke and Imperial Prince Stefan of Austria, Prince of Tuscany, Royal Prince of Hungary and Bohemia, was born on August 15, 1932, in Austria. When the prince was 10 years old he moved with his parents and five younger siblings to live with his first cousin in Castle Bran in Transylvania. Expelled and exiled by the communists in 1947, his family left the country. After living in Switzerland and Argentina he landed in the United States in 1961 and became an American citizen. A graduate of MIT, Baron Stefan worked at GM In Detroit. He married a Boston-born non-royal named Jerrine Soper, who rests beside him.

The prince presumably chose this lovely Bohemian churchyard as much for its Slavic inhabitants (many buried under ornate Czech-style ironwork crosses) as its stunning view of Whaleback and Pyramid Point. Cherry and apple orchards and bee yards surround the church, run by some of the original families that founded the area, while their wives and mothers fill the church hall with kolaches. Just a few steps to the south of the Baron and his wife's gravestone, South Manitou lies big and clear, and looking so close by. A truly lovely resting spot, and fit for a prince!

GS

IT'S 24 MILES ALONG M-72 FROM WEST BAY TO EMPIRE. CHECK OUT WHAT SOME OF OUR UPNORTH FARMERS ARE GROWING ON YOUR WAY WEST. IN ORDER OF APPEARANCE:

JACOB'S

This is the first farm you'll see along your way. One of the older farms in the area, Jacob's has been owned and operated by the Witkop family since 1892.

Jacob himself was from the Netherlands, and like many young men of the time, he set to sea, eventually owning his own merchant ship. An iceberg off the coast of Russia ended that dream, and Jacob spent a year working his way back home. When an opportunity arose to emigrate to America, he took it, and somehow ended up in TC, working for the railroad and paving roads. Jacob sent for his family —— wife, five kids, plus one on the way —— and together the family saved to buy their farm. Jacob's is beautifully maintained, with a market, wagon rides and a 10-acre corn maze.

ROVE ESTATE

Newly opened in May, 2015, Rove is part of the Gallagher family's fifth-generation farming operation. The vines are 5 years old now, and the vineyard boasts some of the biggest views of Benzie county. Stop here for a sample of what the Scots-Irish can do with wine. Snacks also available.

IRIS FARM

With six acres of more than 1,000 different varieties of mostly German hybrids, this farm is a show-stopper in June. Pick a bouquet, or select plants for pick-up or mailing in August.

LIGHT OF DAY FARM

Light of Day uses biodynamic techniques designed by Rudolph Steiner to plant and harvest their selection of teas and tisanes. Tea in Michigan? Yes! Green teas, white teas, black, oolong, matcha, and so much more. There's a shop and classes are available.

Agriculture in Michigan

MICHIGAN IS THE #1 PRODUCER OF FRUIT IN THE U.S. BUT, LIKE EVERYWHERE ELSE, CLIMATE CHANGE IS AFFECTING LOCAL AGRICULTURE. WINTERS COME LATER, AND ARE WARMER. SUMMERS ARE DRIER AND HOTTER.

Temperatures have increased 2 degrees since the 1980s, and are predicted to go up another 5 – 7 degrees by the end of the century. Higher temperatures mean less ice coverage during the winter, and lake levels are expected to drop by 1 to 5 feet.

All of this will lead to less diversity, and probably the end to some of our most beloved crops. Like cherries, for one. Unlike most crops, cherries depend more on air temperature than watering to thrive. Once the cherry trees come out of dormancy — and that can happen in February these days — they are susceptible to freezing temperatures. Michigan has experienced a higher number of extreme spring thaws and freezes in recent years, making cherry farmers skittish about continuing to hoe that row.

Maple syrup farmers are in the same dubious spot. Maple trees need warm days and cold nights to pump out the sap, and springs just aren't cooperating like they used to. Plus, warmer weather makes maple syrup less sweet. In fact, the syrup harvested today is already half as sweet than it was 50 years ago: while it used to take 25 gallons of sap to make a gallon of pure maple sugar, it now takes 50. And that puts pressure on trees already worn out by the warm weather.

Grape farmers, on the other hand, may be seeing sunnier days. The growing season has gotten longer by almost two weeks over the last 40 years, and experts see the season continuing to stretch. There's also a tendency towards milder, wetter winters with lower night-time temperatures.

That said, the weather is pretty crazy. And that's about all you can count on these days.

22% of Michigan's population works on a farm or a farm-related business.

Michigan farmland totals about 10 million acres, but the average farm is only 193 acres. 95% of Michigan farms are owned by single-family or family partnerships. The average age of a Michigan farmer is 56.

Michigan produces more than 300 different farm products, second only to California for diversity.

Source: Michigan Farm Bureau

---

was sitting next to six guys in waders. I could feel their fire slowly opening up parts of my face. There was wet

SLEEPING BEAR DUNES NATIONAL LAKESHORE

THE SLEEPING BEAR DUNES NATIONAL LAKESHORE VISITORS CENTER IS LOCATED ON M-72, JUST OUTSIDE THE VILLAGE OF EMPIRE. STOP IN FOR MAPS, BOOKS AND DIORAMA DISPLAYS OF LOCAL FLORA AND FAUNA.

176

COMPLETE SLEEPING BEAR'S ULTIMATE HIKING CHALLENGE

The Sleeping Bear Dunes averages well over 1.5 million visitors every year, but only a relative handful can lay claim to hiking every mainland trail in the park — that's 13 trails — in a single year.

It's called the Trail Trekker Challenge, the brainchild of two Glen Lake area high school students who pitched the idea to Sleeping Bear officials as part of a senior project in 2011. The TTC was designed to motivate visitors to see some of the amazing places within the National Lakeshore beyond the Dune Climb. While most of the trails on the brochure/logbook — a copy of which you can get when you buy your park pass at the Lakeshore's visitors center — can be tackled in well under an hour without breaking a sweat, only 45 people completed the challenge in 2015. **BB**

THE NATIONAL PARK SERVICE OFFERS 9 FEE-FREE DAYS IN 2017 —

January 18: Martin Luther King Jr. Day

April 16-24: National Park Week's opening weekend

August 25-28: National Park Service Birthday Weekend

September 24: National Public Lands Day

November 11: Veterans Day

sand in my teeth. The board was propped up in front of me to break the wind, half of it anyway. ¶ *"Where's my*

SLEEPING BEAR IS NAMED FOR THE CHIPPEWA LEGEND OF A MOTHER BEAR FLEEING AN ENORMOUS FIRE IN WISCONSIN WITH HER TWO CUBS.

The three swam across Lake Michigan, but when the mother arrived on Leelanau's shore, her cubs were missing. Mother bear waited and waited on top of a high bluff until she was completely buried under the sand. The Great Spirit saw her and was moved by her loss, and to honor her motherhood created two islands — North and South Manitou — to commemorate the lost cubs.

Sleeping Bear became a national park in 1970, after nearly a decade of local controversy. Back then, much of the land now in the park was privately owned, and the landowners weren't happy about losing homes which had been in their families for generations. Area locals were also skeptical about the value of hugely increased tourism.

The federal government, however, felt strongly that the "Third Coast" needed protection. They finally won their case by helping to offset lost property tax revenue by supporting local schools.

In 2014, 32,500 acres of the park were designated wilderness under the federal Sleeping Bear Dunes National Lakeshore Conservation and Recreation Act.

SOME STATS FROM NPS.GOV—

Annual Visits: more than 1.5 million
Employees: 52 permanent, 104 seasonal
Volunteer Hours: 29,595 from 850 volunteers
Area: 71,210 acres
Lake Michigan Shoreline: 65 miles
Inland Lakes: 26
Terrestrial Plant Species: 908
Bird Species: 246
Federally Threatened or Endangered Species: 4
Prehistoric Archaeological Sites: 150

board?", I said. ¶ "Gone", one of them said back. "Gone out into the lake on the current of the river. Probably

THIS 298-FOOT SIDEWHEEL STEAMER MAY BE THE SECRET BEHIND EMPIRE'S EXALTED NAME ... BUT PROBABLY NOT.

Capt. Walker, of St. Clair, set about in 1846 to build the biggest, inland lakes steamer in history. It must have been a rocky road, though, as the ship was sold a couple of times before completion and had three names: *Excelsior*, then *Shakespeare*, and finally *Empire State*. More bad luck followed when the steamer was beached in this yet unnamed, northern mill town during an August gale, only a year after setting sail. The steamer had to be towed to Detroit, but after repairs, it made history for the fastest run between Buffalo, NY, and Milwaukee, WI — a mere 66.5 hours.

That said, the Empire Lumber Company had already been in operation for several years before the steamer showed up. From 1887 to 1917, the mill was the major industry, and one of the largest in Michigan, producing up to 20 million feet of lumber a year. In 1890, more than 1,000 people lived in Empire. Today, there are less than 400.

In 1909, the masted steam barge "Edward Buckley" was employed by the Empire Lumber Company to bring logs from North Manitou to the mill at Empire. The barge then finished the journey by transporting the finished lumber to Chicago.

In the early 1900s, Michigan's mainland forests were a thing of the past, and lumber barons looked to North Manitou's forests. Although much of the timber was already second growth, it was an important source of finished lumber for the building boom in Chicago.

The first Empire mill burned in 1906, and the reconstructed mill burned again in 1917. It was not replaced.

Learn

There's an extensive museum in Empire, built to mimic the Roen Saloon, a prominent watering hole during lumber days. The EMPIRE AREA MUSEUM COMPLEX features the original Roen Saloon bar, a Victorian parlor re-creation, a turn-of-the-century kitchen, a blacksmith shop, a barn display, a railroad exhibit, a covered wagon, and so much more.

Behind the museum is an original one-room schoolhouse. The Billy Beeman Barn contains horse drawn equipment.

Eat

JOE'S FRIENDLY TAVERN is just what its name suggests. Locals eat here.

Play

Get your paddleboards, skateboards, kayaks, sunglasses and suits at **SLEEPING BEAR SURF AND KAYAK**.

Kayak rentals need a one-day notice.

See the SPORTS sections for more info.

VILLAGE PARK IS A SPLENDID SPOT. LOOK SOUTH, AND YOU'LL SEE THE EMPIRE BLUFFS AND POINT BETSIE. LOOK NORTH TO SLEEPING BEAR.

Little kids will love skipping back and forth between Lake Michigan and South Bar Lake. (Beware: the water is deep at the end of South Bar's dock, so watch your kids closely.) There's playground equipment, restrooms and lots of feed-the-meter parking. Lunch and the museum are just around the corner.

For info on surfing in Empire, see page 213.

CALENDAR

EMPIRE ASPARAGUS FESTIVAL || 3rd weekend in May

EMPIRE HILL CLIMB || race your auto up a hill || September 16

EMPIRE HOPS FESTIVAL || 1st Saturday in October

EMPIRE HERITAGE DAYS || 2nd weekend in October

EMPIRE WINTERFEST || ice skating, curling, a polar bear dip into South Bar Lake and a pool tournament || February 17

stuff." ¶ I could feel my head bleeding and one eye refused to focus. ¶ "What in the living hell are you trying

BENZIE COUNTY, JUST WEST OF GRAND TRAVERSE AND SOUTH OF LEELANAU, OFFERS MUCH OF THE ROLLING, GREEN TERRAIN AND LAKES THAT LEELANAU COUNTY HAS. AND IT HASN'T BEEN AS EXTENSIVELY "DISCOVERED" YET. WHAT'S MORE, IT'S HOME TO FOUR DISTINCT AND PICTURESQUE TOWNS THAT CAN MAKE FOR AT LEAST A FULL DAY OF TOURING.

BEULAH is on crystal-blue Crystal Lake. An antiques mall with seemingly endless bays, a well-known cherry-centric restaurant, and a row of unique shops a block off the lake are features of this cozy village of vacation homes hugging the oblong lake's southwestern shore. If you're on U.S. 31, you may want to stop at the CHERRY HUT, with the classic roadside family restaurant feel. They're known for their cherry pie, cherry-ade and other cherry desserts and drinks — plus a menu of homestyle entrees. Turn into town and the MYERS GRANARY ANTIQUE MARKET hosts bays and tables and rows of furnishings and pop culture items from decades and decades past. The row of downtown businesses on South Benzie Boulevard includes a restaurant, a pub, a kosher deli, a gallery and several other shops.

Head toward the public beach on **CRYSTAL LAKE**, known for its clean and deep-hued water. The beach wouldn't be there, except that a canal was dug to connect the lake with Lake Michigan in 1873. In a mammoth whoosh as they connected the two, the inland lake dropped an astonishing 20 feet.

Atop the hill on U.S. 31 south of town lies **BENZONIA**. Just to the south are campgrounds and resorts on the Betsie River.

The drive westward on River Road winds alongside (with fewer twists and turns, of course) through the Betsie River State Game Refuge. If you pack your bikes or want to take a stroll, there's a rails-to-trails path along the way.

On the north side of River Road, about two miles west of Benzonia, you may notice an unusual stone building that subtly rises from the contours of the land. This is the studio of the late **GWEN FROSTIC** which still hosts visitors and sells placemats, note cards, wall-hanging prints and other items bearing the nature-inspired works she hand-carved into linoleum printing plates. There's also a reading room well-stocked with nature books, overlooking a pond that attracts a lot of waterfowl.

A little farther, on the south side of the road is **CRYSTAL LAKE ALPACA FARM AND BOUTIQUE**. In good weather, you may see several of the woolly, South American animals related to the llama and the camel in the pens. Inside, they sell socks, scarves and other items made from alpaca wool.

Farther west and a little south is the town of **ELBERTA**. A striking feature of the town is its Lake Michigan beach, accessible by a steep rise to a scenic lookout and then a steep drop to a relatively low-traffic beach. On Betsie Lake is a landscaped waterfront park near the ruins of an industrial furnace from the town's smokestack past.

BETSIE BAY has marinas where pleasure craft, fishing and charter boats are docked for the more temperamental Lake Michigan beyond the breakwall.

Across Betsie Lake from Elberta is **FRANKFORT**, the biggest of the four towns. Frankfort has, in recent years, grown into a worthy destination for foodies. Take a few minutes to stroll up and down Main Street to see the variety. Among the galleries, gift shops, smokehouse and glasswork studio, there's DINGHY'S retro nautical diner, the seasonal fine dining of COHO CAFE, STORM CLOUD micro-brewery, a grill, a pizzeria, book stores, the GARDEN THEATER for movies and a hot dog emporium, just to name a few. On the outskirts of town is a classic A&W with drive-in bays still there.

Oh, and, if you leave town via highway M-115, check out the cool model of a lake freighter that greets visitors both coming and going at the city limits.

Also, within a short drive of this cluster of Benzie County towns is Crystal Mountain ski resort in Thompsonville to the southeast (see page 145), and Otter Creek (or Esch Road) Beach to the north (see page 182). Also, the Platte River runs through nearby Honor and is a favorite river for canoeing, kayaking and tubing. **TC**

BEE-ING HELPFUL

We all know that bees make honey, but their biggest job is pollination, the transfer of pollen grains from the male anther of a flower to the female stigma.

And all over the world, bees are in big trouble. What's the problem? A tiny insect called the varroa mite is burrowing into the egg-filled cells of a honeycomb. Once there, it attaches to the egg and become a parasite when the bee hatches. Enough of these little critters will wipe out a hive. Last year, Michigan lost 5,000 hives — and each hive supports about 40,000 bees. A U.N.-sponsored report released in 2016 found that "about 40% of invertebrate pollinator species [bees, moths, butterflies] are facing extinction," a fact that could have major implications for the world food supply, because "about 75% of the world's food crops ... depend at least partly on pollination."

Sleeping Bear Farms in Beulah make 100% raw honey products. Their operation of about 6,000 hives pollinate in Michigan in late spring and summer, then move to Florida in the fall, and finally to California around February to help with the state's almond trees.

Really? Doesn't California have its own bees?

Eighty percent of the world's almond trees grow in California, and they need massive amounts of bees, about 1.7 million hives altogether. That's something like 85% of all available commercial hives in the United States.

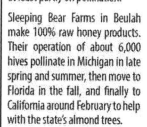

A WRONG TO FIND WRIGHT BY TOM CARR

The incident took place in the sawmill town of Aral, population about 200, a few miles south of Empire. Don't look for it on a map — it only existed for a few decades, when the lumber boom was sweeping the trees from the northern lower peninsula. Perfectly situated for receiving timber, Aral boasted a decent creek for floating logs from inland, a millpond and access to Lake Michigan. When our story begins, it also had a post office, a couple of boarding houses for lumberjacks, horse barns, a school, a church, a meeting hall, a general store and a doctor. And it had a sawmill, operated by Charlie Wright.

Now Charlie Wright was a bit of a Jekyll-Hyde character. People liked him when he was sober, but drunk, he was stinking mean. And he was never meaner than the day the sheriff of Benzie County sent a deputy to discuss a tax dispute.

The deputy didn't get anything but threats from old Charlie Wright, so he headed into town for some back-up and returned with the doctor. Wright wasted no time. He shot them both, left them where they fell and went back to work.

It wasn't long before word got out. Wright realized the town was talking about him and getting pretty worked up. Figuring they might be in the mood for some vigilante justice, he shut down the mill, paid off his workers and ran away into the woods.

But the sheriff was on his way, riding by buggy from Benzonia, then hitching a steamer from Frankfort to Aral. And he meant business. He traveled with a posse of twenty and went straight for the jugular, capturing Wright's right-hand man, a local Odawa man named Lahala.

The sheriff was sure Lahala knew where his boss had scampered to, but he wasn't talking. The sheriff had a solution. He tossed a rope over a tree, hoisted the man into the air by the neck and told him to kick his legs when he was ready to talk.

It's not clear how one avoids kicking one's legs when dangling by a noose, but it wasn't long before Lahala was kicking madly.

---

say. "Bitchin'. I hit one of those smokers just at the pointbreak, man, and started to drop into the curl and then

Photo by Tom Carr

THE NAKED TRUTH

OTTER CREEK BEACH IS PROBABLY THE BEST-KNOWN NUDE BEACH IN MICHIGAN.

But yes, it could also take a big chunk out of your pocket. You know, the one in those wadded up shorts weighted down by a rock.

This long, spacious Lake Michigan beach at the end of Esch Road is the stuff of skinny-dipping legend. Problem is, it's not legally a nude beach. This is the Midwest. Not Europe.

The beach is part of the Sleeping Bear Dunes National Lakeshore and is about a mile off of highway M-22 on the pock-marked Esch Road, three miles south of Empire.

Part of the unparalleled charm of this beach is that you can walk for miles to where you're a pinpoint to those who stay close to their cars. You can find short dunes hiding sandy little bowls where it seems private. You may happen upon people taking advantage of that fact to shed their modesty in pursuit of no tan lines. Or you may get the notion to do so yourself.

But this is land owned by the non-libertine National Park Service. Rangers patrol the area for more than just those trying to park for free. (It's $15; envelopes near the outhouse.) They also write several tickets per month when it's warm enough for a birthday suit. Fines of up to $350 and possible jail for repeat offenders kind of puts a chill on the whole thing. And we all know what a chill can do when we're naked. Yikes! **TC**

This went on, the hoisting and the dropping of the blue-faced Odawa, until the words the sheriff knew were there gasped out. Wright was found and Lahala was released.

It's been said that the hanging tree is still there — just off the dirt road that crosses Otter Creek at the south of Esch Road. Some also say it's obvious which of the trees is the hanging tree. But there are a lot of trees around there that look like they could support a noose, although trees obviously change a lot in 127 years.

There are also supposedly some building foundations still in the woods on the north side of Esch Road. The weather extremes on the sandy shores of Lake Michigan took care of the rest of the buildings over the century since the town ceased to exist.

In looking for the hanging tree, however, one might notice that it's next to one of the most beautiful beaches imaginable.

Excerpted from *Blood on the Mitten: Infamous Michigan Murders, 1700s to Present.*

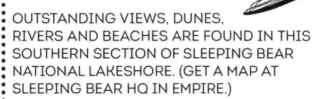

Platte River District

OUTSTANDING VIEWS, DUNES, RIVERS AND BEACHES ARE FOUND IN THIS SOUTHERN SECTION OF SLEEPING BEAR NATIONAL LAKESHORE. (GET A MAP AT SLEEPING BEAR HQ IN EMPIRE.)

TAKE YOUR KIDS TO THE BEACH

Platte Point Beach is a big favorite with kids. Play in the river or play in the Big Lake. Bring an inner tube and float down the river. The park can be very busy in July and August. Restrooms with flush toilets. No pets.

PETERSON BEACH

You'll think you're on the road to nowhere, but we promise there is a secluded somewhere, and it's worth the long dirt road. Peterson Beach has the views, calm waters and not many people. There's a small parking lot, so you may have to park on the road. Pets are allowed on the beach to the left of the boardwalk.

184

WALK THE BLUFFS

Go straight up through a hardwood forest to the big view. Great walking in the spring for wildflowers. Don't go down the bluff. For one thing, it causes erosion. For another, helicopters are expensive.

OTTER CREEK

One of the best walks in the park. Head to the beach —— at the end of Esch Road —— and walk south. Cross the creek and keep going until you start to see the little paths heading up towards the woods. Take any one of them, keep left, and you'll end up on a service road that will once again cross the creek and drop you back in the parking lot. Some of the most varied scenery anywhere. Leashed pets allowed to the right of the beach entrance. More about Otter Creek on the previous page.

PLATTE RIVER

Great for tubing and lazy river paddling from M-22 to Lake Michigan. There's a campground here as well, and it can get very crowded in the high season. Tube, kayak and canoe rentals are available at The Honor Trading Post and Riverside Canoe Trips.

wanted to say. ¶ *Instead I said, "Got a beer"?* ¶ *"Sure", one guy said, shoving one in my fist.* ¶ *"I fished here*

JUST IMAGINE IF THE WILD TURKEY HAD BECOME THE U.S. NATIONAL SYMBOL INSTEAD OF THE BALD EAGLE...

That's what Founding Father Benjamin Franklin lobbied for. In this letter to his daughter, he states his case:

For my own part I wish the Bald Eagle had not been chosen the Representative of our Country. He is a Bird of bad moral Character. He does not get his Living honestly. You may have seen him perched on some dead Tree near the River, where, too lazy to fish for himself, he watches the Labour of the Fishing Hawk; and when that diligent Bird has at length taken a Fish, and is bearing it to his Nest for the Support of his Mate and young Ones, the Bald Eagle pursues him and takes it from him.

With all this Injustice, he is never in good Case but like those among Men who live by Sharping & Robbing he is generally poor and often very lousy. Besides he is a rank Coward: The little King Bird not bigger than a Sparrow attacks him boldly and drives him out of the District. He is therefore by no means a proper Emblem for the brave and honest Cincinnati of America who have driven all the King birds from our Country.... For in Truth the Turkey is in Comparison a much more respectable Bird, and withal a true original Native of America...

The wild turkeys found in the UpNorth are the eastern variety — the same bird the Puritans ate at that long-ago Thanksgiving feast.

But if they're native to the U.S., why are they called turkeys? That's because, when the British ruled, they imported a kind of domesticated guinea fowl to Europe from . . . you guessed it . . . Turkey. The guinea fowl was called, in English, the turkey-cock, and it does look a little bit like our turkey. So, when the American fowl began to show up in English markets it was just another turkey.

Turkeys can be really big — up to 4 feet long from beak to tail. And, although they look rather awkward, even ridiculous, they're powerful fliers over short distances.

Turkeys can be aggressive around humans. The best advice is to keep your distance.

In Michigan, the wild turkey was nearly extinct in 1900, but five different attempts to reintroduce the bird finally paid off. Wild turkeys are now a game species in the state, with a season in the spring and in the fall.

A GROUP OF TURKEYS IS CALLED A "RAFTER." A BABY TURKEY IS CALLED A POULT.

last week", I said. "Landed two steelies just about out in front of where we're sitting, but I gave it up, decided

LOTS OF STUFF TO DO AS WE HEAD NORTH. IN ORDER OF APPEARANCE, THERE'S A BEACH, A PRETTY DRIVE, THE DUNE CLIMB, A VIEW AND A GREAT PLACE FOR DINNER.

ALL OF THE SPOTS MENTIONED BELOW ARE PART OF THE NATIONAL PARK, AND YOU'LL NEED A PASS. JUST BECAUSE YOU DON'T SEE A RANGER, DOESN'T MEAN YOU WON'T GET A TICKET. (PLUS, IT'S THE RIGHT THING TO DO.)

NORTH BAR

Like the Platte River beach (page 184) North Bar is for kids of all ages. Find it by keeping straight on Lacore street where M-22 takes a right-hand curve when leaving Empire. Lacore will become Voice Road, which will then become N. Bar Lake Road. Take a left at North Bar Lake Access. The park paved these roads in the last few years, so it isn't as daunting as it sounds. There's lots of parking now, too, but never enough in the high season, and you may have to leave your car on the side of the road. Now, for the long hike: All those coolers, floats, umbrellas, etc., will need to be lugged down the path to the lake, then around the lake to get to the Big Water. People do it all the time. Bar Lake is warmer than Lake Michigan, and kids will love digging around in the spill-off to the Big Lake. Bring your skimmer for extra fun. No pets.

PIERCE STOCKING DRIVE || M-22 TO 109

A lovely little drive to the top of the bluff and back down. There are several places to get out for views or a picnic. See the next page for other ideas.

DUNE CLIMB || 109

Without doubt, the biggest attraction in the park. Climb up, run down, repeat.

Continue north on 109 to visit the Maritime Museum and the Glen Haven ghost town (page 190). 109 will also take you right into Glen Arbor for lunch and shopping.

INSPIRATION POINT

If you're skipping the Dune Climb and heading towards Glen Arbor, take a sidetrip to Inspiration Point for an incredible view of Big Glen and the islands.

From Pierce Stocking Drive, head across 109 to 616. That will hook you up with M-22. Just before the Narrows between the Glen Lakes, take a right on W. MacFarlane. Just so you know, there are a couple of good restaurants along this road, FUNISTRADA and LA BÉCASSE. Dinner only.

MacFarlane turns into Dunns Farm Road and continues around Big Glen and on into Glen Arbor. It's more scenic, though, to return to the Narrows and M-22.

Over the Top

The Pierce Stocking Drive is a peaceful, rolling road through 7 miles of hilly sandscapes and maple woods. Unfortunately, there is no drive peaceful enough to placate bored, restless kids who have been strapped in a back seat kicking each other for hours.

Well, when you reach the Dune Overlook, there's a chance to work those young legs.

First, walk over to the lookout platform and drink in the scenery. There are pod-shaped dunes and craters — almost a moonscape, if the moon had grass and desert-like plants.

Now notice that you can see a parking lot in the distance to the right, between the golden dunes and the two Glen Lakes. That's the lot for the popular Sleeping Bear Dune Climb. Let's go that way.

The hiking loop, called Cottonwood Trail, heads out into that sandy moonscape. The time-honored INSIDER tradition is to leave the young'ns at the halfway mark while the designated driver(s) return to the car. Let's face it, the kids aren't going to let you enjoy the rest of the drive in peace, so you may as well send them on their sandy ways.

It's good to have an adult or responsible older kid along for the trek — it's about two-thirds of a mile, as the seagull flies. Try to stay on the existing trail so as not to wear new ones in the grassy areas. And take some water and sunscreen.

Keep your eyes on that parking lot, when you can. There are some dips and craters along the way, but also plenty of hilltops where you can make sure you're heading in the right direction for the payoff of running down the Dune Climb's steep spillover.

If all goes well, the trekkers will find their driver at the bottom of the dune, rested up and ready for the next adventure.

Drivers: Take a left out of Pierce Stocking Drive on M-109 and the Dune Climb parking lot is 6.4 miles away. **TC**

DUNES TRAIL

DUNE CLIMB

COTTONWOOD TRAIL

DUNE OVERLOOK & PARKING

ENTRANCE / EXIT
PIERCE STOCKING DRIVE

109
TO THE DUNE CLIMB PARKING LOT

---

once. ¶ Behind him I could see clouds sliding in. West, maybe a little northwest and I was sure I could smell

Leelinau, Delight of Life

Jane Johnston was born on January 31, 1800, in Sault Ste. Marie to an Ojibwa mother and an Irish fur trader. Twenty-three years later, she married Henry Rowe Schoolcraft, who had just been appointed U.S. Indian Agent to the Michigan Territory. Together, the two of them documented Native life in stories and poems. Jane often used the pen name "Leelinau" in her writings.

Henry would become famous for his extensive publications on Native Americans, especially the Ojibwa. Henry Wadsworth Longfellow used Schoolcraft's research as the primary source for his long poem, *The Song of Hiawatha*.

Only recently, however, was Jane's contribution to Ojibwa literature and history acknowledged. In 2008, she was formally recognized as "the first Native American literary writer, the first known Indian woman writer, the first known Indian poet, the first known poet to write poems in a Native American language and the first known American Indian to write out traditional Indian stories." [Parker] Jane Johnston Schoolcraft was inducted into the Michigan Women's Hall of Fame that same year.

But what about the name Leelinau? According to Henry Schoolcraft, the word meant "delight of life," and he liked to call many Native women, not just his wife, by this title. The truth is, he probably made the word up from a combination of Ojibwa, Latin and Arabic, and Jane went along with it. Henry made up a lot of faux Indian words, and many of them live on in Michigan counties —— Alcona, Iosco, Kalkaska, Oscoda and Tuscola are all Henry's inventions.

No matter the origin of the name, we agree that Leelanau County is truly a Delight of Life.

something funny in the wind. I watched set after set break against the sandbar, the waves beginning to build.

MAKING A SAND DUNE

Dunes are hills of sand formed by wind or water, or, in the case of Sleeping Bear, by both wind and water. Most dunes are longer on the windward side as the sand is constantly getting pushed up the hill. In the park, the windward side is always the side facing Lake Michigan.

The Dune Climb faces away from the wind, called the lee. Dunes that face leeward are called slip faces.

WIND DIRECTION

THEN SLUMPS DOWN THE SLIP FACE

THE SAND MOVES UP THE SLOPE FROM LAKE MICHIGAN

CRATERS ON THE DUNES

The large, flat, circular "craters" found on the dunes are actually called blowouts. What has happened is that a tree or large shrub died, and the loose soil was then carried away by the wind.

THE DUNES ARE FRAGILE

Because dunes are made of loose sand, they tend to shift around and change shape. Plants, like the grasses and small shrubs you find on your walks, anchor the sand around them and keep the dune in place. When you stay on the trails, you are protecting the dunes from this erosion.

Also, the dunes are an important buffer zone to the green hills and valleys of Leelanau County. Without the wall of sand, the area would be too windy to sustain the variety of crops that grow there now.

GREAT HORNED OWLS

Inside those dune craters (blowouts) you can often find owl pellets, or the little packages of plant matter, bones, fur, feathers, bills, claws and teeth that an owl can't digest.

The Great Horned (above) is the most common owl resident in the park. Notice the ear tufts that stick up to either side of its head — this owl has excellent hearing and can snatch a mouse up from under a foot of snow.

The Great Horned hunts at night and eats small mammals like mice, rabbits, even skunks. That's normal fare for birds of prey. But the Great Horned stands apart from most owls because it's one of the few which can't turn its head all the way around.

Another interesting fact is that Great Horned owls often freeze uneaten food, saving it for a later date. They use their own body heat to thaw it out when they're hungry again.

A suspiciously mousy-looking owl pellet.

GLEN HAVEN (ORIGINALLY NAMED SLEEPING BEAR) WAS SETTLED IN 1857 AS A DEEP-WATER PORT TO SERVICE THE SHIPPING INDUSTRY WITH FUEL, LUMBER AND SUPPLIES.

By 1911, all the trees were gone, and a new mill was erected on the pond between Little Glen Lake and the current Dune Climb. A narrow gauge steam locomotive track was built from there back to the dock at Glen Haven, where the timber products could be loaded directly onto the ships. You can still see the dock poles near the shore.

MARITIME MUSEUM

It's hard to imagine how dangerous travel was prior to railroads and highways. If you wanted to come to northern Michigan, you simply had to get in a boat. And, while the boat may have been safe enough, severe weather might send even the most ship-shape vessel to the bottom of the lake.

In fact, the terrible winter of 1870 – 1871, and the deaths of 214 people on the Great Lakes, prompted the U.S. Congress to appropriate funds to educate and equip life-saving services on the inland coasts. By the turn of the century, 60 such stations were erected on the Great Lakes. Each station had a full-time keeper, and the keeper hired up to eight "surfmen" to work the shipping season from April to mid-December.

The Maritime Museum and the Boathouse next door present the history of shipping during the 1900s, and display artifacts of life-saving equipment used during that time.

During the summer, there's a rousing re-enactment of the breeches buoy rescue drill every day at 3 PM. Children are welcome to join in.

The Maritime Museum is open Memorial Day weekend through Labor Day, every day from 11 AM to 5 PM. No pets at the museum, but dogs can walk the beach to the right of the museum all the way to D.H. Day Campground.

D.H. DAY

David H. Day was the guy who built that sawmill on Little Glen and arranged for the locomotive transport. He was a good friend of Perry Hannah, down in TC, and often borrowed money from him to fund his business exploits. Like Hannah, he diversified when the timber ran out, establishing the Glen Haven Cannery. By the end of his life, Day owned more than 5,000 acres in the Glen Haven – Glen Arbor area, and was a big promoter of reforestation. Day donated the shoreland between Glen Haven and Glen Arbor to the state of Michigan in 1920. That land is now part of Sleeping Bear National Lakeshore.

For info on the campground, see page 109.

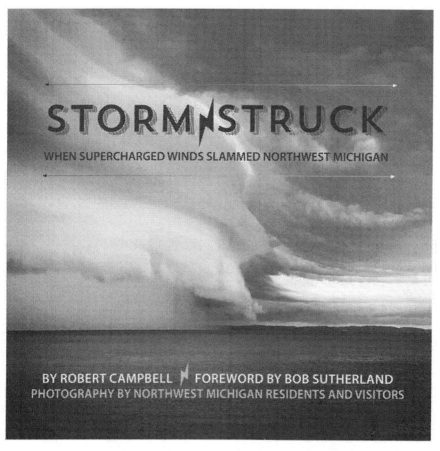

STORM STRUCK

WHEN SUPERCHARGED WINDS SLAMMED NORTHWEST MICHIGAN

BY ROBERT CAMPBELL   FOREWORD BY BOB SUTHERLAND
PHOTOGRAPHY BY NORTHWEST MICHIGAN RESIDENTS AND VISITORS

A HUNDRED-YEAR STORM

AT 3:57 P.M., ON AUGUST 2, 2015, THE NATIONAL WEATHER SERVICE ISSUED SEVERE WEATHER WARNINGS FOR BENZIE, LEELANAU, GRAND TRAVERSE, MANISTEE AND WEXFORD COUNTIES.

Minutes later, the storm slammed the shoreline along the Sleeping Bear Dunes National Lakeshore. Ravaging the land as it went, the storm marched swiftly east-southeast across Leelanau County towards West Bay. It then smashed through the southern half of Old Mission Peninsula and parts of Traverse City before charging across East Bay and battering the northwest corner of Grand Traverse County, including Elk and Skegemog lakes. Left behind was a trail of private and public property damage that reached an estimated $29.7 million in Leelanau and $15.4 million in Grand Traverse.

Evidence of the destructive storm is still everywhere, from Glen Haven to Alligator Hill in Glen Arbor to Maple Bay in Yuba. Mission Point Press produced a book, titled *Storm Struck*, describing the storm and its aftermath. The book full-color is available is stores locally.

---

any fishing today bud", one of them said in my ear. "Just sit tight. Besides, you only got half a board surfer boy".

THERE'S A SENSE OF IF "YOU CAN DREAM IT, YOU CAN BUILD IT" IN GLEN ARBOR. COMPOST HEAPS, SOLAR PANELS, HIPPIE GARDENS AND PONY CORRALS SNUGGLE UP TO HIGH-END HOMES, RETAIL, RESTAURANTS AND RESORTS. IT'S A HODGE-PODGE, AND YOU CAN'T GET A DECENT PHOTO TO SAVE YOUR LIFE – EXCEPT, PERHAPS, IF THE CAMP KOHAHNA JALOPY BUS HAPPENS TO SWING THROUGH, ITS OPEN WINDOWS FULL OF SINGING GIRLS.

D.H. Day did his best to turn Glen Arbor into a tourist destination after the lumber ran out, even building a golf course atop Alligator Hill. A golf course was not enough to make the rugged lumberjack area attractive to visitors. Day's plan came to naught, which may account for the everything-goes, village zoning.

After Day and lumber, Christian Science became Glen Arbor's economic engine. Church members founded the Leelanau School in 1929, and its winter quarters were called the "homestead." Although no longer affiliated with the church, the school is still in business, and The Homestead is an all-inclusive luxury resort.

LAKE STREET

The **COTTONSEED** is a big favorite, and packed to the gills with resort-wear. They have a popular half-off sale every October.

Glen Arbor has more art galleries than any other Leelanau village, and most of them are on or near Lake Street. If you wander out behind the public restrooms, you'll find the the **GLEN ARBOR ART ASSOCIATION** headquarters. GAAA often has shows, and offers classes for all ages during the summer.

COTTAGE BOOKS is a picture-perfect example of book-selling at its best.

He held me at arms length like I was his kid brother and I was trying to hit him in the face, only my arms

CHERRY REPUBLIC got its start in Glen Arbor, and their theme park anchors the south end of Lake Street.

Peek into the BETHLEHEM LUTHERAN CHURCH next to Cherry Republic. The church was built by sailors, and the interior looks like a boat.

Locals love ART'S TAVERN, on Lake and Western Avenue. Ask about the pool table. No credit cards. GOOD HARBOR GRILL in downtown Glen Arbor, open mid-May to mid-October, uses local ingredients in almost everything. Also recommended is the WESTERN AVENUE GRILL.

Lake Street, on the beach side of Western Avenue, has a couple of attractions. BECKY THATCHER DESIGNS makes and displays outstanding jewelry using local and exotic stones. BLU is one of the best restaurants anywhere in the area, and its dining room overlooking the Big Lake is simply spectacular.

PUBLIC ACCESS

There's a boat launch and (tiny) beach access at the end of Lake Street.

There's only one public, motorized boat launch to access the Glen Lakes. It's near the Narrows Bridge on Day Forest Road. Parking is limited.

For swimmers and paddlers, there's a single public access point at OLD SETTLER'S PARK on South Dunns Farm Road. It's a tiny place, and not much beach, but there is an ample dock. The old Methodist chapel was added to the county property in 1917, with the stipulation that the church "shall not be used for dancing." You can rent it for other occasions, however.

SLEEPING BEAR HERITAGE TRAIL

This all-access biking / walking / ski trail starts on Western Avenue (aka M-22) and runs to the Dune Climb, Glen Haven and the D.H. Day Campground to the west, Empire to the south and Port Oneida and Bohemian Road to the east. The Glen Arbor trail was hit hard in the 2015 wind storm.

ALLIGATOR HILL

Look up the hill along the Heritage Trail, this is the Alligator. Totally devastated in the 2015 storm, two of the trails have been cleared for hiking and skiing. The place to go if you like apocalyptic landscapes.

Glen Arbor's fire chief worries that all the downed trees could result in major fires during the dry season, but Park scientists argue that the storm was a natural event, and as such doesn't need fixing. Blow downs are regular events in hardwood forests, and leaving the trees where they fell will encourage a faster, more natural recovery.

CRYSTAL RIVER

Kayaking this shallow river is a total blast for all ages. Read about how to do it on page 111.

194

Port Oneida

This collection of 17 picturesque farms and two schools, part of Sleeping Bear National Lakeshore, puts an idyllic face on catastrophic farming. The buildings are beautiful, but the farming was a bust.

The first farm was built in 1852 by Carsten Burfiend from Hanover, Germany. Several other families arrived from Hanover and Prussia, and the U.S. Census reports 87 people living in the area in 1860. Two years later, there was a dock for loading timber. By 1908, the village center was abandoned.

As you might be able to guess from the wind-swept look of the place, farming conditions are far from ideal. The soil is too sandy, and there's very little in the way of water supply, unless you want to haul it up over the bluff from the Big Lake. Potatoes were the crop of choice, and every farmer knows that potatoes are what you plant if nothing else will grow.

Imagine, though, the work that went into clearing those fields — pulling out all of those stumps! — then finding that your topsoil had all blown away in a few short years. Back-breaking and heart-breaking.

Walk right up and around any of these old homesteads and peek in the windows. The Kelderhouse cemetery on Port Oneida Road is also worth a look, and the old schoolhouse is across the road.

Port Oneida Fair

Held once a year on the second Friday and Saturday in August, the Port Oneida Fair goes all out displaying the crafts, skills and talents that made rural life fun and productive.

Over 100 volunteers demonstrate everything from driving oxen to making soap, trapping for furs, butter-making and hay baling. At the Kelderhouse Farm, you can view a re-enactment of a Civil War camp. Many of the historic sites offer picnic lunch fare. And there's a "Star Party" Saturday night at Thoreson Farm, courtesy of the Grand Traverse Astronomical Society.

A trolley is available to shuttle you around to the different sites. You can also walk or bike. Remember that the Heritage Trail connects all the most popular spots in the Park.

Port Oneida also hosts Antique Apple Day in October. There are over 100 varieties still growing in the Park, and free for the picking.

BAY VIEW TRAIL

Walk or bike the historic district and enjoy the views of Lake Michigan.

THE FARM LOOP is 2.4 miles long, meandering through fields and farms. An easy hike or ski.

THE RIDGE LOOP takes you up the ridge and back. It's a steep climb, but a great view. Please don't go down the bluff. 1.2 miles.

The trailhead for both loops is off Thoreson Road.

who looks so oddly out of place, an ancient creature risen up out of the water and the spray mystified by the

PYRAMID POINT

One of the most popular walks in the park for visitors and locals. It's a climb, but so totally worth the effort. The up and back is a short 1.2-miles. For a longer and even more energetic experience, pick up the trail on the north side of the overlook. You'll climb down through extravagant vegetation, and end up in the middle of a spectacular dune landscape. Follow the top of the ridge and run — RUN! — down the sandy slope to forest. Here, the trees are tall—American beeches and sugar maples loom overhead—and the forest floor is abundant with the glacial till that created the Great Lakes nearly 13,000 years ago. An amazing wildflower show in the spring. You'll end up on Basch Road, which will return you to the parking lot. Pets allowed.

BOBBY'S BEACH

Here's the place to go for sunsets and rock-hunting. Sometimes you'll spot otters bobbing out in the deep water. Plenty of parking and a steep set of stairs down the bluff to the beach. Find this park by following South Port Oneida Road, then left on Lane Road. No pets.

GOOD HARBOR

There are two accesses to the enormous beach in Good Harbor Bay. The first one is off County Road 669. You can park at the end, or take a right on Lake Michigan Road and pick from a variety of beach trails. There's a turn-around and picnic area at the end of the road.

A 2.8-mile trail loop on the wooded side of the road passes over a creek and through a swamp. There used to be homes back there, but you can only pick them out by the plantings that once surrounded them. Many volunteer hours have gone into restoring this trail. Pets allowed on the right side of the beach.

The other access is farther along M-22 on County Road 651. Once upon a time, there was a village here, with a saloon, a hotel, a school and, of course, a sawmill. This beach gets more traffic than the other, and there's poison ivy everywhere. You'll also have to ford Houdek Creek if you want to wander west. (The right side is private.) However, this is a better beach for kids, with shallow water and numerous sandbars. Pets allowed on the left side of the beach.

Both Good Harbor beaches are great for sunsets, and also popular for bonfires. Bonfires are permitted in the park on Lake Michigan beaches between the water's edge and the first dune. Please extinguish your fire with water and sand before you leave.

Common Woodland Wildflowers

WILD OATS

Buttery yellow flowers appear in early spring.

WILD LEEK

Leeks, or ramps, are good for eating in spring. Their white blossoms don't appear until summer.

JACK-IN-THE-PULPIT

Also an early bloomer, the taproot of this plant was a vegetable for Native Americans.

LARGE-FLOWERED TRILLIUM

The most famous UpNorth wildflower blooms in early spring. Flowers are usually white, but are sometimes streaked with green or pink.

EARLY MEADOW RUE

These greenish-white flowers bloom just as trees begin to leaf out in spring. Male plants have yellow stamens, female plants have purple stamens.

FOR MORE INFO ON IDENTIFYING PLANTS, SEE PAGES 247 AND 249.

from the fire coming out of his mouth and at first something in me wanted a fight. I imagined I could hear the

HOW TO
198
find pretty rocks

ROCK, STONES, GEMS ... THEY'RE ALL HIDING IN PLAIN SIGHT ON MICHIGAN BEACHES. BUT IT'S FAR TOO EASY TO WALK RIGHT PAST THEM.

Sarah Armstrong, of Interlochen, has found success finding Petoskey stones, Leland Blue and more with these tricks:

- Look in late winter and early spring. "Fewer people are combing for the same treasures," she says.

- Wear waterproof boots or even waders or hip boots when it's still too cold to get in the water.

- The best beaches are on the west coast, from Frankfort to Leland. The less crowded, the better.

- Look near the line where the waves end on the sand. If you're looking IN the water, there's a chance the waves might wash away the stones "and break your heart before you can get your hands on them." So, while it's not necessary to go into the water, you'll probably get splashed or carried away — hence the boots/waders.

- Take along a little spray bottle to get the dry stones wet. You often can't tell if you're holding a Petoskey stone if it's dry. Some people just lick the rocks; Armstrong's method is a little more hygienic.

- Right after a storm is prime treasure-hunting time.

State Land Rules by the Michigan Department of Natural Resources: It is illegal to remove from state-owned land more than the aggregate total weight of 25 pounds, per individual per year of any rock, mineral specimen (exclusive of any gold bearing material), or invertebrate fossil for individual or non-commercial hobby use. Check out the Michigan Rockhounding Facebook page for info and pics. Collecting rocks IS NOT ALLOWED in Sleeping Bear Dunes National Lakeshore. **JT**

THE BLUE ROCKS COMMONLY FOUND ON LELAND'S BEACHES ARE ACTUALLY SLAG. BACK IN THE LATE 1800S, LELAND WAS A DIRTY, SMOKY CENTER OF IRON ORE SMELTING. THE INDUSTRY FAILED WHEN THEY RAN OUT OF TREES TO BURN IN THE FOUNDRIES. SLAG — BLUE, GRAY, PURPLE OR GREEN — IS THE BY-PRODUCT OF SMELTING AND WAS DUMPED INTO THE LAKE WITH IMPUNITY.

PETOSKEY STONES

BOTH A ROCK AND A FOSSIL, PETOSKEY STONES ARE OLDER THAN THE DINOSAURS.

During the Cambrian period (600–500 million years ago) the Great Lakes area was a warm, salty, shallow ocean. It was during this period that sea creatures began to use minerals to make protective shells for themselves. But it took another 100 million years for coral to develop — and Petoskey stones are fossilized coral.

In the Devonian period (395–345 million years ago) the Great Lakes region began to rise again. Fish crawled out of the shrinking seas and grew lungs and legs. Unfortunately, the coral reefs were left high and dry.

Skip ahead 350 million years to the end of the Ice Age. As the glaciers retreated, they yanked up whatever was loose on the bedrock. Entire fossilized coral colonies were broken up and scattered over the northwestern, lower peninsula.

The illustration from Ernst Haeckel's *Kunstformen der Natur* shows the rogose coral that, fossilized, is a Petoskey stone. For an excellent guide to the area's fossils, see *The Complete Guide to Petoskey Stones* by Bruce Mueller. For children, *Prehistoric Great Lakes* by John Mitchell and Tom Woodruff is a fine, illustrated introduction. ENERDYNE in Suttons Bay has books and displays of area fossils.

my class ring over and punch him as hard as I could but when I looked into his face I could feel something inside

IT'S A BEAUTIFUL DRIVE BETWEEN PORT ONEIDA AND THE EASTERN END OF THE PARK. IF YOU'VE BEEN CLIMBING DUNES, STOP AT LITTLE BASS LAKE AND GIVE YOUR DOGS A DRINK. ACCESS IS RIGHT OFF M-22.

RETURN TO TC ALONG BOHEMIAN ROAD FOR BIG VISTAS

One of the prettiest roads in the county, Bohemian Road showcases working farms and long vistas. The road is named for the settlers who arrived here in the mid-1800s from what is now the Czech Republic and Slovenia. Many of them worked in the foundry in Leland or the sawmill at Gill's Pier.

200

St. Joseph's church, on the corner of M-22 and Bohemian, was built by Catholic Bohemians in 1884, and was once surrounded by the village of North Unity. There's a story that North Unity burned down the same night that Chicago went up in flames in 1871. In fact, there were a great number of devastating fires that night, from Manistee and Holland on Michigan's west coast, Peshtigo on Wisconsin's east coast, and Alpena and Port Huron on Michigan's east coast. Speculation is still alive that Comet Biela caused the conflagrations as it broke up over the Midwest. Westerly winds were strong that night, and the area hadn't seen rain for months.

Biela continued to produce spectacular meteor showers for the next couple of years, but has now faded from sight.

There's no doubt about the coincidence of the Great Fires that October night, but the meteor's part in the action doesn't quite stand up to hard scientific inquiry. It does make the most amazing story, though, doesn't it?

THE GREAT FIRES OF OCTOBER 8, 1871, BEGAN IN THE WEST AND MOVED EAST. ALL FIRES OCCURRED WITHIN THE TRIANGLE.

Peshtigo

Port Huron

Chicago

NORTH UNITY

Even before the fire, North Unity was a tough place to live, particularly the first year. While some of the settlers brought over-wintering supplies with them, everyone was hungry and the wolves were literally at the door. Several of the men walked across the ice to North Manitou island to buy potatoes. A spring migration of the now extinct passenger pigeon saved the day.

Thirty-two families of many nations and faiths eventually gathered in North Unity before dispersing to better farming areas or the big town life of TC. A Michigan historical marker outside the church reads: "Ornate metal grave markers reflect the Bohemian heritage, as do the names Bourda, Houdek, Hula, Jelinek, Kalchik, Kirt, Kolarik, Korson, Kovarik, Maresh, Novotny, Reicha and Sedlacek, which appear in the cemetery."

St. Wenceslaus, on East Kolarik Road, is another Catholic Bohemian church with original, fancy ironwork grave markers in its cemetery. (See page 173)

To return to TC on this route, keep on Bohemian until it ends, turn right on County Road 616, then a quick left on Coleman (669) will take you back to M-72.

ON TO LELAND

Once you're out of the Park, the road to Leland is curvy, as it hugs the coast, but there's not much in the way of views as the private lakeside homes are, well, very private.

GOOD HARBOR VINEYARDS is about the only stopping-off place. It's one of the first wineries established in Leelanau, in what was once an old fruit stand. Some wineries aim for glamour — this one exceeds itself in informality. Inside, there's a free, self-guided tour of the wine-making process. Smell that fruit!

204 TO LAKE LEELANAU

This is the main east-west cross-over north of M-72, and will lead you through the village of Lake Leelanau (see next page) then on to Suttons Bay and back to TC.

WHALEBACK NATURAL AREA

If you're out on the water, or standing on the beach at Good Harbor, or even among the fudgies in Fishtown, this impressive point looks like an enormous beached whale. Formed by a glacier, Whaleback is actually what geologists call a "drumlin," or a long, oval mound of glacial drift that's been molded in the same direction as the ice flow retreat.

Climb the short, steep trail through hardwoods and hemlocks for a spectacular view of Lake Michigan from 300 feet up. Lots of wildflowers in the spring. No views on the loop, but bald eagles, scarlet tanagers, black-throated blue warblers and the American redstart live in these woods. Stay on the trails to avoid poison ivy. Leashed pets allowed.

Whaleback is part of the Leelanau Conservancy and is located at 1639 North Manitou Trail, just off M-22, once you've passed 204. For more on the Leelanau Conservancy, see page 60 and 206.

---

around a bunch of hard-core steelheaders. They were guys who had fillet knives in sheaths on their belts, guys

IT'S LITTLE BIT, CONFUSING, BUT LAKE LEELANAU IS BOTH A LAKE AND A VILLAGE.

THE VILLAGE BEGAN AS A SETTLEMENT FOR FRENCH IMMIGRANTS ARRIVING FROM CANADA. IT WAS ORIGINALLY CALLED "LE NARO," MEANING SOMETHING, THEN PROVEMONT IN 1871, AN IMPROVEMENT, AND FINALLY, AND UNCLEARLY, LAKE LEELANAU IN 1924.

Before the the dam was built on the Leland River in Fishtown in 1854, Lake Leelanau was extremely shallow. Even so, if you wanted to get from one side to the other, you had to wade. There's a story of a tall Saint Christopher-like character who would carry travelers in his arms across the Narrows in the summer. The dam caused lake levels to rise 12 feet, and the giant was replaced by an unofficial fleet of small boats called the Mosquito Brigade. The bridge was built in 1910.

Lake Leelanau, the lake, is 21 miles long and only 1.5 miles across at its max. The lake is navigable from Leland to Cedar. The southern half is much shallower than the northern half, and anglers appreciate its prime walleye and smallmouth fishing. The deeper northern half is better for trout.

Eat

Mario Batali says forget Tuscany and go to TC, but **BELLA FORTUNA** brings Tuscany home. Open from mid-May through October, this fine restaurant has an equally fine wine list and is right in the middle of the village.

Since 1935, **DICK'S POUR HOUSE** has provided libation to farmers and resorters. Family-style dining with parking for both cars and boats.

RED TOP PASTERIA is brand new, specializing in Detroit-style pizza and Finnish pastries. Vegetarian pasties are also available.

who would just as soon eat a piece of raw fish right off their hooks or chew broken glass to let you know that

Visit **LEELANAU PIE AND PASTRY** for croissants, danishes, cookies and pie. Their cherry pie gets high marks.

9 BEAN ROWS is consistently one of the best bakeries in the area, making and serving traditional European pastries. Their bakery is on East Duck Lake Road and the restaurant is in Suttons Bay. You can see their farm from the road. Area schools, from Northport to TC, use their chemical-free produce in their lunchrooms.

PEDALING BEANS COFFEE will happily serve up some additional mojo to help you climb those Leelanau hills.

Drink

BOATHOUSE VINEYARD on the Narrows is a nice spot to sit outside and sip. Drive up in your boat, bring a picnic. Dogs are welcome.

NORTHERN LATITUDES DISTILLERY makes vodka from Michigan grains. They also distill liquors, rum and moonshine, whatever that may be. Try the Apollo Horseradish Vodka and banish those sinus problems.

Shop

BAD PONY makes unique handcrafted accessories for humans, horses and hounds.

BAABAAZUZU crafts hand-made wearables for men and women from vintage materials. Actress Sean Young, who graduated from Interlochen Arts Academy, wore Baabaazuz items when she competed on "Skating with the Stars."

Fountain Point

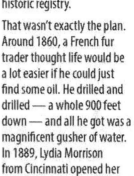

FOUNTAIN POINT is one of the oldest resorts in the state and on the State of Michigan historic registry.

That wasn't exactly the plan. Around 1860, a French fur trader thought life would be a lot easier if he could just find some oil. He drilled and drilled — a whole 900 feet down — and all he got was a magnificent gusher of water. In 1889, Lydia Morrison from Cincinnati opened her Victorian-style Fountain Point House for resorters.

The artesian well is still operating, and the resort is popular with families and wedding parties.

Summer concerts on Thursdays and Sundays. Check out the schedule at fountainpointmusic.com.

THE LAKE LEELANAU ROWING CLUB uses Fountain Point as its base, and offers clinics and camps for all ages.

Winter training is available as well, but you must have a U.S. Rowing membership to participate.

you were in their part of the world. On my way to the car I could still hear them laughing, kicking the remains of

LELAND

LELAND SITS ALMOST SMACK-DAB ON THE 45TH PARALLEL NORTH – OR HALFWAY BETWEEN THE EQUATOR AND THE NORTH POLE.

WE GET A LOT OF SUN HERE IN THE SUMMER – A WHOLE 15 HOURS AND 37 MINUTES DURING SOLSTICE. IT ALSO GETS REALLY DARK IN THE WINTER, WHEN, AT THE WORST, THERE ARE A LITTLE LESS THAN NINE HOURS OF LIGHT.

LELAND WINE & FOOD FESTIVAL
JUNE 10, NOON
NON-STOP LIVE MUSIC

the board toward the fire, "to keep it away from their lines," they hollered after me. ¶ I sat in the car and

THERE'S A WORLD OF DIFFERENCE BETWEEN GLEN ARBOR AND LELAND.

Although both of them experienced logging, Leland got even dirtier with the addition of an iron smelter and charcoal kilns, besides the normal, sooty sawmill.

Leland cleaned up its act fast, though, when wealthy families from Chicago, Cincinnati and Indianapolis began to appear around 1900, building "summer cottages" and ultimately transforming the community into the picture-perfect tourist destination it is now.

Because of that early resorter settlement, the village of Leland is much more organized — and conservative — than Glen Arbor. Many of those families still maintain summer homes, and they're deeply hidden. Leland's tourist industry is focused narrowly around the few blocks of Main Street (M-22) and Fishtown. It's a zoo in the summer, but a contained zoo. Once you're off the beaten track, Leland is the peaceful, picturesque destination that attracted tourists in the first place.

THE OLD ART BUILDING

It isn't hard to escape the madness of Leland's Fishtown. Walk south across the bridge to the Old Art Building. There's always something going on, so take a peek inside. Outside, pretty gardens surround the building and little paths lead to the river.

LEELANAU HISTORICAL SOCIETY MUSEUM

From the Old Art Building, continue down Cedar Street to the Leelanau Historical Society and Museum. Across the river, you can see the RIVERSIDE INN, now 116 years old and still serving elegant dinners during the summer. Check out their home-made charcuterie and artisanal cheeses.

VILLAGE GREEN

For another pleasant walk (about 45 minutes — don't drive), go north on Main and turn left on Pearl Street, next to the gardens of the Village Green. Pretty cottages are all around here, as well as the stately Leland Lodge. Pearl Street ends at Bartholomew Park for views of Lake Leelanau (not good for swimming). Continue walking Juniper Trail, then cross back on any of the little streets, and you'll end up back in the village.

Fishtown Fudgies

ASK THE DARNDEST QUESTIONS:

Where is the whale-viewing platform?

Ummm... No whales in Michigan. No sharks, either. Both of those guys live in salt water, and we don't have any of that here.

We do have the snakehead bass, though. It can grow up to 3 feet long and walk — yep, walk — from one body of water to another. It can even breath out of water for up to seven days.

The sea lamprey also lives in Lake Michigan. Unfortunately. They got into the Great Lakes in the 1950s and decimated the trout population. The sea lamprey looks like an eel, and has a round hole for a mouth, completely ringed with sharp teeth. The lamprey is a parasite, meaning that it attaches itself to the side of a fish and sucks the life out of it. Sea lampreys can grow up to four feet long and live in both fresh and salt water.

watched the wind die down, the lake going flat as a mirror. I watched all six of them head into the lake together,

Beaches, Cliffs, Dunes

LELAND HAS AMAZING AMOUNTS OF PUBLIC
BEACH ACCESS, AND BEAUTIFUL BEACHES THEY
ARE – LONG AND WHITE AND, THE FARTHER
NORTH YOU WALK, THE BIGGER THE CLIFFS.

IN-TOWN BEACHES

Walk right out onto the beach from Fishtown. It's that easy. There's also access at Van's Beach, just beyond Van's Garage, and a bit farther south, Christmas Tree Cove. North Beach is also public, but parking there is the size of a handkerchief.

CLAY CLIFFS NATURAL AREA

Those big bluffs along Lake Michigan are made of sand, gravel and clay —— very different from the National Park's dunes. There's no way up or down —— unless you own a home there and have built a staircase —— but the Leelanau Conservancy has made the area a park now, so you can walk the bluff and take in the big sky views of the islands. There's more up there than big views, though. Old homesteads, huge trees and wide-open meadows make the short, 1.5-mile hike one of the more diverse. Lots of wildflowers in the spring. Leashed pets are allowed.

then each once took his turn casting toward the horizon, my board smoldering in the ashes of their fire. I kept

HOUDEK DUNES NATURAL AREA

A bit farther along the Clay Cliffs, you'll find this delightful park. A completely different landscape from the Clay Cliffs area, Houdek is all white birches, sand dunes and wetlands. Two loops of .75 and 1.5 miles. Leashed pets allowed. Houdek Dunes is also managed by the Leelanau Conservancy. No beach access.

ABOUT THE LEELANAU CONSERVANCY

Since its formation in 1988, the Leelanau Conservancy has preserved more than 11,500 acres of farms, wetlands and view properties in each of the county's 11 townships.

Working with over 200 area families, The Conservancy has created 25 natural areas and 15 miles of hiking trails for public enjoyment. Guided tours are also available. Check the schedule at LeelanauConservancy.org.

The Leelanau Conservancy has about 2,800 members, and relies heavily on volunteers to maintain protected areas and trails.

If you've enjoyed one, or many, of their natural areas, consider a donation.

MICHIGAN LAW AND WALKING THE BEACHES

Over 70 percent of Michigan's third coast is privately owned, and the public has always had the right to walk any Great Lakes shoreline as long as they had their feet in the water. That changed in 1998, when Joan Glass filed a lawsuit against her neighbors for harassing her as she walked in front of their Lake Huron property. The suit went all the way to Michigan's Supreme Court, and came out the other side (highly contested) with citizens getting the right to walk any beach as long as they stay below the "natural, ordinary high-water mark."

So, where is the high-water mark? Water levels go up and down — sometimes fast and drastically — and invasive grasses can disguise and confuse even further. According to attorney Jim Olson, president of Traverse City-based FLOW (For Love of Water), the best practice is to play it safe and stay as close to the water's edge as possible. Of course, if your feet are wet, then there's no problem at all.

Fishtown Fudgies

ASK THE DARNDEST QUESTIONS:

You're so isolated: Do you have to homeschool your kids up here?

Nope. Not if you don't want to.

Both Traverse City Area Public High Schools (CENTRAL and WEST), LELAND PUBLIC SCHOOL, and high schools in BENZIE, CADILLAC and ELK RAPIDS all rate in the top 100 Michigan schools according to *U.S. News and World Report*.

Excellent private schools include PATHFINDER SCHOOL in TC, an independent day school since 1972 and THE LEELANAU SCHOOL in Glen Arbor serving students with attention-deficit-related learning differences and is ranked among the top 20 American non-profit, college prep boarding schools.

In Benzie county, there's INTERLOCHEN CENTER FOR THE ARTS, the highest profile pre-professional arts boarding school in the world.

EAT

Visit the VILLAGE CHEESE SHANTY and CARLSON'S FISHERY in Fishtown.

Tourists love THE COVE, above the dam. Open only in the summer.

Locals love THE BLUEBIRD, and it's open all year around.

BOGEY'S 19TH HOLE is part of Leland Lodge and also open year-round.

Fine dining at RIVERSIDE INN.

Oh, the shopping in Leland

ALL THE SHOPPING IS CONCENTRATED AROUND FISHTOWN AND THOSE FEW BLOCKS OF MAIN STREET (M-22).

MAIN STREET GALLERY, two blocks south of the bridge, has original paintings, woodcarvings and the delightful metal sculptures of Bill Allen.

LEIF SPÖRCK'S beautiful tile art is on display and for sale in Fishtown.

BENJAMIN MAIER also displays his handsome ceramics for the home on Main Street.

Painter BRENDA J. CLARK and photographer MEGGEN WATT have studios in Leland.

TWO FISH GALLERY has ceramics, jewelry, watercolors by Michigan artists and photographs by Ken Scott.

HAYSTACKS makes uniquely designed bias-cut skirts, cut and sewn in their Suttons Bay studios.

GOOD OLD BOOKS stocks rare and used books, specializing in Michigan and the Great Lakes. LEELANAU BOOKS has bestsellers and children's books.

Go to THE DUNE BERRY for Lilly Pulitzer resort wear. And MOLLY'S for Eileen Fisher.

TSONGA USA invests in rural South African communities for the production of handmade leather shoes, bags and accessories.

Hundreds of hats at DIVERSIONS.

For jewelry, TAMPICO and BECKY THATCHER DESIGNS have you covered like a queen.

SISSON'S MAIN STREET SPECIALTIES makes the best cookies ever.

for a couple of hours, running may hands back and forth over the defroster vents, dead silent, no lip synching,

Leland Heritage Festival

SEPTEMBER XX

OGLE THE CARS AND BOATS, PLUS LOTS OF END-OF-SEASON SPECIALS AT THE STORES AND RESTAURANTS.

LELAND CLASSIC CAR SHOW

This annual "invitation only" exhibition continues to grow since its inception, and now numbers about a hundred vehicles from many eras. Sponsored by Van's Garage.

13TH ANNUAL WOOD BOATS ON THE WALL

One hundred years of area vintage wood boats, including Chris Craft, Century, Lyman and Garwood. Sponsored by Leelanau Historical Museum.

OTHER AREA ROAD AND WATER SHOWS:

MAY 26 || **NORTHERN MICHIGAN HEARSE CRUISE** || GAYLORD

MAY 27 || **CARS IN THE PARK** || NORTHPORT

JULY 2 || **OLD TOWN CLASSIC CAR SHOW** || TC

AUGUST 13 || **ALDEN CLASSIC SPORTS CAR SHOW** || ALDEN

AUGUST 3 || **CRUISIN' FRANKFORT** || FRANKFORT

AUGUST 26 || **OLD 27 MOTOR TOUR** || GAYLORD

ASK THE DARNDEST QUESTIONS:

Are those real fishermen or actors?

The largest, oldest community in Leelanau County of Ottawa Indians settled around Fishtown. They worked cooperatively: the men made nets — from fibers gathered by women — and they did the actual fishing while the women smoked or dried the catch on triangular racks.

Fishtown is still a thriving fishery and center for the charter industry, and if you see someone who looks like a fisherman, chances are pretty good that he's the real deal.

Those two tugs parked out on the river, however, are just there for show, and are owned by the Fishtown Preservation Society. In 2004, the Carlson family sold the tugs and Fishtown property to the Preservation Society for $3 million dollars.

no shouting out the window, "Well I'm not braggin' babe, so don't put me down, but I got the fastest set of

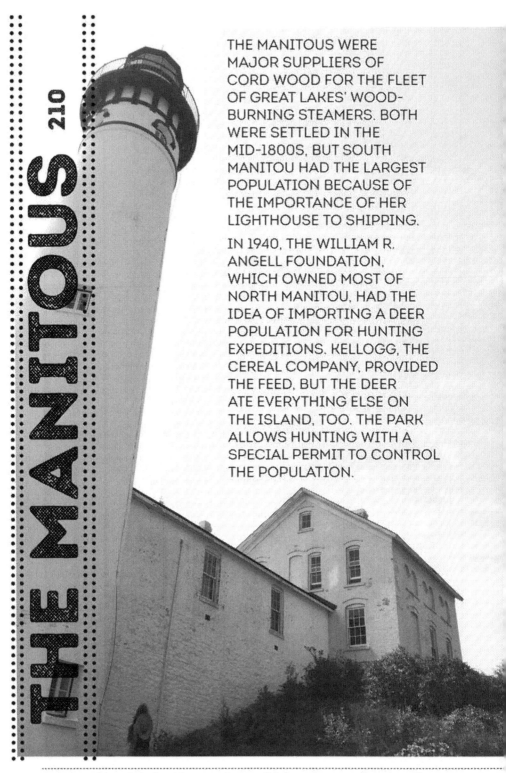

THE MANITOUS WERE MAJOR SUPPLIERS OF CORD WOOD FOR THE FLEET OF GREAT LAKES' WOOD-BURNING STEAMERS. BOTH WERE SETTLED IN THE MID-1800S, BUT SOUTH MANITOU HAD THE LARGEST POPULATION BECAUSE OF THE IMPORTANCE OF HER LIGHTHOUSE TO SHIPPING.

IN 1940, THE WILLIAM R. ANGELL FOUNDATION, WHICH OWNED MOST OF NORTH MANITOU, HAD THE IDEA OF IMPORTING A DEER POPULATION FOR HUNTING EXPEDITIONS. KELLOGG, THE CEREAL COMPANY, PROVIDED THE FEED, BUT THE DEER ATE EVERYTHING ELSE ON THE ISLAND, TOO. THE PARK ALLOWS HUNTING WITH A SPECIAL PERMIT TO CONTROL THE POPULATION.

wheels in town." Instead, I hunkered down, stayed quiet and all the way home it was "I Get Around" humming,

NORTH MANITOU ISLAND and South Manitou Island are about as different as siblings can get! Take the ferry from Leland, and bring all the gear you'll need for the day——if you're hiking——or the night——if you're camping. North Manitou Island has over 22 miles of trails, over wetlands and beaches, past historic homesteads and through old apple and cherry orchards. With the island's introduced deer population, you'll want to check yourself for ticks at the end of the day. Infected ticks can cause Lyme disease.

Camping on North Manitou is open, so you choose your own spot — although it has to be at least 300 feet from the water's edge. You can also stay in the Village Campground, and that's the only place you're allowed to make a fire. Potable water available only in the village. No dogs.

SOUTH MANITOU ISLAND has only ten miles of trails, but since it's not home to any large grazing mammals, its ecosystem is markedly different from that of its big brother. Here, there are three campgrounds, two ancient cemeteries and an old lighthouse——now defunct. The lighthouse was quite useful back in the day, however, as any avid Great Lakes diver could tell you. There are more than 50 shipwrecks surrounding the Manitou Islands. If you've packed a snorkel, you can paddle around the *Morazan* wreck.

There are three first-come, first-serve campgrounds on South Manitou. Water and restrooms — or outhouses — are available at all the campgrounds except Popple. No fires at Popple, either. No dogs anywhere.
ZV

The Crib

The North Manitou Shoal Light was built in 1935 in the most dangerous shallow waters of the Manitou Passage. For over 40 years, the Crib was manned by three Coast Guardsmen who rotated duties — two weeks on, one week off. In the 1970s, the Crib was the last manned offshore lighthouse on the Great Lakes. But by 1980, technology had made the Crib redundant and it was shut down.

The Crib was sold in 2016 to a group of people calling themselves the North Manitou Lighthouse Keepers for $73,000 at a government auction.

GET TO THE ISLANDS

North Manitou Transit has been in operation since 1917, and a jolly one it is. Enjoy a Bloody Mary on the way to where you're going and back! The company also offers sunset, shoreline cruises, and dogs are allowed.

Open from mid-May through the first weekend in October. Kayak transport costs $35, canoes and tandem kayaks are $70.

low and steady, my hand on the five-speed hoping for a dry patch of highway, just one place to stop dead and

Remembering Archie Miller

THE MANITOU ISLANDS–SPLITTING THE WATERS IN THE MANITOU PASSAGE–EMBODY PRISTINE ISOLATION, AND ARE A PLACE TO BE IN SOLITARY NATURE.

Today, few residents, and even fewer visitors to the area, would ever suspect that at one time the Manitous boasted a booming population. Aside from post offices, hotels, wharves, docks, fishing and agricultural enterprises, there was a railroad on North Manitou!

At a time when snowshoe priests were thrashing through the frozen cedar swamps of the Upper Peninsula, the interior of both Michigan peninsulas was a wilderness. The long stretches of open water in the Great Lakes made the earliest exploration most feasible by boat, and the Manitous were ideally located between Chicago and Roger City — perfect for restocking vessels with firewood, fresh water, fish and venison. In time, thriving communities grew up around the docks and lumber camps; churches, schools, hotels and the lighthouses were built and food production was set up, with grain, fruit and fish exported to the mainland. The agricultural research department of Michigan State University used South Manitou for the isolated production of pure Rosen Rye seed. The seed was sent to farmers all over the Plains states, and was, in-part, responsible for the Dust Bowl.

By the 1950s, the population had declined sharply. Nonetheless, the Manitous' placement in the straits made the lighthouses vital to safe shipping. At this time, both North and South Manitou were almost exclusively privately-owned. South Manitou had more people: a few homesteaders and a small store for tourists. The lighthouse, as well as many other structures and docks, had to be maintained and looked after. Lumbering was still a source of income for those with ships to move timber. On North Manitou, deer hunters from Detroit, Chicago, and beyond were guided to the plentiful game during hunting season. In the wake of the human exodus, however, the deer population exploded to unsustainable numbers. With no predators and limited food, hard winters often found them starving to death. In the early 1960s, North Manitou looked like a manicured park — every scrap of foliage up to the height the deer could reach, stretching on their hind legs, was gone. They were even starting to manifest signs of island dwarfism.

Archie Miller, a cantankerous Mack truck of a man who would walk calmly past the "No Indians" sign in the Hotel Northern, spent decades of his life in the Manitou Straits. He was a caretaker of the lighthouse, a lumberjack and one of the most sought-after hunting and fishing guides. Miller lumbered with his brother Ivan in the early years, hauling big timber to the beach for shipping. Hunting and fishing was good, especially the bass fishing on Lake Florence on the south island. He talked of harsh winters, of stuffing game with a dressing made of oatmeal and onions. He said raccoon was okay, but porcupine was good eating if you could drain off the grease.

Archie was a great reader, a legacy of early Catholic schooling and his study with the Trappist brothers. His great indulgence when on South Manitou was to go into the glassed-in lighthouse tower in the afternoon when it was warm with sun, taking an apple and a book.

212

Archie's youngest son, Anthony Miller, remembers the winter of 1959 when he and his dad were the only people on North Manitou. Anthony was four years old. Archie had been contracted to stay on the island during that harsh winter to feed the deer and to clear snow away. A barn was filled with hay, and Anthony sat on the toboggan while Archie pulled it through the woods, dropping off feed here and there. Anthony remembers that the house was comfortable and he was happy to be with his dad.

In later years, the whole Miller family spent time in the Straits, living in a house behind the dock on South Manitou. There were long curving beaches and tiny coves to be explored, Seagull Point with its thousands of nesting gulls, dunes to climb, and fishing and playing in the often empty lighthouse.

Photo by Minnie Wabanimkee

Archie was also on South Manitou the fall of 1960, scouting out the wreck of the *Francisco Morazan* as soon as the weather permitted (see next page). Although already stripped of its brass navigational instruments and fittings, there was plenty of other scavanging to be done. The Alberto V05 hair-gel packets washing up all over the beaches were interesting, but the tinned chicken was a godsend. The early 1960s were tough times in Peshawbestown, and the chicken was a welcome addition to the diet of many village children. That summer, South Manitou became a kind of summer camp for Peshawbestown children. Every two weeks, a new group would arrive to the island for the feast.

Archie passed his love of the islands down to his children and grandchildren. He maintained lifelong relationships with many people from Leland and the islands: Bill Carlson, who met when Bill was a boy; the Grosvenors; the Reikers; and the Jelineks. Today the islands are a special legacy to us all. A refuge to man and millipede, the island's beauty awes visitors and offers solitude. But it's also intriguing to look past the regrown forests and empty beaches to try to imagine scores of masts, the horses hauling lumber from the interior, the schools ringing with voices and so many stories of lives lived on these islands, our Manitous — a true treasure of Leelanau County. **GS**

COMING UP NEXT .... *THE NIGHTSWIMMERS by TODD MERCER*

LOST AT SEA

BEFORE THE ADVENT OF THE AUTOMOBILE AND THE AIRPLANE, TRAVERSE CITY AND LEELANAU WERE THRIVING MARITIME CENTERS.

THE BAYS ARE NO LONGER FILLED WITH THE SAILS OF SCHOONERS AND THE BILLOWING PUFFS OF COAL SMOKE FROM THE BIG STEAMERS. BUT BENEATH THE CLEAR UPNORTH WATERS, IF YOU SHIMMY INTO A WETSUIT AND STRAP ON A SNORKLE OR TANKS, YOU CAN FIND THE RUINS OF MANY WRECKS. BOTH THE MANITOU PASSAGE UNDERWATER RESERVE AND THE GRAND TRAVERSE UNDERWATER PRESERVE BECKON MORE AND MORE DIVERS TO EXPLORE THE DEPTHS BENEATH THE WAVES.

The Manitou Passage, the 282-mile area between the Manitou Islands and Leelanau County, has been a shipping shortcut for the past two hundred years. However, due to the shifting sands and shoals, the passage can be a dangerous timesaver. Within the passage, at least 130 ships floundered in the waves. Most of the submerged wrecks were quickly covered with sand, and still wait to be uncovered.

The most visible and famous of the wrecks is the hulk of the 246-foot long, iron FRANCISCO MORAZAN, which sank just off the southeastern shore of South Manitou. While some of the *Morazan* rises above the waves, the bulk of the hulk lies in 15 feet of water. Ironically, the *Morazan* rests atop the wooden WALTER L FROST.

Two other easily accessible wrecks are the 194-foot ALVA BRADLEY, which can be found in the waters between South and North Manitou, and the most recently discovered THREE BROTHERS, which went down in a storm off Sleeping Bear Point.

In addition to the carcasses of cargo carriers, you can easily access the pilings and remains of the piers that once welcomed big ships. In both Good Harbor Bay and Sleeping Bear Bay there are pilings that still resist the waves.

In the more sheltered waters of Grand Traverse Bay, 4 miles off the tip of Old Mission Peninsula, one can visit the A J ROGERS. And just a few leagues away, in East Bay, the 125-foot METROPOLIS went down. In West Bay, off the shore of Power Island, a 54-foot tug rests on the lake bottom.

All of the wrecks and remains in both the Manitou Passage State Underwater Reserve and the Grand Traverse Bay Underwater Preserve are protected by state and federal statutes. You can dive and explore, but you may not take any artifact from the cold and silent resting places of the ships that once plied the deceptively beguiling waters of UpNorth. **DM**

DIVE THE GREAT LAKES

Scuba North began in a gas station at Old Mission's Bowers Harbor in 1971. They now have two locations in TC, and offers full-service instruction, sales, service, charters and group travel. Scuba North also has snorkeling equipment, full scuba diving gear, underwater cameras and lights.

change-over went long. Laid off, the Nightswimmer landed atop the tall chair at the East Bay beach, armed with a

GILL'S PIER RANCH || M-22

This agrotourism farm raises Tibetan yaks and Suri alpacas for meat and fiber. Farm tours and dinner are available, as well as sporting clay shooting.

GILL'S PIER BEACH || GILL'S PIER ROAD

Only some old pylons are left to prove that Gill's Pier is another ghost town from the lumber era. There's public access to an okay beach near the end of Gill's Pier Road. It's rather weedy, and hemmed in by private housing on both sides, but not a bad spot for a picnic. Gill's Pier got its mojo back during the terrible winter of 2014 when gigantic ice caves formed along the shore. News of the caves spread by social media and hundreds of people showed up to slip and slide.

FISCHER'S HAPPY HOUR || M-22

A favorite local spot since 1971. Feels like an old-time country club, except everyone gets in. Burgers, clams, fried chicken dinners. Full bar.

GREEN BIRD ORGANIC CELLARS AND FARMS || E. ENGLES ROAD

A communal farm run by friends and family, this is Michigan's only organic vineyard, orchard and winery. They also make beer, cider and rum. Very kid friendly and an interesting group of people in a pretty spot.

HOW TO
live in a lighthouse

YOU CAN BE A LIGHTHOUSE KEEPER. YOU WILL, HOWEVER, HAVE TO PAY ... AND YOU HAVE TO WORK.

Both the Grand Traverse Lighthouse north of Northport and the Mission Point Lighthouse at the tip of the Old Mission Peninsula host guest keepers. At the Grand Traverse Lighthouse, keepers stay in the former assistant keeper's quarters on the north side of the lighthouse. The quarters have a fully equipped modern kitchen, two bedrooms (both with twin beds), a living room and one and a half baths. The Mission Point Lighthouse has a similar setup, and includes wi-fi and cable TV.

A log entry from the Mission Point Lighthouse said the keepers had 2,381 visitors over the course of a July week but had time to visit seven wineries, three breweries and four restaurants. They saw the sunset every night and the space station two of the evenings. They kayaked and paddle-boarded and still enjoyed each other's company at the end of seven days.

Keepers at both lighthouses bring their own food, sheets, pillows and blankets. The Mission Point Lighthouse can accommodate two people; the Grand Traverse Lighthouse fits up to four.

During your stay, you'd be responsible for cleaning the lighthouse, greeting guests, working in the gift shop, keeping up the grounds at the Grand Traverse Lighthouse and helping out in the museum admissions. At the Mission Point Lighthouse, you need to be able to climb 37 stairs to the light in the tower to wash the windows, sweep and vacuum. Chores change throughout the season; keepers in the spring and fall may be asked to paint and repair more than keepers at the height of the season.

The Grand Traverse Lighthouse hosts keepers from April to December for either one or two weeks. A stay costs $150 per person per week and keepers get either Tuesday or Wednesday off each week. The Mission Point Lighthouse gives a price break if you stay for two weeks (and meet the qualifications) — $200 for one week or $370 for two consecutive weeks. You get one day off each week. Wintertime stays at Mission Point, from November to April, are weekends only; the gift shop is open in November, then closed the rest of the time.

Training on everything you'll need to know at either lighthouse is provided when you arrive. Children are not allowed to stay as lighthouse keepers and friends and family are not allowed to sleep over. Animals are not allowed and smoking and alcohol are prohibited. Keepers are expected to be neat and properly groomed while on duty and are free to leave when the lighthouse closes for the day, although they are expected to sleep onsite. **JT**

WHEN FISHTOWN AND GLEN ARBOR EXPLODE WITH TOURISTS, HEAD UP TO NORTHPORT FOR LUNCH, A WALK AND SOME ECLECTIC SHOPPING.

Before Northport, there was Waukazooville. Joseph Waukazoo was born in the North Dakota, Red River territory, and was chief of a tribe of fur traders around Lake Winnipeg. In 1837, when the federal government was anxious to encourage the idea of private property, Waukazoo received an annuity to purchase land for farming near Holland, MI. It didn't work out very well. The tribe's nomadic lifestyle didn't settle with the drudgery of farming. As they told an official Indian agent, they would rather "take their rifles and get it [food]; and when they returned to their wigwams, lie down and rest, instead of waiting upon and feeding their dumb brutes." In 1849, as more and more Dutch were moving to the area, they sold their land and moved again. "They said they were going to Grand Traverse Bay, which the Dutchmen couldn't find," reported the wife of Rev. George Smith, who went with them.

The Waukazooville street names are still there — Shabwasung, Nagonaba, Waukazoo and Smith — but the village was annexed to white Northport in 1852, which is why the streets don't quite line up.

For a time, Northport was the largest village in the area — even bigger than TC — but its poor soil, isolation and lack of year-round industry resulted in decades of hard times. Recently, those two latter reasons for Northport's decline have worked in its favor, as some of the nation's very rich and famous have chosen to build summer homes in the area.

Northport is built around its newly renovated marina, so a lot of visitors arrive without a car. People (and dog) watching is good fun at **THE GARAGE BAR AND GRILL** on Waukazoo. Sure enough, the walls roll up and most of the seating is outdoors. Plus, nothing says "vacation" like an open-air bar.

Good food can also be had at **THE TRIBUNE** and **NORTH END EATERY**. There's often live music at **SPICE WORLD CAFE**, featuring menu items from India and Pakistan.

After lunch, check out the many galleries and curiosity shops. **DOG EARS BOOKS** is the largest new, used and rare bookstore in the area. Next door, artist **DAVID GRATH** displays his rich, dreamy landscapes. The Dennos Museum in TC is hosting a one-man show of Grath's work the summer of 2017.

Rounding the corner to Nagonaba, and then left on Mill Street, there's ice cream, a wedding venue, a bakery and lots of very pretty gardens. If you're in the market for ceramic cats, a crucifix or a some extra crystals for your chandelier, try **POT OF GOLD**, aka Dead People's Stuff, also on Mill Street.

PETERSON PARK

Take Mill Street north to Peterson Park Road for 1,000 feet of beach, big views, a beautiful green area, studded with ancient, windblown trees, picnic areas, grills and a playground. The beach is rocky, but the rocks are interesting.

Those totally gorgeous barns on Peterson Park Road belong to **IDYLL FARMS**, maker of award-winning goat cheese. (See page 237.) The operation is owned by "Wall Street's most bearish" hedge funder, Mark Spitznagel. (He's worth Googling.)

Just past Peterson Park Road on Mill Street, you'll find **CHRISTMAS COVE FARM** on Kilcherman Road. The Kilchermans have been farming for four generations, and specialize in antique apple varieties. They also claim the largest pop bottle collection in the world.

WOOLSEY AIRPORT

Heading north on Mill Street, the first item of note is a small fieldstone castle next to two grass runways. The airport is named for native son Clinton F. Woolsey, one of the pioneers of long-distance flight. Tragically, he died during the Pan-American Goodwill Flight of 1926 – 1927, when he collided in mid-air with another plane over Buenos Aires. Every year, Woolsey hosts a fly-in, car show and pancake breakfast. Join them this year on August XX at XX pm.

NORTHPORT POINT

East of the airport is an exclusive — very exclusive — 100-year-old resort community. Residents enjoy a yacht club, a 9-hole golf course, a clubhouse, restaurant, and there's a chapel on the property for family weddings. U.S. presidents have been known to vacation there.

CATHEAD BAY

Continuing north, there are great walks to be had at Cathead Bay. Part of Leelanau State Park, the trails wind and roll through mature forest down to the dune-covered Lake Michigan shore. Lots of migrating birds come through here. No biking on the trails, and dogs are not allowed on the beach.

GRAND TRAVERSE LIGHTHOUSE

At the end of the road, there's a lighthouse —which is also a museum — a gift shop and a campground. The beach is rocky and the wind never stops. Lots of ships went down in the Manitou Passage and there are some good photos of the wrecks on the way to the lantern room. The exhibition for 2017 focuses on Lake Michigan Aircraft Carriers. Plenty of books in the gift shop, too. If you're a diver, Scuba North in Traverse City can help you explore. For camping info, see page 109.

OTHER STUFF IN NORTHPORT

- A farmers market every Friday morning in August. Music in the park every Friday night through Labor Day.

- **CARS IN THE PARK ||** May 27

- **WINE FESTIVAL ||** August 13

- **LOBSTER FEST** at the lighthouse on August 16

- The Northport Community Arts Center usually has a theatrical production running during August and again in December.

- **LEELANAU UNCAGED**, free fun on the last Saturday of September.

Gull Island

WHAT'S ON THAT CREEPY ISLAND OUT IN NORTHPORT BAY? THE ONE WITH THE CHIMNEYS STICKING UP?

Fifty years ago, when some of the walls were still standing, local kids swear they could see curtains waving in the breeze like a ghostly surrender to the birds, THE BIRDS!

Byron Woolsey, father to the pilot of Woolsey Airport fame (page 219) built the cottage around 1911 for Harvard Professor Lee Ustick. The Ustick family used the island as a summer retreat until the end of the Depression, often bringing Harvard fellows along with them from Cambridge. There was never any beach, though, and nests were everywhere, protected ferociously by swooping gulls.

That's the problem with Gull Island — the gulls were there first. And the cormorants, and, once upon a time, the terns. Dr. William Scharf, professor of biology and Gull Island researcher, says the birds have used the island as a nesting spot since the end of the ice age. Scharf has spent decades studying the birds on the island: his research was instrumental in the banning of the pesticide DDT. Gulls are a top-of-the-food network predator, and their study exposes the health of everything below, like the fish gulls eat, the water they drink, and whatever else — like garbage — they're picking up.

The gulls of Gull Island, however, are herring gulls — not the ring-billed gulls you see hanging out at the dumpsters in TC. Herring gulls are larger, and prefer to live in dense vegetation, and when protected from human interference they eat dead and dying fish, keeping our UpNorth beaches clean.

The Leeanau Conservancy began action to purchase Gull Island in 1994, adding the island to its sanctuary lands the following year.

Gull Island has had many names over the years. Officially, it is now called Bellow Island. According to the Leelanau Conservancy, there are about 2,000 active gull nests on the island and 100 cormorant nests.

Nightswimmer's love of life renewed itself when the girl gasped, spit out foam, called for her mother. It gave

CORMORANTS, LIKE THE RAVENS, BALD EAGLES AND THE PILEATED WOODPECKER, WERE EXTREMELY UNCOMMON IN THE UPNORTH 50 YEARS AGO. PESTICIDE USE, WATER QUALITY AND HUMAN DISTURBANCE NEARLY ERASED THEM FROM THE ENTIRE GREAT LAKES REGION. THAT'S ALL CHANGED. SINCE 1977, CORMORANT NESTS HAVE INCREASED EXPLOSIVELY, FROM A HANDFUL TO OVER 30,000.

Cormorants are fish-eaters. Alewives, perch, smelt and suckers are a big part of their Great Lakes diet, although they'll also eat insects, reptiles, crustaceans and amphibians.

It's the fish eating that gets them into trouble, though. Cormorants are incredibly attracted to an easy meal and will flock quickly around a school of fish, leap-frogging over each other to make the kill. Quite often, the school is part of fish-stocking program. Sport-fish populations of smallmouth bass and yellow perch can also be dramatically affected by cormorant populations. Both of these concerns have led to culling programs to control the population.

The awkward, somewhat prehistoric cormorant you see in the UpNorth is the double-crested species, and they live all over North America, from Alaska to Florida. Cormorants swim low in the water, then dive to fish. What's truly distinctive is the way they perch and extend their wings. Cormorant feathers don't have the oils that duck feathers do — a heavy bird is a better diver — so they're not very water-proof and need to air-dry.

Double-crested cormorants make large, bulky nests of sticks and whatever else catches their fancy, like rope, plastic bags, fishnet and dead birds. Rocks are also commonly found in cormorant nests, which the birds treat as eggs.

him fuel, same as swimming out too far to be assured of a return. ¶ He leads the series versus the Great Lakes,

WRITERS UPNORTH

EVERY UPNORTH WRITER KNOWS THAT THE YOUNG ERNEST HEMINGWAY SPENT HIS SUMMERS AROUND PETOSKEY AND BASED HIS NICK ADAMS STORIES ON THOSE EXPERIENCES. MAYBE THAT'S WHY SO MANY WRITERS MOVE HERE, HOPING A LITTLE OF THE OLD MAN'S FAME WILL RUB OFF. OR, MAYBE THEY JUST LIKE THE FISHING.

JIM HARRISON is our greatest treasure. Start at the beginning, with *Wolf: A False Memoir*. Jim wrote this first book after he fell off a cliff while bird hunting. Both Jim and his wife Linda passed away in 2016.

Our most recent literary sensation is TC's own DOUG STANTON. Doug is a magazine writer, screen writer and the author of *New York Times* bestsellers *In Harm's Way: The Sinking of the USS Indianapolis and the Extraordinary Story of Its Survivors; Horse Soldiers: The Extraordinary Story of a Band of US Soldiers Who Rode to Victory in Afghanistan*; and the newly released *The Odyssey of Echo Company: The Tet Offensive and the Epic Battle of Echo Company to Survive the Vietnam War.* "Horse Soldiers" is also a movie starring Chris Hemsworth and Michael Shannon, produced by Jerry Bruckheimer. Stanton is also a founder of the National Writers Series and the Traverse City Film Festival. (See page 31.)

GET WRITING

MICHIGAN WRITERS is a TC non-profit with a mission to support writers of all ages and skill levels with workshops, critique sessions and professional development. The group also sponsors the Interlochen Public Radio show, "Michigan Writers On the Air," which presents interviews with local and visiting authors once a month.

INTERLOCHEN CENTER FOR THE ARTS presents adult writing programs during the summer and winter. Mystery writing, memoir writing, poetry, blogging and programs that combine sketching with writing are regularly offered.

LISTEN / PERFORM

THE BEACH BARDS share storytelling and songs around the campfire every Friday night during the summer at the Leelanau School in Glen Arbor.

Terry Wooten hosts STONE CIRCLE, 10 miles north of Elk Rapids on Stone Circle Drive. Poetry, songs and storytelling around a campfire every summer Saturday night.

HEAR:SAY is a live (and lively) storytelling event held the third Monday of every month at the Workshop Brewery in TC.

More about local writers on page 249.

one to nothing, meaning even with a future failure he will at least tie. Beat a force of nature and you're a

NORTHERN STARS

WHERE THE FAMOUS COME TO PLAY

Madonna's dad bottles and sells wine here. The singer and '80s icon grew up in Bay City and then high-tailed it to New York. But after she became a worldwide legend, she's said to have bought the land near Suttons Bay where her father now operates Ciccone Vineyard & Winery. She also made an appearance at the Traverse City Film Festival several years ago when she had developed a featured movie.

OK, so you're not likely to run into the pop star around here, but she's just one of several celebrities with local ties.

Up the shore in Northport, Mario Batali, celebrity chef and a co-host of ABC's The Chew, often gets away to his property up here and boasts about the area on network TV. But he also entertains here, and such stars as actor John C. Reilly have been known to join Batali's enviable dinners.

There's also TV fix- and remodel-it heartthrob Carter Oosterhouse, who's a buddy of Batali's. He grew up here, now owns a winery on Old Mission Peninsula where Batali designed the eats (see page 83). If you don't run into him, you're pretty likely see his eternally be-stubbled face on a billboard or other ad.

The infamous have also sought out the charms of the scenic peninsula.

Al Capone is said to have had a hideout two miles south of touristy and stylish Leland. Local residents of the 1920s and '30s said they'd seen him in town, though most of his time was spent inside the compound that a previous owner had named Heart's Ease. Armed guards stood watch at the gate and there was a lookout tower on a hill, which presumably gave the famous gang boss's heart a little bit of ease.

Tim Allen brought attention to the area when he filmed an episode of "Home Improvement" here in the 1990s. The episode was about a Traverse City family vacation and was shot in several locations, largely in Leelanau County. Allen set the episode here because he was a frequent visitor himself, having grown up downstate.

Not all stars are as eager to tell the world about the area as Allen and Batali are. Seems they may have come here to get away from it all.

Others said to have had homes in Leelanau now and in the past include Julie Kavner, the voice of Marge Simpson; Bruce Willis and Demi Moore, when their daughter Rumer Willis was a student at Interlochen; and Allan Melvin, who played Sam the butcher from the Brady Bunch and whose jovial face was on dozens of 1960s and '70s sitcoms in supporting roles.

In addition, for years, hunters have boasted about Ted Nugent sightings in the north woods.

And, of course, hang out downtown during the Traverse City Film Festival and Michael Moore, who has lived in Antrim County, is probably nearby. Also, you'll have a better than usual chance of seeing other stars. In addition to Madonna, past years have seen appearances from Jeff Daniels, Susan Sarandon, Kristen Bell and others. **TC**

rare colossus. Steal back from the undertow? That earns rent on earth. It establishes a new account to save

You Don't Say!

IN 1852, THE REVEREND PETER DOUGHERTY LEFT THE OLD MISSION SETTLEMENT AND LANDED IN THE PHENOMENALLY BEAUTIFUL NATURAL HARBOR OF OMENA.

Considered one of the best in the state, this bay is deep and clean and sheltered from the westerlies off the Big Lake. The area was already home to a population of First People, so many of the Native families accompanying the Reverend settled along the north shore, towards the village of Northport. Indian Beach and Indian Camp roads are reminders to this day.

Omena, (Oh-me-nah) is an Ottawa word, much like the modern expression "You don't say." The story is that Reverend Dougherty used the English phrase often when the Indians told him something. It is just as likely that the Natives used "omena" to respond to Dougherty's pronouncements.

The Mission Boarding School was founded at Omena Heights in 1852. The Grove Hill New Mission Church was dedicated in 1858; the post office was established that year as well. The copper bell in the church steeple is noteworthy for being forged from English pennies given by the Native congregation. Two-hundred, ninety unmarked stones representing the burials of native and white inhabitants are scattered throughout the cemetery grounds. You'll also find the white headstone of an unnamed Civil War veteran, a member of the Company K Michigan 1st Sharpshooters, a famous all-Indian company and the largest Native company in the Union Army. Members of Company K, imprisoned in the Andersonville POW camp, bravely stood up to the infamous gang of Union

against the day a wave breaks barely on the unlucky side of the divide, when he swallows more than he can

soldiers who had been brutally terrorizing their fellow inmates and are credited with their demise. The Grove Hill New Mission Church and graveyard were placed on the Michigan Historic Register in 1971 and on the U.S. National Register of Historic Places in 1972.

The first hotel in Omena, Hotel Leelanau, opened in 1885, two years before the Grand Hotel on Mackinaw Island. The Omena resorts advertised themselves as providing a more intimate and personal experience than other UpNorth resorts. They were also rumored to be more tolerant of Jewish visitors. Elegant cottages in lovely gardens were available just steps away from bathing, canoeing, sailing and fishing. Clean country air, fresh food and home-cooked meals were all strong selling points. In 1887, the Michigan State Board of Health registered Omena on its list of summer resorts...and sanitaria.

At the peak of the Omena Resort era, seven resorts opened simultaneously in 1897. Many of these establishments featured large main lodges, libraries and stages for summer performances. The Shabwasung, the Clovers, the Oaks, Sunset Lodge and the Omena Inn were among them. The Clovers, closed in 1955, enjoyed a brief incarnation as a Christian commune from from 1972 to 1976. Manna House was part of the House Church Movement of the 1970s.

Before his death, Col. George A. Custer and his wife, Libby, sold their family's land one mile south of Omena to the Society of Jesus. An intensely scholarly order, the beauty and solitude was considered to be conducive to contemplation. The original Victorian farmhouse was moved to its present site at the center of the village, and is now the OMENA HISTORICAL SOCIETY'S PUTNAM-CLOUD TOWER HOUSE MUSEUM.

In 1936, the Cloud family donated the land south of Omena to the Jesuits, which became VILLA MARQUETTE. It is still in use as a retreat and place of worship.

The nearby OMENA BAY COUNTRY STORE has been in operation since 1889.

Today, the micro-climate of the farmland surrounding the bay produces world-class fruit and wine grapes. It has been compared, by those who would know, to the Provence region of France! **GS**

LEELANAU WINE CELLARS

Making wine since 1977, Leelanau Wine Cellars produces 30 different affordable varieties. Their tasting room overlooking Omena Bay is worth the view alone. Friendly service. Park your boat.

The home-style restaurant next door, KNOT (JUST A BAR) has a good selection of beer and an ample deck for outside dining on the bay.

TAMARACK GALLERY

Tamarack Gallery was started in 1972 by David and Sally Viskochil and is the go-to gallery in Leelanau county...the go-to gallery anywhere in the UpNorth, for that matter. A seriously delightful selection of two- and three-dimensional art, furnishings and jewelry for every budget. Open year around.

spit out and there's no one on the chair.

Cut Flowers, Nurseries, Tours

CUT FLOWERS || OMENA CUT FLOWERS || SUTTONS BAY

Just south of Omena, off of M22, you'll find 23 flowerbeds of over 40 varieties of flowers for you to cut and arrange. Omena Cut Flowers provides customers with scissors, water and a container, or bring your own. Ready-made bouquets also available from the fridge in the shed. Open from dawn to dusk during the growing season.

CUT FLOWERS || OLD MISSION FLOWERS || TC

This hilltop half-acre garden off Center Road contains roses, peonies, dahlias, lilies, gladiolas and dozens of other perennials and annuals to round out your bouquet. Old Mission Flowers also provides scissors and a bucket. Open from dawn to dusk. Ready-made bouquets are also available at Oryana Natural Foods Market in TC.

CUT FLOWERS & NURSERY || IRIS FARM || TC

Six acres of rainbow glory. Pick a bouquet or order for your own garden. Daylilies, too. On M-72, west of TC.

NURSERY || BARKER CREEK || WILLIAMSBURG

The mother of all area nurseries is way out yonder on M-72, just past the turn-off to Sand Lakes Quiet Area. Ninety acres of shrubs, trees, perennials and water plants. Most of the plants are grown on site, so they're not ahead of the rest of your garden.

NURSERY || WILDFLOWERS || GLEN ARBOR

A tiny place with an interesting selection. Lovely silk flowers inside.

LEELANAU BY TODD MERCER ¶ *He believes he can do anything, after stepping into the big lake at Eastport,*

NURSERY || PLANT MASTERS || SUTTONS BAY

The best selection of annuals and exotics, baskets and houseplants. Lots of perennials, too.

NURSERY || PINE HILL NURSERY || TC

This is the go-to nursery for townies. Perennials, shrubs, some nice indoor plants, lots of herbs, succulents and terrarium items. The friendly, knowledgeable staff will order whatever you need. Pine Hill has a nursery in Torch Lake that's easily four times bigger.

NURSERY || FOUR SEASON NURSERY || TC

Native Michigan plants are the specialty at Four Seasons, including trees, ferns, vines and wildflowers. They also have a fine selection of conifers ans shrub roses. Compost available here, as well as major landscaping design.

NURSERY || MANITOU GARDENS || TC

TC's oldest nursery, and getting a bit run-down, but worth a trip or two for daylilies, roses and a nice selection of hostas. Good stuff not found anywhere else. Big sale in the fall.

TOUR || FRIENDLY GARDEN CLUB
TRAVERSE CITY GARDEN WALK || JULY 21

Wear your big hat on the 35th annual Garden Walk featuring eight gardens on TC's east side. Tickets are $8 in advance and $10 the day of the walk.

TOUR || JUNIPER GARDEN CLUB WALK || JULY 19

The Juniper Garden Club of S. Torch Lake presents "Life is a Garden – Dig in!" View six beautiful gardens from Alden to south of Rapid City, including a recovering garden from the August 2015 storm and the gardens at Charity Hill. Ticket are $8 in advance and $10 the day of the walk.

TOUR || CRYSTAL MOUNTAIN RESORT GARDEN TOURS || THOMPSONVILLE

Once a week throughout the summer, Crystal Mountain's master gardeners offer tours through the resort's gardens. Designed by award-winning architects James Van Sweden, Mark Johnson and Sandy Clinton, the grounds feature hundreds of perennials, shrubs, bulbs and native plants. Every Thursdays at 10 a.m. Tours are free but by reservation only: 855.995.5146.

Wine Country North

THE AREA SOUTH OF OMENA, BETWEEN WEST BAY AND LAKE LEELANAU, IS WHERE YOU'LL FIND SOME OF THE FINEST LAND FOR GROWING GRAPES. THE 45TH PARALLEL PASSES RIGHT THROUGH THE AREA, JUST LIKE IN BORDEAUX, FRANCE AND NORTHERN ITALY.

RAFTSHOL VINEYARDS

The Raftshol brothers were the first to risk commercial planting of red *vinifera* in 1985, thus producing one of the first reds in northern Michigan. Just off M-22, north of Suttons Bay. No charge to taste. Open year around.

FRENCH VALLEY VINEYARD AND BISTRO

A fancy place on the beach surrounded by cherry orchards. The barn was moved and rebuilt by Amish craftsmen and can seat up to 400. Both the barn and the Bistro are great spots for a wedding. Also north of Suttons Bay, off M-22. Four wines for $5. Small plates. Open daily in the summer. In winter, by appointment only.

SILVER LEAF VINEYARD AND WINERY

A new place, well off the beaten track, started by a couple from downstate. There's a nice, 2-mile walk through the woods with bridges and a waterfall. Also a cabin for rent on the property for $150 a night. Take Stallman, south of the casino, off M-22, then right on Peshawbestown Road. Open May — November.

45 NORTH VINEYARD AND WINERY

Want to retire and start a winery? Meet the Grossnickles of Indiana. In production since 2006, they've got 35 acres of grapes plus a few of raspberries. Yum. It's a very pretty spot on a pretty road. There's also a pergola set up for weddings and a small barn for events with up to 80 guests. Take 204 towards Lake Leelanau, then right on E. Horn. $5 for 5 samples. Open year around.

AURORA CELLARS

Right down the road from 45 North, Aurora Cellars serves reds, whites and two sparklings. They also have hard-pressed apple, cherry and bourbon ciders. Two different event spaces for weddings, depending on the amount of guests, plus a three-bedroom Victorian home for the bride and her entourage. Tuscany-style architecture for the tasting room. $5 for 5 wine selections. Open May — November, Fridays and Saturdays in the winter.

where P.J. and her man present as more puzzled than charmed by his knock at 4 a.m., swimsuit dripping on

BLUSTONE VINEYARDS

A modern design, serving reds, whites and cider. Big views are especially nice in the fall. Try the RED-HEADED SISTERS hummus plate with your selection. Off 204 on N. Sylt Road. Open year around.

LAURENTIDE WINERY

Named for the great sheet of ice that carved out the contours of Leelanau county ten thousand years ago, Laurentide whites are award-winning wines. Pass through Lake Leelanau, then take a left on S. French Road. Open April – November.

Return to TC along French Road, one of the prettiest drives in the county. (If it's high-summer, you'll also miss the traffic on M-22.) Stop off at tasting favorites **CHATEAU FONTAINE** and **BEL LAGO** on the way (see page XX). Follow French Road to Schomberg. Pick up County Road 651 in Cedar to get to M-72 and back to TC.

CIDER

TANDEM CIDERS was born when owners Dan Young and Nikki Rothwell toured the cideries of England on a tandem bicycle. They decided that the cider apple-based beverages of the United Kingdom, bright with acid and richly bitter, were far superior to the often cloyingly sweet, dessert apple-based ciders of the states. Dan and Nikki brought the lessons they learned abroad to their own operation, back home in Michigan. Tandem favorites include the sharp and tannic Crabster; Pomona, an apple brandy and cider "pommeau" aged in oak; and Pretty Penny, a blend of over 30 heirloom varietals from Kilcherman's Christmas Cove Orchards!

see page XX

their carpet. ¶ You push across open water, he said, still light-headed while they dressed for the day. The fear

PESHAWBESTOWN, RESTING IN THE PATH OF TEMPESTUOUS NORTHERN WINDS, CAN BE COLD AND BLEAK IN THE WINTER. THIS IS A SHARP CONTRAST TO THE COOL GREEN SUMMERS AND THE RICH COLORS OF THE FALL.

NATIVE AMERICAN TALES TELL OF THE SPIRIT NEENABUSHOO SPILLING HIS PAINT POTS OF CRIMSON, RUSSET AND GOLD OVER THE HILLS AND THE SURROUNDING WOODS OF THE AREA, IMAGERY THAT HOLDS TRUE TO THIS DAY.

Although you can't miss Peshawbestown with its location on M-22, it existed for nearly a century before the truckline-turned highway was built. The village was founded as a Catholic missionary for Ottawa and Chippewa Indians in 1849 — the same year the Waukazoo people arrived in Northport. Tough times followed. In 1911, the *Detroit Free Press* wrote that Peshawbestown "was the only pure Indian village in all of Michigan." Also according to the article, Peshawbestown had only "two long rows of log cabins" showing "the battering of nearly three-quarters of a century of tempestuous northern winds and snows... broken window panes [are] stuffed here and there with rags to keep out the cold... the doors of the houses all fasten with a latch string, a piece of bent wire hooked over a nail or an occasional padlock."

Fortunately, life has gotten better since federal recognition in 1980 and the building of the casinos. (See page 124.)

Peshawbestown's KATERI TEKAKWITHA CATHOLIC CHURCH is dedicated to Saint Kateri Tekakwitha (1656 – 1680) who was the fourth Native American to be venerated in the Roman Catholic Church and the first to be canonized.

THE EYAAWING MUSEUM AND CULTURAL CENTER is also an opportunity to take in the history of the area. The building was designed in the image of the Mother Earth and Father Sky. The museum has a gift shop with tribal art and crafts and educational materials.

The annual PESHAWBESTOWN TRADITIONAL POW WOW is the major cultural event, with a long tradition of food, art and dancing. Celebrated the third weekend in August. Admission is free.

LEELANAU SANDS CASINO is open year-around with 400 interactive slot machines, blackjack, craps, roulette and progressive 3-card poker. There's also a 50-room Lodge and a restaurant.

The Grand Traverse Band of Ottawa and Chippewa Indians also owns and manages Turtle Creek Casino and Hotel in Williamsburg and the Grand Traverse Resort & Spa in Acme.

Photo by Minnie Wabanimkee.

Minnie Wabanimkee cards are available at Brain Storm, Ways to Wellness and Dog Ear Books.

Minnie Wabanimkee

man, unflappable, says, let's get down the road. ¶ *The Nightswimmer as passenger asks him not to tell people*

The train, stuck on the track between TC and Suttons Bay, 1913.

SUTTONS BAY WAS ANOTHER MILLTOWN, SUPPLYING CORDWOOD TO STEAMSHIPS ON THE BAY. LATER, IT WAS A MAJOR STOP ON THE RAILWAY BETWEEN MANISTEE, TC AND NORTHPORT. THE DEPOT IS STILL THERE, BUT THE LAND AND TRACK WERE SOLD IN 1995 TO MAKE THE LEELANAU TRAIL, PART OF THE TART TRAIL SYSTEM FOR BIKING, HIKING AND SKIING.

READ ABOUT HOW YOU CAN BIKE FROM TC TO SUTTONS BAY AND BACK ON PAGE 94.

Suttons Bay is named for the first white settler, Harry Sutton, but a more appropriate name would have been Bahle's Bay. Lars Bahle arrived in the area from Norway in 1876 and subsequent generations of Bahles have made their mark on the village. Lars bought a farm, then built docks and warehouses on the Suttons Bay shore for shipping produce as well as the dry goods store that still carries his name. The only movie theater in the entire county, the **BAY THEATRE**, is owned by Bob Bahle. And there's also a very nice golf course, **BAHLE FARMS**, southwest of town (see page 134). In 1929, a descendant of Lars reported that Norwegian was still spoken on the streets of Suttons Bay.

Suttons Bay can present something of a bottleneck during the high season, so drive slowly. Better yet, park your car and get out for a walk. There's a nice beach down on the bay, and a pleasant meander around the marina and through the wetlands on boardwalks. **INLAND SEAS EDUCATIONAL ASSOCIATION** has its headquarters along there, and its museum maintains exhibits covering everything from invasive species to sea lampreys and the Asian carp. (See more on page 117.)

Above the beach, the village rises up along the hill with a little creek cascading here and there and pretty houses with gardens.

that he swam to Leelanau. This is how I work on staying present in the world, he explains to P.J.'s man, a natural for

Eat

9 BEAN ROWS, in the old fire station, uses as much local food as possible, from their own farm as well as others. Open from 3:30 to 9 p.m. Monday through Saturday, the menu changes with the local produce available. Mario Batali loves the frites with rosemary aioli and the lamb burger.

Everything's made from scratch at **MARTHA'S LEELANAU TABLE**. Dinner every night. Breakfast and lunch available Wednesday – Saturday, brunch on Sunday.

Locals swear that **ROMAN WHEEL** pizza is the best.

The **VI GRILL** has been serving food since 1871. And you can sit on the sidewalk, sip a brew and watch the cars go by at **STREETSIDE GRILLE. PARALLEL 45 CAFE** is nice for breakfast.

The brewpub **HOP LOT**, just south of town, also has food and outdoors seating in the woods. A great place for families with kids.

Shop

Lots of locals make the trip to Suttons Bay just to visit **ENERDYNE**. They have wonderful, science-based toys and games, all sorts of stuff for watching the weather or your garden, and the most complete optics shopping in the area. Enerdyne also has a fine display of Petoskey stones and books about the geography of the area.

Suttons Bay is where **HAYSTACKS** got started. Check out their comfy, colorful, bias-stitched clothing.

BAHLE'S OF SUTTONS BAY specializes in high-quality clothing for country living, from Harris Tweed to Barbour to Patagonia and Dale of Norway.

WILL CASE DANIELS has been crafting outstanding jewelry and weather vanes for almost 50 years.

THE PAINTED BIRD is loaded with arts and crafts by more than 60 different artists.

CALENDAR

JUNE 16 || ART AND WINE WALK

JULY 16 || LEELANAU WINE ON THE WATER FESTIVAL

JULY 21 || TOUR DE TART

AUGUST 5 – 6 || SUTTONS BAY ART FESTIVAL

AUGUST 11 – 12 || SUTTONS BAY SIDEWALK SALE

SEPTEMBER 9 – 10 || HARVEST STOMPEDE

OCTOBER 20 || ART AND WINE WALK

unsolicited confidences. The cabin of a car—a confession booth for travelers.   ¶ *What that guy knows but*

Wine Country South

BETWEEN TC AND SUTTONS BAY, ON THE HILLS ABOVE WEST BAY, IS ANOTHER PRIME GROWING AREA FOR GRAPES. THESE WINERIES GET THE MOST TRAFFIC, AND SOME ARE VERY CLOSE TOGETHER, MAKING A PLEASANT AFTERNOON LOOP, AS LONG AS YOU DON'T GET LOOPY.

WE'LL START WITH THE WINERIES FARTHEST FROM TC AND WORK BACK.

BOSKYDEL VINEYARD

Kind of a kookie place along the west shore of Lake Leelanau. Bernie Rink, self-proclaimed Wine Nazi and retired library director at Northwestern Michigan College, was the first True Believer in Upnorth wines. You'll either love it or hate it. Open year around.

BLACK STAR FARMS

If you like your wine with a dog and pony show, this is the place for you. There's a petting zoo, horses, an inn, dining and a lofty tasting room. You can't miss the big, red spread off M-22 on Revold Road. Open every day. Tasting is not free.

To visit a cluster of four vineyards, take a right out of Black Star to S. Elm Valley Road and turn left.

L. MAWBY VINEYARDS

Larry Mawby is famous for SEX. That's right, and it's a sparkling wine. A laid-back, happy tasting room, perfect for the bubbly. Open year around. From M-22, take Hilltop Road to S. Elm Valley. Two samples are free.

CICCONE VINEYARD AND WINERY

A lovely place, perched on a hill overlooking vineyards and the Bay beyond. Yes, this is Madonna's dad's place. Now that that's over with, enjoy a glass of Dolcetto — Ciccone is the only winery in Michigan that makes the Italian delicacy. The barn is a great place for a wedding, too. Open all year, weekends only in the winter. On Hilltop Road. Tastings are not free.

WILLOW VINEYARD AND WINERY

Right across the road from Ciccone's is Willow with hands-down the prettiest entrance, situation and views in the area. Event space for up to 50 people. Open summer only.

CHATEAU DE LEELANAU

Another one that's hard to miss with its in-your-face signage right on M-22. Staff is friendly, there's hard cider and a Tiki bar, too.

SHADY LANE CELLARS

Located halfway between TC and Suttons Bay on Shady Lane Road, this winery is carved out around an old farmstead. A nice place for a wedding with a large, outdoor patio and lawn games. Wine tasting in a former chicken coop costs $5 for five. Open all year round.

BRENGMAN BROTHERS

Quite the spectacular spread at the top of Crain Hill Road. This is the closest winery to TC, near M-22. Tasting on the expensive side at two for $5, and if you're in a large party of 20-somethings, don't expect a warm welcome. Events can seat up to 200 people.

CIDER

SUTTONS BAY CIDERS has just about the best view in northern Michigan, and it's a view made even better when there's a pint of crisp, clean cider to enjoy it with! While you gaze out over West Bay, sip a Power Island, made from Rhode Island Greening and Jonathan apples; a Cherry Fest, with wild apples and Montmorency cherries thrown in the blend mix; or a bourbon-barrel aged Sumac with—you guessed it—wild sumac berries. For an added kick, try one of their flavor blends (like the Power Fest) or even design your own blend at their tasting room!

HOP LOT, a collaboration between brothers Steve and Drew Lutke, is one of the best places to get your brew on in Leelanau. Steve, the head brewer, cooks up marvelous concoctions like the silky 8 Cord oatmeal stout; the Rough Sawn amber ale, made with Leelanau hops; and the Highway Robbery blonde ale, with Leelanau hops and Michigan barley malted at the Pilot Malt House. Drew, the GM, will be serving these pints—and more—along with barbacoa nachos, pork tacos, and mac and cheese!

Hop Lot is very kid-friendly. Bring along a game — we recommend "In a Pickle" or some Madlibs. Parking can be tough in the summer, and you may have to leave your car out on the highway.

need returning. THE END

Let's Make Dinner

EVERY VILLAGE IN LEELANAU COUNTY HAS SOME KIND OF GROCERY STORE GOOD FOR THE BASICS. <u>HANSEN'S</u> IN SUTTONS BAY IS THE MOST COMPLETE.

YOUR BEST BET IS TO SHOP FOR FISH IN LELAND OR PESHAWBESTOWN, THEN HEAD TO THE NEAREST FARMERS MARKET.

Farmers Markets

BENZONIA || Mondays from 3 – 7

CEDAR || Fridays from 3 – 7

EMPIRE || Saturdays from 9 – 1

FRANKFORT || Saturdays from 9 – 1

GLEN ARBOR || Thursdays from 9 – 1

LAKE LEELANAU || Sundays fro 9 – 1

LELAND || Thursdays from 9 – 1

SUTTONS BAY || Saturdays from 9 – 1

HILLSIDE HOMESTEAD

Experience dinner, cooked from scratch in a 1910 kitchen. A truly tasty and unplugged journey into the past. Host and food historian Susan Odom can accommodate 6 – 20 guests. Fun for the whole family.
3400 Setterbo Road, Suttons Bay

U-PICK

ALPERS BERRY FARM
Suttons Bay || Raspberries

CEDAR SOL HYDRO FARM
Cedar || Strawberries

CLEARBROOK FARMS
TC || Peaches & Chinese Chestnuts

CROSS FARMS
Northport || Saskatoon berries

GALLAGHER'S
TC || Cherries, Pumpkins & Veggies

GOOD NEIGHBOR
Northport || Apples

JACOB'S
TC || Apples, Pears, Peaches, Raspberries, Pumpkins & Veggies

LEABO FARMS
Suttons Bay || Strawberries

NORTH STAR ORGANIC
Frankfort || Cherries

PUTNEY'S
Benzonia || Raspberries, Saskatoons, Rhubarb, Currant, Gooseberries & Veggies

RENNIE ORCHARDS
Williamsburg || Apples, Apricots, Cherries, Pumpkins

SHANGRI-LA TOO
Old Mission || Cherries, Apples, Raspberries

WESTOVER MARKET
Maple City || Blueberries, Raspberries & Pumpkins

CHEESE PLEEZ

LEELANAU CHEESE

Leelanau Cheese specializes in raclette, a melting cheese with a long, alpine tradition in France and Switzerland.

Raclette is made with cow's milk, and Leelanau Cheese uses milk from the Garvin Farm in Cedar.

Leelanau Raclette bested close to 3,000 cheeses from across the globe and became one of only two American cheeses to earn a Super Gold Award at the World Cheese Awards in San Sebastian, Spain. Along with the award, Leelanau Raclette was also named "one of the world's 66 best cheeses."

You can visit their creamery, just south of Suttons Bay on M-22, to watch the cheesemakers at work or to try one of their tasting platters.

Leelanau Cheese also makes fromage blanc, spreads and some different varieties of raclette, including aged and black truffle. Cheeses are available locally and throughout the state.

IDYLL FARMS

Forget that sour, dry, salty goat cheese sold in grocery stores — you won't believe how deliciously creamy, or fluffy, or sweet goat cheese can be when professionals are involved.

Idyll Farms raises pasture-fed alpine goats and is a Certified Humane® farm. Their seven varieties of goat cheese have been winning medals in the World Championship Cheese Contest since 2014. There's no best in class — all of them are different and wonderful in their own ways.

Idyll Farms cheeses are available locally and across the state of Michigan, as well as in Illinois and New York.

TWO AWARD-WINNING WINERIES ARE FOUND INSIDE THE COUNTY. BOTH OF THEM WILL TAKE YOU THROUGH CEDAR.

BEL LAGO VINEYARDS AND WINERY

Bel Lago got started early, in 1997, and was able to import its Auxerrois root stock from France before that became illegal. A small tasting room and a pretty view of Lake Leelanau. Their Chardonnay is a big award-winner. A winery for connoisseurs. Tasting is free. Open Saturdays and Sunday, 12 – 5.

CHATEAU FONTAINE

Award-winning wines here, too. High marks for its friendly, knowledgeable staff and reasonable prices. Open May – November and most Saturdays in the winter.

CEDAR ‖ POLKAFEST JUNE 22 - 25

Cedar is best known for its POLKAFEST, celebrating the Polish settlements of Schomberg, Bodus and Isadore. Most of the Poles arrived around 1868, after first stopping off in major cities like Chicago and Detroit to earn enough money to buy land through the Homestead Act.

Cedar's a nice stop for an ice cream cone after a day at the beach. Fantastic paddling at Cedar River Preserve. (See page 110.)

THE GALLERY, in a restored gas station, houses three retail establishments.

WOOL & HONEY is a knitter's paradise, specializing in locally grown, dyed, spun yarns and fibers. There's a big table in the back for classes and socializing.

PLEVA'S MEATS has been making sausages since 1946. Ray Pleva began adding cherries to his products in 1987, and they became a national sensation, leading to Ray's appearance on "Oprah."

THE POLISH ART CENTER carries everything from Polish paper cups to Polish Forest mushrooms.

MAPLE CITY

From Good Harbor Beach, it's a straight shot back to TC along County Road 667, through Maple City.

Breakfast and calzones at this local hang-out, PEGTOWN STATION.

FUNISTRADA, on MacFarlane Road, prepares fabulous Italian dinners using local dairy, produce, meats and specialty products.

LA BÉCASSE has been serving authentic French cuisine for more than 30 years.

The Roads of Leelanau County

WINDING THROUGH FOREST, ORCHARD, HAY FIELDS
AND VILLAGES, THE ROADS OF LEELANAU COUNTY
LEAD ALWAYS TO SCENIC VISTAS. FROM THE ROLLING
HILLS ONE SEES THE WATERS OF LAKE MICHIGAN,
CLOUDS BANKS AND SUNSETS, THE MANITOU AND
THE FOX ISLANDS,

M-22 is Leelanau's iconic highway. The black signs with white numerals have come to represent all that is best about UpNorth. Hugging the shore from one corner of the county to the other, M-22 heads north,east, west and south, no matter which way one is driving. A 70-mile V, M-22 takes you from Empire, through Leland, to Northport, then south to Suttons Bay and Traverse City. Along the way you pass wineries, cheese shops, farm stands and neighborhood taverns memorialized in art and fiction.

The roads south of M-22 tend to follow a general grid pattern , though they will often dog-leg to avoid a barn or swamp, only to straighten again a half mile farther on. But you can rest assured that at some point you will come to a sign pointing the way to somewhere you have always wanted to be.

North of M-22 the roads tend to wander with less geometrical but more geographical rationale. Getting lost in the northern third of the county is always easier than you think, even if you've driven the roads each summer of your life. The roads wander around rolling drumlins and captured dunes, and often seem to double back on themselves. Yet since the peninsula narrows the farther north you drive, at some point you will come to a stop at M-22. The only challenge is to figure out which side of the county you are on.

Some of the most scenic byways are the roads less traveled by the day tourist. On French, Schomberg, Jelinek and Kolarik roads you'll see the county the locals cherish, a landscape steeped in its ethnic enclaves and agrarian past. Quintessential white farmhouses and red barns are nestled behind cherry orchards that delight the eyes no matter the season. Along the way you will pass one-room school houses renovated into homes, unique churches whose graveyards host stones inscribed in Polish, Bohemian or Ottawa, and the hidden wineries and organic CSA farms that support the farm-to-table culture that represents the Grand Traverse area today.

Driving the backroads of the county, you should turn onto the dirt roads, those seasonal two-tracks the county does not plow in the winter. On these roads you might catch a glimpse of a fox , a bobcat or a hidden lake where only canoes or kayaks can go. And always the dirt roads lead you through the maple and beech forests that, cool and quiet, are timeless reminders of the northwoods in myth and memory. **DM**

LEELANAU, OLD MISSION, CHARLEVOIX, HARBOR SPRINGS AND CADILLAC ARE ALL PRIME COLOR TOUR TERRITORY. THE BEST COLORS ARE FOUND WHERE THE MOST MAPLE TREES GROW.

A TOUR OF THE WINERIES WILL ALSO TAKE YOU THROUGH THE FALL COLORS ON OLD MISSION AND LEELANAU PENINSULAS.

HOW DOES IT HAPPEN?

As temperatures cool and the days become shorter, the veins that carry fluid in and out of the leaves begin to close off, stopping the flow of chlorophyll, water and minerals. Chlorophyll is what makes leaves green. It also is the agent that captures the sun's rays and turns that energy into food for the tree. Leaves begin to change from the edges inward; that's why you'll often see colored leaves with green veins.

YELLOW AND ORANGE

These colors are always present in the leaves of hickories, ash, maple, poplars, birches and others — we just can't see them under all that green chlorophyll. The color comes from carotenoids, the same pigment found in carrots and corn and canaries.

RED AND PURPLE

The pigment group, anthocyanins, creates the scarlets, rubies and purples. Not found in leaves before the end of summer, the presence of these pigments depends on growing conditions. The more sunshine we have in the fall, the more brilliant the display. Anthocyanins also like chilly but not freezing temperatures. Only 10 percent of trees in temperate areas produce this pigment, but UpNorth is lucky to have so many maples, oaks, dogwoods and sumac that fire up the hillsides in the fall.

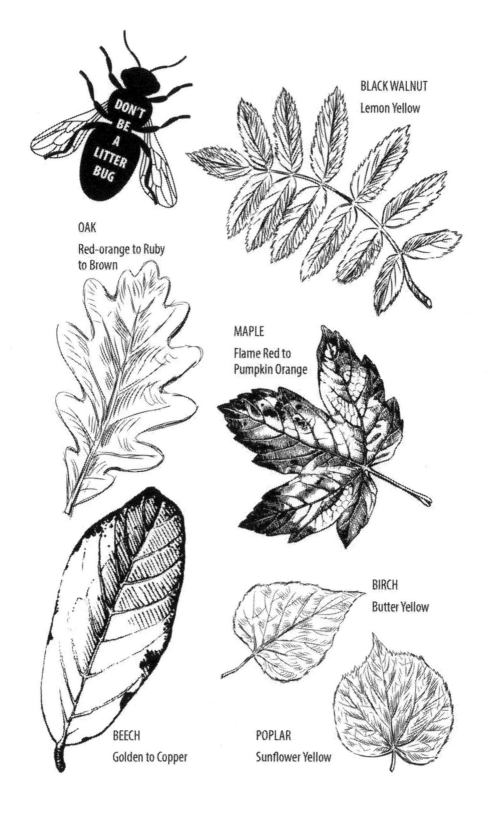

DON'T BE A LITTER BUG

BLACK WALNUT
Lemon Yellow

OAK
Red-orange to Ruby
to Brown

MAPLE
Flame Red to
Pumpkin Orange

BIRCH
Butter Yellow

BEECH
Golden to Copper

POPLAR
Sunflower Yellow

HOW TO
242
make maple syrup

CAN YOU PEEL THE BARK OFF THAT
MAPLE TREE IN YOUR FRONT YARD?
IF YES, THEN IT'S PROBABLY NOT A
GOOD CANDIDATE FOR SYRUP.

Mike Street, who has been tapping his 300 "hard maple" trees near Kingsley for a decade, says trees with firm and rigid bark have the highest concentration of sap.

You also want to make sure the tree can handle it, so don't tap anything with a diameter of less than 15 inches. And a smaller tap, or spile, like a 5/16th size, is more tree-friendly.

First wait until the temperature reaches 40 degrees, with colder nights (preferably below freezing). Street says if it's been a really cold winter, with lots of snow, you have to let the roots warm up enough, so one day of 40-degree weather won't cut it. The sap comes from the roots and is making its way upward, like a hydraulic pump, to feed the leaves for the summer. Tapping a tree — as long as it's old enough and you don't use too many taps — won't hurt the tree, he assures.

Once the tap is in the tree, you can expect up to four gallons of sap over a 24-hour period. It takes 40 gallons to make one gallon of syrup.

Street doesn't recommend boiling that precious sap in the house. He has a sugar shack in his sugar bush and boils over a wood fire, with all the windows open because of the humidity. And you'll want to filter the syrup before you bottle it. A regular coffee filter will work in a pinch. If you're not going to filter it quickly, you'll have to process it in a 180-degree water bath, as if you're canning vegetables.

The sap season is over when the trees begin to bud. Street says a good season is four to five weeks. **JT**

 AMERICAN INDIANS TAUGHT THE EUROPEAN SETTLERS HOW TO TAP AND PROCESS MAPLE SAP.

DURING THE CIVIL WAR, MAPLE SYRUP BECAME A NORTHERN SUBSTITUTE FOR CANE SUGAR AND MOLASSES IN PROTEST TO SLAVE LABOR.

GLEN ARBOR CEMETERY

In the woods just south of Glen Arbor is a lonely pioneer cemetery where a young mother and her youngest child are buried. The husband/father, who died in a farm accident in the 1920s, is said to have haunted the site where his loved ones rested out of guilt for abandoning his other two children. The tale of that ghost is the subject of *Aaron's Crossing* by Linda Alice Dewey. She says it's based on her true experiences with the spirit. The trail to the cemetery is near a stone gate entrance at Forest Haven Rd. and M-22. To get there, park on the north side just inside the gate and walk in at least 1/8 mile. When the trail forks, take the path on the left.

GRAND TRAVERSE LIGHTHOUSE MUSEUM AT LEELANAU STATE PARK, NORTHPORT

This red-roofed navigation light has kept watch over the nail of Michigan's pinky since 1852. It is said to have one particular resident who occasionally raises goosebumps on the skins of those who work or visit. Employees have heard voices and footsteps on the hardwood floors or when climbing up the tower. Some have felt a presence brushing past them and others have even seen a man appear. It's all believed to be the ghost of Captain Peter Nelson, a Danish ship captain and keeper of the lighthouse who died in 1892 at the age of 81. In October, the lighthouse hosts ghost walk tours. The park and lighthouse are at the northern end of County Road 629, also known as North Lighthouse Point Road. **TC**

A-Mazing Fall Fun

GET OUT OF THE CAR AND ENJOY THE COLORS AND TASTES OF AUTUMN UPNORTH.

GALLAGHER'S FARM MARKET || TC
A fun stop for little kids, Gallagher's has a corn maze, a pumpkin patch, farm animals and petting zoo.

HOXSIE'S ORCHARD HILL FARM MARKET || WILLIAMSBURG
More fun for kids with u-pick apples and pumpkins, farm wagon rides, a haystack in the barn and a giant corn maze.

JACOB'S CORN MAZE || TC
Jacob's is great for all ages with three, yes, three corn mazes! One for tiny tots, a haunted maze for the brave and the humongous 10-acre monster maze. Plus, u-pick pumpkins and apples and horse-drawn hay rides.

PAHL'S PUMPKIN PATCH || BUCKLEY
U-pick pumpkins in the field patch, a minimal-pesticide corn maze, a haybale maze, tractor-pulled hay rides and farm animals.

CLARK'S FAMILY FARM || TC
A family farm with a haunted house and a corn maze. Clark's also sells Christmas trees.

244

HOW TO
deal with leaves

HOW FUSSY (ANAL) ARE YOU ABOUT HOW YOUR LAWN LOOKS? IF YOU NEED IT SPOTLESS, WITH NARY A LEAF OR TWIG, THEN CARRY ON. RAKE, BLOW AND HAUL THE LEAVES TO THE CURB AND LET SOMEONE ELSE BENEFIT FROM THEIR GOODNESS.

But if you want to help your lawn, fertilize it and save time for lovely walks in the woods — then mow those leaves.

Sure, homeowners of yore did rake, bag and (mmm, the smell) burn their leaves. And sure, you have to get them off the grass because piles of soggy, snow-covered leaves don't do anyone any good. But researchers at Michigan State University —home of a turf grass program that has grown the heads groundskeeper at Comerica Park, among others — back up the mowing theory. Here's how to do it:

- Dry leaves mow best.
- Set your mower at its highest level.
- Plan to go over your leaves at least once, possibly twice.

You'll probably have to do this once a week. Depending on your mower, you may be able to handle six inches or so of leaves.

If you have a bagging mower, mow the first time without the bag and leave the leaves on the lawn. Thereafter, bag the mulched leaves and put them elsewhere in your yard, on shrubs, your garden or the compost pile.

Among the benefits of mowing your leaves are:

- Winter annuals won't germinate
- It's a nice organic addition to any garden
- Fewer weeds. Seriously, MSU researchers found that after three years of mowing leaves, there was a 100 percent decrease in dandelions and crabgrass.

There will still be little bits on leaves on your lawn, but you won't see them for long because they'll filter down through the grass and start fertilizing it. By springtime, even the little bits will be gone. **JT**

HOW TO
246
find morels

MARK RINGLEVER HAS A KIT HE TAKES INTO THE WOODS WITH HIM EACH SPRING. IT CONTAINS MESH BAGS, POCKET KNIVES AND COMFY SHOES.

HE COMES OUT OF THE WOODS WITH SACKLOADS OF MOREL MUSHROOMS.

Ringlever says it helps when looking for fungi to know the science of mycelia, which grows just under the surface of the earth — everywhere. It takes the right combo of mycelia to sprout a mushroom, but Ringlever, a boat captain with a background in environmental science, offers a few tips for finding the wily morel.

- Wait until the end of April and continue looking into May. If you're a beginning hunter, Mother's Day is a good time because the mushrooms will be big enough to stand out.

- "You have to cover a lot of ground. When you find one, make a concentric circle. If you don't find more within a few minutes, move on."

- Don't go where there are lots of cars. However, if you see a car in one spot, go back 4 or 5 days later. Mushrooms grow fast.

- The best hunting is in the morning after a nighttime rain, when temperatures are 50 to 60 degrees.

- "Key in on burn areas. If you know a spot that burned last year, look there."

- Look for ash, hemlock, maple and beech trees, but mushrooms will grow in most any kind of area, even if there aren't trees. They don't grow well in high areas (hills) or low areas (swamps). They don't like sandy soil either.

- Gather responsibly. Take a pocketknife and cut the stem of the mushroom above the ground.

- DO NOT yank the whole mushroom out of the dirt.

- Put your picked mushrooms in a mesh bag as you continue to hunt to help spread the spore.

Know your mushrooms. Take a book with pictures to help identify them. **QUICK ID**: Slice a mushroom in half vertically. The cap should attach to the stem. If it doesn't, it might be a "false morel," which could make you sick.

You don't need water to clean morels; a soft brush should work unless they're really sandy.

Ringlever recommends hunting morels in Benzie County. He would not be more specific. **JT**

WHITE MORELS

We highly recommend the *GRASS RIVER NATURAL AREA'S FIELD GUIDE TO NORTHWESTERN MICHIGAN: ITS FLORA, FAUNA, GEOLOGY, AND HISTORY* by James Dake.

This well-designed, portable and full-color guide will help you identify mushrooms, trees, wildflowers, birds, butterflies and so much more.

Show your mushrooming skills at the MESICK MUSHROOM FESTIVAL, May 12 – 14.

FALSE MOREL

CHANTERELLES

CHICKEN OF THE WOODS

MEET THE INSIDERS

HEATHER SHAW grew up on a cherry farm in Yuba, MI. She was once a downhill ski racer, but when she wiped out the entire scoring apparatus at the finish line one year, her parents let her move on to other occupations.

Heather is Director of Design and Marketing at Mission Point Press.

JODEE TAYLOR is a Traverse City native and the author of **TAYLOR'S ENCYCLOPEDIA OF LOCAL KNOWLEDGE.** Jodee worked one summer at Bardon's Wonder Freeze, where she invented the Hot Fudge Marshmallow Milkshake. She learned to ski at Mt. Holiday when it was still a hill, and found out the hard way how to not sail in an offshore breeze. Jodee handles digital media marketing for Mission Point Press.

Sometimes referred to as the 4,846th Monkee, **TOM CARR** enjoys playing guitar, long walks on the beach and ....wait, what is this, "The Bachelor"? Carr reported for the *Traverse City Record-Eagle* for two decades. His work has been on NPR, the *Detroit Free Press, New York Daily News*, Interlochen Public Radio, traverseticker.com and several other media. Carr lives in the greater Buckley metropolitan area with his wife Maria.

THE STORYTELLERS

BOB BUTZ moved to the TC area in 1995, and has been writing about it ever since. His story, THE DOGMAN, is published in *An Uncrowded Place: A Life Up North and a Young Man's Search for Home.*

MICHAEL DELP, an award-winning creative writing instructor at Interlochen Arts Academy, is the author of eight books and has his own Wikipedia entry. Delp's story, "A BUSHY, BUSHY BLOND HAIRDO" appears in print here for the first time.

TODD MERCER won the Dyer-Ives Kent County Prize for Poetry (2016), the National Writers Series Poetry Prize (2016) and the Grand Rapids Festival Flash Fiction Award (2015). His digital chapbook, *Life-wish Maintenance*, appeared at Right Hand Pointing.

CONTRIBUTORS

BOB BUTZ, DUNCAN MORAN, ZACH VELCOFF, GABRIELLE SHAW, HART CAUCHY, LIZ & MOLLIE, STEPHEN LEWIS, ANNELLE KASPOR, TAJIN ROBLES, T. DORMAN, MINNIE WABANIMKEE AND GLENN WOLFF.

LOCAL WRITERS
LOCAL TOPICS

An Uncrowded Place by BOB BUTZ is about moving to the area as a young man. BUTZ contributes regularly to area magazines.

MICHAEL DELP'S *Lying in the River's Dark Bed* brings together in one collection two of Delp's most beloved (and often hilarious) characters, The Deadman and the Mad Angler.

JERRY DENNIS is an award-winning author of many books about fishing, paddling and the local environment, some of them illustrated by local artist GLENN WOLFF.

BOB DOWNES' *Biking Northern Michigan* is essential Upnorth reading and there's a forthcoming novel, *Windigo Moon*, an epic saga of love and war among the Ojibwe.

JACK DRISCOLL'S newest collection of stories, *The Goat Fish and the Lover's Knot* is set in the area. Driscoll's stories have frequently appeared on NPR's *The Sound of Writing*.

MARDI LINK investigates true crime in Michigan, and was the winner of the Michigan Notable Book Award for her memoir *Bootstrapper: From Broke to Badass on a Northern Michigan Farm*.

STEPHEN LEWIS has two books about murder on Old Mission. FRANK SLAUGHTER'S trilogy about an Upper Peninsula family spans continents and generations.

STEPHANIE MILLS is an ecological activist and author of many books about living close to the land.

ANNE-MARIE OOMEN has several memoirs about growing up on a rural farm in the 1950s and 60s. Two of her books have been chosen for Michigan Notable Book Awards.

LYNNE RAE PERKINS is a Newbery Award-winning author and illustrator of many children's books.

HEATHER SHUMAKER'S brand new book is called *Saving Arcadia: A Story of Conservation and Community in the Great Lakes*.

AARON STANDER'S best-selling series of murder mysteries set in Leelanau county is now in its tenth volume.
PETER MARABELL also writes a series of novels starring a private eye and set in Petoskey and Mackinac Island.
And ELIZABETH BUZZELLI writes cozy mysteries where murder happens in the UpNorth.

KATHLEEN STOCKING, has published two books of essays about the people and places of Leelanau county.

• RESOURCES •

HORIZON BOOKS in TC has a huge selection of books about local topics, from area history and ecology to trail guides. Horizon Books — also in Cadillac — is a strong supporter of local writers and we Insiders say thank you.

The OLD MISSION HISTORICAL SOCIETY has quite the collection of documents and photos. Their newsletters are always a good read as well. Visit them online at omphistoricalsociety.org.

SLEEPING BEAR NATIONAL LAKESHORE publishes complete lists of area flora and fauna that you can access online:
www.nps.gov/slbe/learn/nature/upload/SLBEchecklist_WEB.pdf.

Michigan's DEPARTMENT OF NATURAL RESOURCES is a treasure-trove of information about hunting, fishing, camping and licensing. Check out their website at www.michigan.gov/dnr/.

The NORTHERN EXPRESS is a free paper published weekly and provides an up-to-date events calendar.

If you like to get stuff by email, sign up for the DAILY SPLASH from MyNorth.com.

THANK YOU FOR STOPPING BY!

For suggestions, comments and contributions to the 2018 edition of INSIDE UPNORTH, write to Heather@missionpointpress.com

MORE BOOKS FROM MISSION POINT PRESS

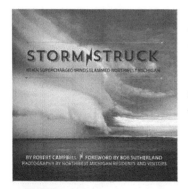

STORM STRUCK:
When Supercharged Winds Slammed
Northwest Michigan

By Robert Campbell; Foreword by Bob Sutherland
Photography by northwest Michigan residents
and visitors

POISON ON TAP:
How Government Failed Flint and the Heroes
Who Fought Back

A Bridge Magazine Analysis of the Flint water crisis.

Sometimes truth is stranger and scarier than
fiction—such is the case with the Flint Water Crisis.
Bridge Magazine staff painstakingly document
one of the most significant cases of environmental
injustice in U.S. history. ——Marc Edwards, Virginia
Tech professor whose work helped prove that the
regulators were wrong

BLOOD ON THE MITTEN:
Infamous Michigan Murders
1700s to Present

By Tom Carr

In this hugely effective debut, Tom Carr sheds keen
illumination upon a regional inventory of killers,
kooks, cutthroats and the aggressively unhinged. The
tales are horrific and humorous by turns —— grisly,
goofy, poignant dispatches expertly summated by a
skilled veteran reporter who's no stranger to the back
stairs habituated by a true sleuth. Story telling at its
fully imagined best." —— Ben Hamper, bestselling
author of *Rivethead*

MISSIONPOINTPRESS.COM

AN UNCROWDED PLACE:
A Life Up North and a Young Man's Search for Home

By Bob Butz

Originally published in *TRAVERSE: The magazine*, this collection of essays features the quiet musings and hilarious contretemps of a self-proclaimed mountain man. Butz takes readers hunting, trapping, bushwhacking, and fishing. He falls in love, rebuilds a house, and raises a boy. A charming and insightful account of living the dream of the Up North life.

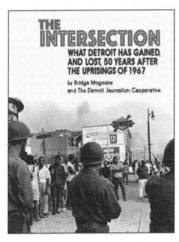

THE INTERSECTION:
What Detroit has gained,
and lost, 50 years after the uprisings of 1967

By Bridge Magazine
and The Detroit Journalism Collective

Fifty years after anger and frustration over police-community relations boiled over into a rebellion in Detroit, there are lots of people asking what we've learned, how we've changed.

…There are so many ways that the factors that led to the uprising are still with us. There are so many reminders, both physical and metaphorical.

If there is good news, 50 years after the 1967 uprising, it is probably that we are all much more honest about the ways in which the problems of then still haunt us now. There's nowhere near as much gloss or self-kidding as we used to indulge.

This book, a collection of the coverage by the Detroit Journalism Cooperative during 2016, is a testament to that. —— From the Foreword by Pulitzer Prize-winning, Detroit native Stephen Henderson

NATIONAL CHERRY FESTIVAL:
Generations of Fun

More than 90 years of celebrating cherries in eye-popping full color.

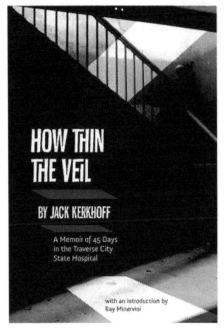

HOW THIN THE VEIL:
A Memoir of 45 Days in the Traverse City State Hospital

by Jack Kerkhoff

with an introduction by Ray Minervini

How Thin the Veil is a 45-day account of Kerkhoff's treatment, his conversations with the nurses and doctors (some of them with their real names), his interactions with the inmates, and his trips to downtown Traverse City watering holes. There's also romance in the form of Suzy, a pretty, lisping waif whose "bad spells" had kept her hospitalized for eight years.

First published in 1952, *How Thin the Veil* shines a "hard-boiled" light on the mid-century conditions of patients of mental illness.

Ray Minervini, who restored and developed Building 50 of the old Traverse City State Hospital, provides an insider introduction to this classic memoir of mental illness.

MISSION POINT PRESS

QUALITY BOOK EDITING, DESIGN AND MARKETING

MISSION POINT offers aspiring and veteran authors a combined 66 years of experience in writing, designing, and publishing the written word. We are an affiliation of talented professionals who have worked on every kind of book you can imagine—from two *New York Times* best-sellers about war to a series of gorgeous cookbooks to a superbly written, self-published cancer memoir that has garnered dozens of rave, five-star Amazon reviews.

Mission Point Press can also help large or small institutional clients publish their own commemorative books. We understand that publishing a book, especially within a complicated organization, is no small undertaking. We have deep experience in helping to facilitate the planning and process of pulling a book's content together into a coffee-table-style book or other form.

No matter what your book—fiction or nonfiction, whimsical or serious—our mission is to help you achieve literary excellence and publishing success.

Visit our website at www.MissionPointPress.com

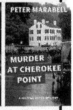

89763287R00152

Made in the USA
Columbia, SC
25 February 2018